Oops, My Team is Toxic

Transforming the Negative Veterinary Team into a Team of Unicorns

Amy Newfield, MS, CVT, VTS (ECC)

This Page Intentionally Left Blank

Oops, My Team is Toxic

Transforming the Negative Veterinary Team into a Team of Unicorns

For permission requests or speaking inquiries, email: vetteamtraining@gmail.com
Printed in the United States of America
ISBN: 9798526382724

First Edition

Dedication

I would not have been so crazy to publish a second book if I did not have the support and encouragement of my closest friends and family members. Every time I said, "I can't," they said, "you can." Thank you to everyone who kept pushing my imposter syndrome away and telling me I could do it.

My parents are my biggest support, and my mother is one of the best proofreaders anyone could ever hope to employ. Being supported unconditionally beats any support a publishing company could provide someone. Every book I write is dedicated to them.

A small army of colleagues and friends read the raw version of this book and provided their candid feedback, which helped shape the content. Their names are spread throughout this book as a thank-you.

Lastly, countless animals have touched my soul over my entire lifetime. Each one got me to where I am today. My love of the veterinary profession all started with a dog named Molly. This book is dedicated to all the animals that have touched my life.

Thank you to everyone who helped get me where I am, provided feedback, told me I could, and genuinely provided love when I needed it. This book is for you.

About the Author

Amy Newfield has a master's degree in leadership and management and has spent more than 20 years in the veterinary profession as a credentialed veterinary technician. Amy's career has been diversified, starting in a general practice owned by one owner in a small town in Massachusetts. From small to large, Amy has worked in general practice, specialty medicine, private, government, and corporate environments. Her leadership skills have included owning her own business, managing both general practice and specialty hospital teams, operating a non-profit spay/neuter clinic, and holding various board positions.

In 2020 she published her first book, "Oops, I Became a Manager," which focused on the key ingredients to creating a happy and healthy veterinary team. Reaching best seller status in its first few months, the veterinary community started talking, and they let Amy know there was still a gap. One of their biggest unanswered questions was, "How do you turn a toxic team into a happy one?"

To answer their question, Amy set out to write a sequel that focused on just that. Her real-world experience, combined with her honest leadership approach, provides readers with practical tools to help hospital teams and their leadership transform into more positive, productive teams.

www.VetTeamTraining.com
www.Linkedin.com/in/amynewfield
Email: VetTeamTraining@gmail.com

VETERINARY

TEAM TRAINING

Like this book? Help to support it by reviewing on Amazon.

TABLE OF CONTENTS

Introduction
What's Up with The Unicorn?

Why the hell is there an angry unicorn on the cover? One could easily say it is because there is a unicorn on my first book, *Oops, I Became a Manager,* but it goes deeper than that. You are likely reading this book because your team isn't happy. Perhaps negativity and gossip run rampant. You want a better team. You want a team of superstars.

Superstars are your unicorns. They are rare, wonderful, and hard to come by. The truth is, for many of you, you likely had superstars at one point, but they have turned angry and toxic. The mission of this book is to get your team back to their happy, rainbow spreading unicorn-selves.

Kevin Daum, best-selling author, and contributor of Inc.com, described 11 traits that superstar unicorns have. I agree with all these traits and encourage leaders to share this list with their teams. Why shouldn't the team learn about what traits make up a unicorn? Teams can more readily aspire to become unicorns if they understand what they are made of, which, it turns out, is not just rainbows and magic dust. Unicorns are the following:

- They are natural researchers. Unicorns want to know why and they seek to find answers. They refuse to let ignorance stand in their way of progress. They are some of your smartest individuals.
- Their ego is low. Unicorns never allow their ego to be a source of disruptive drama. Instead, they are comfortable with their ego and exude modesty at most times.
- They inspire others. Of course, they do! They are unicorns! They lift others, motivate, and have a "yes you can" attitude.

- They freely teach and give their knowledge away. The unicorns on your team love to share their knowledge and help others grow.
- They are efficient. They can rock out a clinic floor, manage ten cranky clients at once and slam dunk the most difficult surgeries. They know how to do their jobs easier and usually faster than others.
- They are happy to assume any role asked of them. A unicorn understands that they may be asked to do something they may not be excited about at times. They will assume that role because it is best for the team and the hospital. Unicorns trust their leaders will work to get them back to the role they are happiest in within a reasonable amount of time.
- They are problem solvers. Your unicorns see a disaster coming before it strikes and work to avoid it. They tell you about their heroics afterward in a "not a big deal, but I did this" kind of way.
- They strengthen a team. I know you are thinking, "Isn't that the manager's job?" Unicorns do this too. They build networks between departments, individuals, and teams.
- They are the voice of the team. A unicorn is a leader in that team. Their fellow coworkers see them as such and often look to them to advocate on behalf of the team. A unicorn can professionally advocate for the team while also looking to develop a solution for the issue at hand.
- They believe in the polite, kind, and honest (PKH) communication approach. For unicorns, communicating in the PKH way comes naturally. They maintain that communication style with everyone on the team.
- They come to work because they want to, not because they have to. True unicorns are driven by their work. It motivates them and provides a sense of purpose.

(Daum, 2015)

I was not quite prepared to start the journey of writing a second book after I had just published my first book. And yet, here I am. The first book was meant to introduce and lay the foundation for what a successful and healthy veterinary team looks like. While it dove into some pressing issues of gossip and negativity, it only grazed the surface of these deep topics. Due to the request of many who reached out asking for more resources on how to handle their toxic team, I dove into writing this second book just a month after the first one was published.

If you pick up this book before reading *Oops, I Became a Manager*, no worries. You will still gain much insight from this book alone, but I would encourage you to read my first book, which introduces salary ranges, career paths, reducing gossip, and elevating your team. It's the building block on which this book was written. If you have not set up your hospital for success or laid a solid foundation, it will be difficult to implement the suggestions in this book.

For example, you can introduce polite, kind, and honest (PKH) communication (introduced in Chapter Six) to your team, but if the team finds out you aren't paying fairly (a concept introduced in the first book), you can kiss all your hard work goodbye. You must have solid organizational practices established in your hospital, or you will never get rid of the toxicity.

I hope this book will complement the first book, and together we can find more unicorns within our veterinary hospitals. And should your unicorns be angry, this book will get them back on track.

Chapter One

Oops, My Team is Toxic

I had just joined my new veterinary hospital only two weeks earlier. It was a general practice that was in the process of expanding to offer emergency services to the community. In addition to adding emergency services, the hospital was looking to expand even further in the future by offering other specialty services like neurology and cardiology. I was beyond excited because I was hired on to eventually be the technician manager for the brand-new shiny emergency and specialty hospital addition. I was like a kid in a candy shop.

The leadership team wanted me to work on the floor and develop a relationship with the team for the first six months. Then, as the emergency hospital was being built, I would be pulled in for the larger discussions on the hospital's design and flow. I was thrilled! This would be the second leadership role of my career and significantly bigger than the first one. The problem was I knew my team was toxic within two weeks into my new role. It was not just a little toxic. It was the vat of toxic water that Joker accidentally fell into that turned him into the arch-nemesis of Batman and the root of all evil in Gotham. It was the epitome of all things toxic.

I hoped that my assessment of the team was wrong. Surely my prior management role gave me the tools needed to solve all the problems in this hospital, right? Unfortunately, I knew less than I thought when it came to toxic teams. In my prior role, I had a few cranky individuals, but they were largely manageable. I assumed that all I needed was my prior leadership experience. That's when I was slapped in the face by this new team's toxicity. As I suffered through my first and only year at the hospital, I kept praying a unicorn would come and save me. No such unicorn came. I ended up quitting.

I Started Offering Suggestions

The general practice side of the hospital had a veterinary technician manager. When I was hired on, it was determined that she and I would work together since some staff would be shared between the specialty and general practice hospitals. Since the team was undergoing significant change, the owner and leadership felt it best not to announce my new management role for at least six months to allow me to be integrated into the team first. I can hear your screams of, "Nooooo, don't do it!" from here. Unfortunately, the younger version of myself was unaware that employers sometimes lie, so I agreed to the plan.

Six months in, I inquired about when my management role would be announced. I was told there had been construction delays, and they wanted to put off announcing it a little bit longer until they were closer to opening up the new addition of the hospital. I was frustrated but wanted to do what was best for the hospital and the team.

Knowing that my ability to act as a true manager had been stifled for a few more months, but eager to showcase my leadership skills, I thought I would offer suggestions to help improve the morale and culture of the team. I requested a meeting with the medical director, general practice technician manager, and owner. In my mind, we needed to address the toxicity of the team sooner rather than later, regardless of my role.

I voiced my concerns about the issues and highlighted examples of the daily toxicity that ran rampant throughout the team.

"The cursing is out of control."

"The gossip never ends."

"Everything is centered on their hatred of working at the hospital."

"They bash clients and yell at the pets."

"There is only negativity."

"Something gets thrown across the treatment room every day."

"Actual screaming occurs frequently."

I thought the reaction would be one of gratitude or even acknowledgment that there was an issue. I half expected the owner of the hospital to say, "Thank you, Amy, for bringing this up. You are right. We need to fix these issues immediately. Let's get you in your new role so we can work on the team."

What I did not expect him to say was, "I'm shocked by your accusations. Our team works exceptionally hard, and many are good friends outside this hospital. We have several employees who've been with us for more than ten years. I'm not sure we need to change anything because I think we're doing a pretty amazing job already. I am, however, questioning our decision to put you in a leadership role."

After the owner defended his hospital and team, I didn't argue and recognized that he could not acknowledge the damaged team because he was part of the damage. He was unaware that the entire hospital team talked about how they disliked him as an owner. They called him a micromanager, sexist, liar, annoying, and incompetent. That meeting showed me that the hospital team was not only toxic but also very poorly managed.

Every month that passed, it was promised that I would eventually be moved into a manager position, but it was not a good time for some reason or another. The lack of promotion continued until the construction ended and the new building was done. We were set to open the hospital doors to the new building within a week when I finally put my foot down and asked when I would be promoted. After all, that's what I was promised. They told me they wanted to give the team time to adjust to the new building, and then they would announce my new role.

And so, approximately one year from the day I was hired, I turned in my notice to my manager and said I would be ending full-time employment exactly two weeks from that day. I offered to stay part-time because my heart bled for those caught up in the toxicity. Most were wonderful veterinary professionals trapped in a toxic workplace environment. I enjoyed many of the veterinarians that I worked with and wasn't quite ready to say goodbye to them. My manager informed me that the owner did not believe in part-time employees. He wanted only employees who were fully committed to the hospital. Yes, the list of things done wrong by this hospital continued to grow.

About one week later, I received a call from the owner, who asked if I would stay on if I was given the manager role that very week. "Amy, we've thought about it and believe the team can benefit from you as their manager. We hope you will continue to stay on full time with us in the role you were promised." Shockingly to him, I declined.

He then offered me part-time hours, stating he had thought about it, and since I was the hospital's only veterinary technician specialist, he thought keeping me part-time would be okay with the team. I thanked him for his offer but let him know that I had already accepted a position elsewhere and did not want to renege on the new hospital.

I thought it kind of him to call me personally, as that was not something he was known to do, but it didn't change my mind. I was leaving not just because of the team but largely because of the leadership. I realized that it wasn't that the hospital couldn't be helped, but that it could not be helped by me alone. To date, it was the most toxic hospital I have ever worked in. Every dysfunction lived inside its walls, which was an eye-opening experience for me. Despite being there for only a year, it provided me a humbling look at my leadership skills.

The Two Parts of Toxicity

While the team was certainly toxic, they were not the only toxic part of the hospital, making this an extremely difficult situation to correct. The hospital owner was set in his ways and micromanaged the hospital even though he no longer practiced as a veterinarian. He frequently walked through the hospital, and if something was out of place or not to his liking, he would bark out statements such as, "Doesn't anyone else have respect for my hospital?" or "This is not how it should be done. It's my hospital!" As a result, the team felt disengaged, as if it was not their hospital, because he constantly reminded them it was not.

The general practice technician manager had been there for an extensive period of time and had learned to adjust to the owner's cranky, archaic ways. The two of them felt it was normal to have a team that was so unhappy. The hospital leadership prided themselves on how they paid above-industry standards and offered above-average benefits. They truly did have some amazing veterinarians, so they bragged about their medicine and how they were cutting edge. Unfortunately, they failed to see the high turnover they had in their hospital. They also never recognized their reputation within the local veterinary community, which depicted them as a bad place of employment. The leadership only saw the good aspects of the hospital. They filtered out the unpleasant issues and chalked them up to things that occurred in every hospital. Despite my telling them that the daily pen and chair-throwing was not normal in most hospitals, they had blinders on. Since they saved ten pets that day, it did not matter to them because the good outweighed the bad.

The team was a whole other issue. It is difficult to have a positive team in the face of poor leadership, but it is possible. I have been part of a few amazing teams that were led by terrible leaders. As a team, we were close-knit and managed ourselves in a way that made us successful. We created an environment in which bad leadership didn't matter to us. Those teams are rare to find. More commonly, you find bad teams because of bad leadership, as was the case with this particular hospital.

Every other word in this team was a curse word. F-this, S-that, everyone was a B or C. It was never-ending. I'm no prude, but it was to the point of being unprofessional and difficult to function in. I tried talking to the team about it and attempted to put a curse jar in the treatment area. Every time someone cursed, they had to put $0.25 in the jar. My goal was to get enough money to buy dinner for the team. It turned out that not many people carried change, and those that did told me to take my curse jar and F-off. Since I was not their manager, I felt powerless to do anything. I doubt asking them to Venmo $0.25 would have gone over any better.

It wasn't just the cursing. It was the constant negativity, drama, and gossip that occurred all the time every day. Even if I managed to go to work feeling good, I always felt emotionally drained by the end. The negativity sucked all the happiness from me, leaving me feeling exhausted and dreading coming back the next day.

Defining Toxicity

What exactly is a toxic team? Toxicity is largely defined as the degree to which something is poisonous. Therefore, when we use the term toxic or toxicity to describe our veterinary team, we are essentially calling out traits or habits that are poisoning the health of the hospital and/or team.

We think of several key traits immediately when we hear the term "toxic team." Gossiping, negativity, and even backstabbing are just a few of the common traits that people associate with a toxic team. But what about someone who feigns their level of expertise or the person who feels they need to be authoritative all the time? Those individuals are just as damaging to a team as someone who is gossiping. The list of toxic traits can also include selfishness, the fear of speaking up, emotional leeching, or lying.

Some of the traits I just listed are ones that leaders don't typically identify as being toxic. They are also harder to correct because they are often hidden. For example, approaching an employee and talking to them about their constant gossiping is easier than having a conversation with an employee about being selfish or overly emotional. Toxicity is anything that is poisoning our teams and causing them to be in a negative state of mind. When you look at the definition from this perspective, it might appear overwhelming. Never fear, I'll break it all down in the next chapter.

Chapter Two

The Cycle of Toxicity & The Players in It

No one wants to be unhappy at work. People largely gravitate to a certain industry or field because they feel a passion for that industry. In veterinary medicine, this is most definitely true. Most who go into this industry like animals more than people. There's no shame in saying it. That's predominately why most of you and I went into the veterinary industry. We connect with animals on a deeper level than we do with people.

I often joke I remember more pet names than I do their owners. I can tell you about Jellow the cat, who was a 15-year-old domestic short hair in renal failure. She had the most beautiful green eyes. Jellow was a patient of mine 20 years ago. Jellow was named by the daughter, who was five when she named her. The daughter's favorite color was yellow, but she pronounced it "jellow." She named the cat after her favorite color. I don't remember the owners' names at all.

When most of us started in the veterinary profession, we had delusions of saving all the animals and it being a rewarding profession for us. Unfortunately, no one entering the veterinary industry is prepared for the hardships of client's financial constraints, animal abuse, high caseloads, and being overworked. It is an exhausting industry that can take a physical and emotional toll on even the best veterinary professional. That said, most veterinary professionals can navigate those difficulties fairly well. In this modern era of the Internet, the veterinary community has bonded together to help provide support to each other for the many difficulties that veterinary professionals face every day. There have been many industry-wide studies focused on burnout, the rate of suicide, and compassion fatigue within veterinary medicine.

Many conferences have started to add health and well-being as a conference track. There are even conferences solely dedicated to the health and well-being of veterinary professionals. In addition, individuals can read blogs, listen to podcasts, and purchase books, all dedicated to helping find outlets and ways to destress in this high-stress industry.

Every individual working in veterinary medicine needs to be responsible for caring for themselves. I'm thrilled to see such a movement encouraging people to do so. As a profession, we must recognize that health and well-being are as important as saving a pet's life. If we do not have a healthy mindset, it is difficult for us to be the best version of ourselves for our patients and clients.

While all of that is exceptionally important, none of it addresses the toxic team. There is almost too much over-emphasis on well-being that it is taking away from what to do if a hospital is already in a bad place. Too many believe that the negativity will disappear if you add in a yoga class and some salads for lunch. While I will discuss how to create a well-being plan for your hospital, it's important to note that it alone will not solve your hospital's issues.

Focusing on our well-being teaches us to navigate our emotions a little better when it comes to dealing with argumentative clients or even handling a high caseload. Still, when we are faced every day with the negativity of a team that continues to bring us down, it is hard to maintain a good mental state. For this reason, I will make this statement: unless we focus on cultivating happier teams, individual mental states will never improve. Focus on getting rid of the toxicity, and we will decrease the stress, anxiety, and negativity that the individual veterinary professional experiences simply because they work in a happy workplace environment.

Blame the Salary!

I have seen the cycle of toxicity time and time again. At some point, the team becomes so toxic that they start blaming all of their issues on the fact that they're not getting paid enough. Hospital leadership eventually believes this to be true.

Salary is an easy scapegoat to blame, especially if a corporation owns the hospital. The leadership reaches out to the corporation and states that their team is unhappy because they are not getting paid enough. Since the corporation often sets the payroll budget, that absolves the local leadership of any responsibility. They blame the corporation for not increasing their payroll. "If we paid them more, they would be happier," the hospital leadership team argues. I have heard from technician managers, medical directors, and practice managers alike that money is the root cause of their team's unhappiness. It certainly is an easy thing to blame.

Before we go much further, I have never been one to sugarcoat anything. Most everyone in veterinary medicine should be making more money. There are many reasons why this doesn't occur. First, there is a high cost of overhead in running a veterinary hospital. Unfortunately, most pet owners do not have pet insurance in the United States. Health insurance helps to increase the salaries of those that work in that industry. The human healthcare hospital or doctor's office can charge exceptionally high fees that the consumer never sees because it gets billed through health insurance. The employer partially pays the health insurance, so the prices seem reasonable to the consumer.

The pet owner cannot afford the human healthcare price of knee surgery. An average cruciate repair billed cost in human healthcare is about six to ten times more than the average billed cost in veterinary care. Yet, the surgery supplies cost roughly the same. Therefore, veterinary professionals will never make as much money as human health care professionals unless most pet owners have pet insurance.

Another reason salaries for veterinary technicians/nurses/assistants are low is because they are archaic. The field of veterinary technology and nursing started by a veterinarian asking their family friend or neighbor's kid to help restrain pets. These individuals were paid very little and under the table. In the 1970s, the first United States Veterinary Technology program was created in New York. By the 1990s, there were a little over 50 AVMA accredited schools, but most veterinary technicians that were employed in the hospitals at that time were still on-the-job trained.

Fast forward to 2022, and the face of the veterinary technology/nursing profession has drastically changed. Veterinary technicians are asked to do more now than ever. Veterinary technicians today perform epidurals, develop anesthesia plans, monitor anesthesia for heart-valve replacement surgeries, administer dialysis, run CPR codes, place arterial lines, and much, much more. And yet, the salaries are largely still that of the on-the-job trained salaries.

My original 1990s starting vet tech salary of $6.50/hr would equal $12-14/hr today, depending on the inflation calculator used. The salary of $12-14/hr is what many starting credentialed veterinary technicians in the United States earn. In short, veterinary medicine is still paying the original 1990s salary for on-the-job trained individuals who were doing little to nothing in the hospital at that time. Veterinary medicine must pay a salary worthy of educated veterinary technicians/nurses. This actual profession has driven the revenue up in veterinary medicine to very high levels, all thanks to their expert skill and knowledge.

Sadly, most businesses strive to keep payroll at a certain low percentage. These percentages have been documented as the best way to run a veterinary hospital and have been largely unchanged over the last two decades. Unfortunately, many hospitals believe these percentages to be the key to success. If they set the payroll budget at 15% of gross revenue for non-DVM staff, they stick to it. These numbers from experts cause many hospitals to get stuck, unable to think outside the box about what is best for their hospital. Salaries are stuck in a rut from the "it's always been done this way" mentality.

I know that changing an entire industry will take a lot of time, but I have seen a shift, particularly in the last few years, that salaries may be improving. However, changing an entire industry will need to come from industry leaders and big businesses. For example, a few companies are now starting to pay a credentialed veterinary technician a percentage on top of a base salary for revenue they generate for the hospital.

Is salary to blame for all the toxicity within our hospitals? No. But is it a contributor to unhappiness in individuals? Yes. We should all be earning more money, but the reality is we also accepted these low salaries when we entered the workforce. We were excited when we placed our first intravenous catheter, the first time we performed a surgery, or the first time we made a pet feel better so it could go home to its people. It felt amazing the first time we had any of those moments.

We went home to our friends and family and wanted to share the amazing experience we had at work. In that moment, we loved our job regardless of the salary. That's what most of us experienced in the early days of our veterinary career. Financial rewards are a satisfier, but they are not the driver of why anyone loves doing what they do in any profession.

We must admit that everyone in this profession loved their job at some point and accepted the salary even if we weren't happy with it. By the time a veterinary professional blames the salary as the root of their issues, the toxicity or burnout within that individual is likely beyond repair.

The Cycle of Toxicity

Does the cycle above look familiar or resonate with you? Employees didn't enter veterinary medicine because they wanted to hate their jobs. They entered veterinary medicine because they love animals and medicine. However, because of the culmination of several events within a hospital, eventually, that team becomes angry and bitter. They start saying things such as, "This hospital doesn't deserve us. We work too hard, and no one cares. We deserve to be paid more!" At some point, when an employee or a team continues to be disgruntled, they will eventually shout their war cry about their salary. While I want everyone to get paid more, money will not fix the many issues that caused them to start talking about how they're not getting paid enough.

Unfortunately, I see managers using money as a Band-Aid when they have failed to deal with the cultural issues within the hospital. Many times, when money is thrown at an unhappy employee, they are bitter about it. They wonder why they had to fight so hard to get a nominal increase in their salary. It may placate them for a short while, but it hardly addresses any of the other issues. Throwing money at an employee instead of managing the issues cheapens them. It says, "I don't care about your concerns of why you are unhappy. Here's some money." Managers need to be more willing to invest in their employees as people by developing them and caring about them deeply. With that said, let me be clear. If you aren't compensating your team well, then the low salaries absolutely are contributing to the toxicity within your team.

This cycle can apply to an individual or perhaps a team. Sometimes we have a single employee somewhere in the middle of the cycle of toxicity. Other times it may be more than one employee. At worst, it's the majority of the team. We must figure out how to get employees back to enjoying and loving their jobs. The medicine and pets are still there, so what changed in between?

Before we go much further, I'm going to define culture versus climate. For those who love to geek out on organizational change and health, you know there is a difference. But, for the sake of this book, I'm going to use them interchangeably, and I will explain my argument as to why.

Organizational culture is essentially the hospital's identity. It is the values of the hospital that have arisen over time. Some of these values were created purposefully, and some arose organically. For example, culture might include values like quality, excellent customer service, or kindness to all pets. Organizational culture is a broader concept that includes most of the employees' experiences. If you want to dive into the roots of organizational culture, consider taking a course that describes various types of organizational culture, including clan, adhocracy, market-oriented, and hierarchy.

Organizational climate is the way in which employees experience the workplace environment. What is the climate like to work there? What is the mood of most of the employees that work there? How engaged are the employees? The climate is the shared perceptions and attitudes of the veterinary hospital. Organizational climate is the narrowed definition of employees' perception of the culture. Most veterinary hospitals strive to offer a people-oriented climate in which the hospital focuses on the perception of individuals who are working in the hospital. A people-orientated climate considers the team's perception to determine if the employer is successful or not. If the team is unhappy, the hospital fails. If the team is happy, then the hospital is a successful employer.

Most veterinary hospital leaders focus on organizational climate. They work to ensure that their employees are engaged and enjoy coming to work. It tends to be something that can be measured based on engagement surveys and performance reviews. Unfortunately, these surveys and reviews often cause employers to realize that the problem is cultural. The culture (the values and identity) helps to drive the climate (how people truly feel).

In *The Handbook of Organizational Culture and Climate,* this statement summarizes it best. "A climate can be locally created by what leaders do, what circumstances apply, and what environments afford. Culture can evolve only from mutual experience and shared learning

(Ashkanasy, 2010)." If the culture is driven by mutual experiences based on what leaders do, then are they not equally important and not mutually exclusive?

Climate and culture are dependent upon one another. Edgar Schein is considered one of the world's organizational culture and climate leaders. He has authored numerous books and argues that 90% of the behavior in our organization is driven by the cultural rules that have been set (Kuppler, 2015). These behaviors then drive perception, which drives the climate. It is the people in the hospital that drive the culture rules, which sometimes include gossip and negativity. This results in a toxic feeling climate.

It is for these reasons that I will be using climate and culture interchangeably. I have had leaders argue that the organization's culture, values, and beliefs are not the problem and that only the climate is the issue. To me, that is never the case. For example, a large veterinary company could argue its culture is solid, but the climate will fail if it's not effectively transmitting its culture to its employees.

I recently had a conversation with a veterinary owner who showed me a list of core values, a mission statement, and even a hospital slogan. "See," she pointed out, "the culture here is amazing. I can't understand why they are so unhappy. How do I fix the climate?" I responded, "A living culture is different from one on paper. Your team hasn't bought into the culture you are selling. That's why the climate is broken. Their perception is that the current values are none of these things you have on this paper."

Understanding the difference between the two and how they impact your hospital team is important. However, I'm not going to be grammatically correct when using these terms throughout the book. If your culture is broken, so is your climate, and vice versa. Regardless of whether or not a team's perception or the values instilled by leadership are causing issues, all veterinary hospitals just want their team happy.

You say tomato; I say tom<u>ah</u>to. In the end, we both just want a less toxic workplace environment.

But It's Only a Few People Who Are Toxic

You may only have a handful of bad apples in your hospital. However, while 90% of your team is a bunch of unicorns, the 10% is still causing significant harm. Does one bad apple spoil the entire team? Answer yes, and there's some interesting research to back it up.

Doctor Will Felps is an associate professor at the University of South Wales in Australia. He teaches and conducts research on a wide range of management-related topics, including how human behavior affects team dynamics. Doctor Felps' wife was particularly unhappy at work and told him how she noticed that her cold and unfriendly behavior seemed to have "infected" her coworkers. She noticed many were also displaying unfriendly behaviors after she came in to work a few days in a funk. This made Felps want to investigate the question of whether one person could influence an entire team's behavior.

He put together an experiment to see what would happen when a bad worker joined a team. Participants were divided into small groups, and each was given a task. In each group was an actor portraying a very loud characteristic such as a slacker, cheerleader, or negative depressive. For example, the slacker overpowered the group and exclaimed they thought the task was dumb and put their head on the table. The negative depressive voiced how there was no way the task could be completed and how they were sure the group would fail.

Remarkably, within 45 minutes, the rest of the group started behaving like the bad apple. The group that had the cheerleader actor was successful. However, several other participants in the group with the slacker actor also rested their heads on the table and gave up. The negative actor's team ended up thinking it was a stupid task. The study concluded that yes, one bad apple does ruin an entire team (Felps, 2006).

It's hard to believe our smart teams could be susceptible to one loud negative person. Still, multiple studies have found a single toxic team member can be the catalyst for the downward spiral of an entire team. These other studies have shown similar results, concluding that one negative team member causes teams to experience more conflict, have worse communication, and refuse to cooperate with one another. Employee behavior is contagious, and leaders need to understand the importance of curing it before it infects the entire team.

Different Toxic Traits

I think it's important that every manager or supervisor takes the time to get to know each one of their team members and what makes them tick. You should consider having teams take personality tests like DiSC or Myers-Briggs. These easy-to-take and often free tests will provide insight into each member's personality. How I communicate may be vastly different from how someone else communicates. Understanding these differences will help foster a more trusting and beneficial relationship. Learning about each one of your employees and truly caring about them will help you with difficult conversations when their behavior slips and moves into the undesirable category.

There is a myriad of different toxic team members. Each of them will require a similar but slightly different action on your part to pull them out of their toxicity. Not all team members who may contribute to issues within a team will have glaringly obvious toxic traits. Some are more subtle. The vast majority of team members causing issues within the hospital or team are not even aware that they are doing so. However, most teams will continue to deal with these toxic behaviors until they are beyond repair.

Each one of the toxic traits listed in the next box causes harm to a veterinary hospital and the team.

1. Territorial	9. Self-Entitlement
2. Controlling/Micromanaging	10. Gossiping
3. Overly Confident	11. Favoritism
4. No Voice	12. Bullying
5. Lack of Motivation	13. Lying
6. Discriminatory	14. Victim and Blamer
7. Emotional Leech	15. Doom and Gloom
8. Burned-out	16. Drama Lover

Arguably, each of these traits causes different degrees of harm, but regardless, they are all harmful. Recognizing any of these traits within your team member is the first key to adjusting these traits in the future. Never fear. We will dive into how to have tough conversations with employees exhibiting these traits and how to modify the behavior in future chapters. For now, let's identify the toxic players in our team.

Territorial

This trait is often pretty harmful to other employees. Teams may embody this trait, or it may be an individual. Often the team member or entire team exhibiting this trait has a level of seniority in which they believe they have a right to be possessive about some aspects of their job. The toxic traits manifest in conversations like these:

- "Why is that technician working on my patient? They better stop."
- "The surgery department better not come over to oncology and take our stuff."
- "It is none of the manager's business to ask me about my patient. They need to go back to their office."
- "That's my chair at the front desk. They better move."

- "Who touched my food bag and moved it? There better not be anything missing inside it!"
- "What is that doctor doing with my patient?"

This individual or team usually feels like they are above the rest of the team or hospital. They feel entitled to a certain territory within the hospital. They've put in their time and deserve to sit in the same chair daily. They don't see it as an issue because the area, chair, and computer belong to them. After all, they worked hard to earn that right. The team earned the right to store their supplies in the best drawer of the cabinet. No one better open it up except them.

Unfortunately, toxic territorial behavior causes riffs in the team. This member of the team doesn't trust others, and this causes a disconnect. Often the team or individual doesn't recognize that their behavior is malicious. After all, they deserve whatever it is they think belongs to them. Being territorial doesn't make others feel welcome, and it certainly is not a trait that represents belonging to a cohesive team.

Controlling/Micromanaging

These two terms are the same. This individual likes to control everything and does not like when things do not go according to plan. This may be a surgeon whose schedule has been derailed by a gastric dilatation volvulus now requiring emergency surgery. The results of this derailment include snapping orders at the team and being angry that their day is no longer in control.

This person is often a micromanager because that's how they maintain control. They like things done in a certain way or a certain order. They like to control their area of the hospital, team, or a particular case. If they need to request the help of others, they give detailed instructions and expect them to be followed so that control is maintained.

This person suffers from a lack of trust. They do not trust their team. As a result, their team often doesn't want to work with them because they feel like this individual does not trust them. "That's not how we do it here" is a common saying this individual likes to tell new hires. "Let me do it" is another frequently used sentence. Another slogan of the micromanager is, "It's easier if I just do it, so it gets done right." The team feels disconnected from the micromanager.

They often have a sense of pride and focus on meticulous detail in their work. They want to make sure it's done to perfection. They don't see the root cause of this toxicity is their inability to trust others.

Overly Confident 😎

This person is often a danger to themselves, the client, and the pet. They may or may not know that they lack skill or knowledge. Any person working outside their level of skill and knowledge in a medical hospital is dangerous. It is always better to have someone on the team who asks for help and knows what they don't know.

The overly confident person may think they know something when they do not. The other possibility is that the overly confident person lacks actual confidence and puts on an external appearance in an effort for people to like them. They prescribe to the "fake it until you make it" mantra.

Often this individual is not transparent and may even tell fibs to protect themselves. They never admit ignorance and always seem to have the answer for everything. They never admit mistakes. Regardless, if this person honestly believes they are skilled or whether they know they are faking it, it is harmful to the hospital.

No Voice

An individual who does not have a voice carries a silent toxic trait. This individual is always afraid of speaking up. They may see a problem and just ignore it. They dislike any conflict, so they figure it's best to keep their mouth shut and keep on doing the job to the best of their ability. Everyone has moments where they fear voicing their opinion, but this individual always has this trait.

This trait is almost as dangerous as the overly confident individual. This toxic trait causes a team member to see a medical mistake has been made, but they fail to speak up. They usually suffer from extreme imposter syndrome (where they doubt themselves), rendering them silent for fear of saying the wrong thing. They may also have given up on having a voice because they have learned that no one will listen or acknowledge them.

At meetings, when opinions matter, this individual rarely speaks up. As a result, they may become disgruntled and upset because they feel like no one cares about them. Every employee has an opinion, but this one simply never voices theirs.

This is a tricky toxic trait because, on the surface level, it seems quite benign. But this is not a healthy trait for a team member to have. Their opinions are valid. They probably have amazing thoughts and ideas, but they are poisoning the team and themselves because they remain silent.

Lack of Motivation

Yes, having a lack of motivation is a toxic trait. These individuals work at your hospital just to take home a paycheck. They provide a barely average job performance. The lack of motivation causes this individual to do just below the required amount needed to be considered an employee and earn a salary.

When the hospital gets busy, these are the people that are often seen moving at a snail's pace. This builds resentment and anger among the rest of the staff, who are working hard to keep up with the increased demand. Sadly, many individuals with a lack of motivation may also be burned-out. They have given up trying because they are crispy.

However, as leaders, we see them sitting more than anyone else. As a result, the complaints from their colleagues pile up. A lack of motivation frustrates everyone except the person who has it.

Discriminatory / Bias 😕

Unfortunately, these are two more prevalent toxic traits than many practices realize. Until we as leaders start to recognize that discrimination and bias are lurking in our hospitals, we will be blind to it. While they are different traits, they are also very similar. Sometimes they occur separately and sometimes together.

Bias is a belief that a group is inclined towards something. This bias suggests that a certain group has a predisposition towards a trait. For example, middle-aged white women complain a lot (sorry to everyone named Karen).

Discrimination is the actual act against someone because of a belief about a certain individual that usually falls into a category (race, religion, sex, etc.). A bias may cause someone to discriminate, but even in the lack of doing so, it is damaging as it perpetuates harmful beliefs towards individuals, resulting in obstacles for them.

We often think that discrimination and bias are obvious. We assume discrimination is when one employee walks up to another and tells them they can't work with them because of their race, religion, or gender. We assume bias is glaringly obvious and mean. That's rarely what happens.

More often, biased statements are rooted in off-color jokes focused on a certain race, religion, or sex of individuals. These bad statements are often centered around stereotypes which are incorrect and harmful. Discrimination often occurs subtly. For example, a woman isn't hired into a leadership role because she may get pregnant, which would cause project delays. Instead, the less qualified man is hired, and the woman is unaware of why she was passed up.

Those with one or both of these toxic traits are often unaware that they are causing harm. They can't see that others feel uncomfortable and that it's causing the workplace to be an unfriendly environment. For example, these individuals might have been brought up hearing jokes and conversations centered around a certain group. Now well into adulthood, a white employee may joke with a black colleague and say, "It's so nice outside we should hit the beach and go for a dip in the ocean. Oh, wait, you don't swim because you're black. Just kidding. Do you want to go?" They may not realize this is bias and socially unacceptable, especially in a workplace environment. We must address any discrimination or bias we hear about or see first-hand immediately. These traits will completely break down an entire team because it does not promote a psychologically safe work environment.

Emotional Leech

Everyone has a personal life outside of work. As human beings live their lives, tragic things happen. Human beings routinely suffer from losing loved ones, abuse, marital disagreements, illness, monetary issues, and child problems. For many, going to work is a reprieve from the daily drama in their personal lives. They get comfort from their wonderful work family, who is ready to accept them with open arms, make them laugh, and listen to them when they need it.

That said, many teams have one or more individuals who are emotional leeches. These individuals treat the team as if they are their personal psychologist or counselor. While teams are always willing to support their team members, the emotional leech drains the team daily with no end in sight.

Veterinary medicine is hard enough. It is an emotionally charged profession where life and death play out daily. Most team members are amazingly supportive individuals because they have great compassion and empathy, which has driven them into the line of work that they are currently in. However, when a team member airs all their emotions every day onto the team for weeks to months, it can become a toxic problem.

The team members don't want to tell this individual to stop because they recognize their struggle. However, they also no longer enjoy having conversations with this individual. The emotional leech has become solely dependent on the team for support and spends most days showcasing their wide range of emotions while expecting their teammates to listen and support them.

Burned-out

Burnout is perhaps one of the most common toxic traits veterinary professionals experience. Burnout is a cumulative process in which the individual slowly lacks empathy for a situation. They just stop caring about work. Usually, this is due to increased stress or workload. The increased workload and stress are combined with a lack of support or appreciation, resulting in a no f-bleeps-given attitude.

Interestingly, many of those who burnout are the top performers. They are the ones who stay later than most, pick up extra shifts and go the extra mile, often to the detriment of their well-being. Leaders don't recognize it in employees because the person is performing great, except their attitude starts to fumble. Surely someone who does so much isn't that burned-out? Sadly, they often are.

Burnout is probably one of the main reasons employees quit and leave a particular hospital or even the veterinary field entirely. They often take this burnout home with them, and it causes dysfunction in their personal lives outside of work.

Because the employee is often angry and negative, it leads to major disruption on the team and also contributes to the stress and negativity of others. Too often, hospitals think that burnout is "normal stress." It is not. There are many reasons why burnout may occur, but ultimately, recognizing that an employee is suffering from burnout is key.

Self-Entitlement ♛

This employee is difficult to deal with because they are often a high-performing individual. If I had to give it a percentage, I would say that, in my experience, 50% of self-entitled individuals are also burned-out. These two go hand-in-hand because those who are burned-out feel overworked and underappreciated. They start to give permission to their maladaptive behaviors because they feel they are entitled.

After all, they worked two extra shifts. "The reason why I'm so cranky today and biting everyone's head off is because I worked 60 hours this week." Are they not entitled to coming in late, complaining, and being rude to others? Of course not, but those that become self-entitled often do so because they feel their maladaptive behaviors are justified from all the extra hard work they did.

I was guilty of this. When I burned-out from one of my roles, I found myself showing up a few minutes late every day. When the hospital would call to see if I was available to come because someone had called out, I would purposely delay my response. I gave myself permission to do these things because I felt unappreciated. Certainly, these are not the worst self-entitled offenses, but they are just that.

This becomes particularly damaging when the self-entitled individual starts being a detriment to the rest of the team. They are late, and now the rest of the team is behind. They don't see as many appointments because they have been there for 10 years, so they deserve an easier schedule. Employees start to say things like, "They are allowed to do XYZ because that's just how they are. They've been here for a decade."

Self-entitled behavior is a toxicity. It tells the other hard-working employees that leadership permits certain individuals to misbehave. Should employees not be expected to perform at the same level and expectations year in and year out? Just because someone has been at the practice for a long time, are they awarded extra perks and permitted self-entitled behaviors?

When dealing with this toxic trait, we must figure out why employees feel self-entitled. The individual may not even notice that they're doing it because it's occurred gradually over months or years. Addressing this toxic trait sooner rather than later is the key to making sure it gets corrected quickly. It's much harder to get Dr. ABC to show up on time if we've allowed them to always come in late for five years. That is the fault of leadership.

Gossiping

This toxic trait remains one of the most prevalent in almost every veterinary hospital. In fact, when over 100 employees were polled as to what their least favorite thing was in their last job, it was gossip. Gossip is exceptionally damaging to an entire team. It can ostracize an individual or a group of people. It can divide the hospital and cause individuals to quit or even leave the profession entirely. It is the toxic trait everyone acknowledges exists in their hospital, yet very few people know how to stop it because most enjoy doing it.

In *Oops, I Became a Manager*, I addressed this topic in detail and even provided an example of how to create a no gossip agreement within a hospital. I would encourage you to review the information in my first book since it is helpful for reducing gossip in any hospital. Without question, this trait needs to be stopped for the team to be healthier and happier.

Favoritism

We all have people we connect with better than others in our hospital. There's no shame in saying that, and that's not necessarily a toxic trait. The toxicity comes into play when there's actual favoritism played towards the individual to the detriment of others. It may even be favoritism towards a group of individuals like a team.

When individuals work within a certain team, like the front office or a surgery department, it's hard for them not to play favorites towards their own. Unfortunately, toxicity comes into play when there is favoritism. It can be very damaging when a veterinarian feels ostracized by a group of technicians who prefer another veterinarian over them. The technicians treat one veterinarian well and will offer to help with client callbacks but give the cold shoulder to another and never offer help. When a manager gives a raise to an employee that may be their friend outside of work, that's favoritism.

Sometimes the individuals doing the favoritism are not even aware they are doing so. They are unaware they are causing harm or division with a particular individual or group. Other times it's maliciously intentional. Regardless, this toxic trait must be addressed.

Bullying

The bully is an individual who humiliates and uses abusive action or language to get the desired result. The bully's main desire is to humiliate, belittle, devalue, demoralize, or ridicule another in order to inflate their own ego or agenda. The bully may purposely sabotage a new employee from being successful. This is often considered a hazing ritual by more senior staff who don't even recognize that they are bullying. "No one helped me, so this new person needs to figure it out by themselves" is a form of bullying.

Often the person doing the bullying feels like they are performing some type of social justice. They ensure that the underperforming front desk employee knows they are doing a terrible job. They want to make sure that the new veterinarian knows exactly what the pecking order is. They must keep everyone in their place because they know what is best for the hospital.

I was recently a victim of bullying in a hospital. With 20+ years of experience, most of them in emergency medicine, and VTS credentials you would think I would be immune. No one is immune. I arrived for a shift at a hospital I had not worked in before but was there to observe the team and help out in the process. There had been some concern from leadership that the culture was not doing well. Most of the team greeted me with a friendly hello. Shortly after arriving, a pet owner rushed into the hospital with their dog who had just had a seizure. The dog was done having the seizure but was confused and disoriented, stumbling and falling down.

I offered to restrain the 65 lb (29.5 kg) dog while another veterinary technician placed the catheter. It was like restraining a bucking bronco. I was on top of the dog with it flailing around. Other veterinary technicians stood and watched, not offering to help, even though I smiled and said, "I could use some help here." The veterinary technician placing the catheter snapped at me, "Have you never restrained a dog before? I need you to keep it still so I can get the catheter in!" I explained I was doing my best, but the dog was post-ictal, and if someone else could help that would be great. She snapped again at me. "Well, it could be your skills." Wow.

After we successfully managed the catheter and dog, I saw the veterinary technician laughing, looking at me, and gesturing towards me while others laughed with her. One of them bent down and pretended to restrain an invisible dog while getting thrown around. They kept laughing and looking at me. I felt humiliated. Suffice to say this group of bullies was one of the big reasons for the hospital's culture issues.

Bullying ruins teams through its toxicity and causes individuals to quit or leave the profession. We need to stop the bullying so it doesn't lead to physical altercations, lawsuits, harassment, and the permission for others to bully.

Lying 😕

Lying occurs for many reasons, but the most common one is because of self-preservation. The liar is often trying to save face. Less commonly, the liar may be trying to become the center of attention for popularity reasons. Unfortunately, many leaders have created a culture of lying without even knowing it. For example, when employees constantly get in trouble over small things, like failing to take out the garbage, they resort to lying to avoid being written up.

Unfortunately, many liars are not even aware that they are lying. Brené Brown (*Dare to Lead*, 2018) wrote about individuals who suffer from confabulation. These are individuals who believe the lies to be true. Unfortunately, we find that confabulators can also get others to believe the lies. To stop the confabulation from happening, we need to listen to the fear or anxiety the individual is having. This can be a struggle when trying to reduce this toxic trait. First, the liar must have the emotional intelligence to recognize that they are, in fact, lying. It may seem obvious to us, but to the liar, they believe they are telling the truth.

Regardless of why it is happening, lying should not be accepted in any veterinary hospital. Often, the way to reduce this toxic trait in a hospital is to ensure that leaders reward honesty instead of punishing it.

Victim & Blamer 👉

This person is never at fault. They blame everyone else for any perceived injustice. This is a toxic trait because this individual lacks personal accountability. They are never responsible for their actions because they are the victim.

This toxic trait usually happens because the individual is very insecure. It's similar to the liar, except they blame others more frequently to downgrade their mistakes or showcase that they are the victim. The liar just lies. The blamer can't see their responsibility in the situation.

Leaders often feel bad for individuals with this toxic trait. "The other team couldn't get an IV catheter in. That's why I had to leave the patient I was monitoring under general anesthesia. We need better-trained staff so I can focus on just one thing!" It's never their fault, and there's an excuse for everything. It may take a long time for a leader to recognize that this individual can't always be the victim.

Doom & Gloom

Every hospital team has a doom and gloom individual. This is someone who sees nothing but negativity in every situation.

The toxicity of this trait starts the minute the individual walks through the hospital door. The weather is terrible, their personal life is terrible, it's going to be another terrible day, and the world is terrible. This toxic trait is exhausting to the rest of the team. The doom and gloom individual sucks the positivity out of the room and infuses negativity wherever they go.

Negativity is like a disease in that it spreads quickly. As a leader, it is important to quickly recognize if a team member is exhibiting this toxic trait in order to deal with it as soon as possible.

Drama Lover

Most everyone I know has worked with someone who loves drama. They thrive on it. Often this person is a big gossiper or at least loves hearing it. The more emotions, the better.

Many times, this individual doesn't realize they are doing themselves harm. By always living in drama, they rarely get to relax and struggle with letting the small things go. Everything is a crisis. Everything is a problem. There is often a high level of anxiety with this toxic trait. Why is everything a crisis to them? It often stems from the worry of the what-ifs that have not occurred.

The printer runs out of toner. Normally this would result in a few curse words, some quick troubleshooting of who could run to the store, and that would be the end of the situation. The drama lover brings in the emotion, the exaggeration, the chaos. "We've run out of toner! How are we supposed to print invoices? No one has the time to run to the store. This is going to cause a backup in discharging pets! Our doctors will be angry. I hope no one quits over this!" It's just ink. No drama needed. Unfortunately, this person now has others believing it to be a crisis and feeding into the drama.

Leaders need to get to the root as to why everything is a perceived crisis. This toxic trait can be difficult to manage because the offender doesn't see the harm. They see the benefit they are providing by alerting the team to what is or could be happening.

What Do We Do with the Toxicity?

I recognize that there are probably other toxic traits that I have missed on this list. However, those listed are arguably some of the most prevalent in veterinary hospitals. Recognizing that not all toxic traits stem from negativity and gossip allows us to identify harmful characteristics that poison our veterinary teams without us knowing it. All toxic traits will slowly or quickly decrease the team's or individual's overall happiness and health at the hospital. Recognizing toxic traits is the first step to improving the team's culture. The second step starts with leadership.

Chapter Three

It Starts With Leadership

"Why am I Babysitting Adults?"

This thought crossed my mind numerous times early on in my career after taking my first leadership role. It seemed like all I did was one counseling session after another. I found myself having to repeat the same policies over and over throughout any given year. I felt like I was babysitting adults.

- "Who left an empty roll of toilet paper in the bathroom?"
- "This is the third time you ran out of gas coming to work. Let's brainstorm ways for you to remember to fuel up."
- "Please stop watching *Keeping Up with the Kardashians* on your phone while at the front desk in front of clients."
- "I know you say you're sick, but you posted on social media that you were out all-night drinking and partying."
- "No, you cannot bring your boyfriend to work and have him wait for you in the treatment room while you monitor anesthesia on a spay."
- "Can you please change your scrub pants to ones that don't have giant holes in the knees?"
- "Yes, if the shift starts at 7:00 am, that does, in fact, mean you need to be ready to work at 7:00 am."

- "No, you cannot smoke marijuana on your lunch break. Yes, you are correct. It is legal in this state, but no, it's not the same as smoking a cigarette."

The list of statements similar to these that have come out of my mouth over the years goes on and on. At some point, all leaders question whether or not they are babysitting adults and make the following statement, "I did not sign up for this."

It goes beyond statements like these as well. I cannot recount the hundreds of hours I spent counseling employees on personal life issues. I have listened to so many sad stories about hardship and how it has crossed over into their work performance. While I have great compassion and empathy for these individuals, I found myself in my early leadership roles saying, "Why is this my problem?"

I wanted these employees struggling with work-life balance to simply "get their shit together" and just do their job well. I felt like it was beneath me to listen to their issues. After all, my only job as a leader was to make sure employees performed well in their role at the veterinary hospital. Providing coaching on personal life matters was above my pay grade. Life outside of work wasn't my concern, but somehow, it became mine. Why couldn't they just act like adults and do their jobs?!

Reshape Your Thinking

Does the above resonate with you? Are you having similar thoughts? Do you wonder why you even took on a leadership role because you now have become both a counselor and a babysitter? I have some disheartening news for you. That is what being a leader is all about. Sadly, too many leaders are unaware that mentoring and coaching individuals are their primary responsibilities.

So many of us who moved from the floor to a leadership role still perform medical or front office duties in conjunction with our leadership functions. Our first love that drove us to veterinary medicine was the animals. This is also true for many of those who are customer service representatives. They were driven to work in veterinary medicine because they have a "help the people, help the pets" mentality.

It can be a struggle for us to balance between the medicine and coaching a team. We have the same stresses as those working on the floor, but we have the additional stress of coaching and mentoring a team.

Liane Davey (2013), the author of the *New York Times* Bestseller *You First*, writes that to change a toxic team, leaders must start with positive assumptions. Unfortunately, too many leaders think poorly or negatively about their teams. They talk and think about their team as if the team is a burden to them. As a result, the team has become a hassle to the leader. The reality is that any time a leader feels that the team is a bother or a hassle, they need to rethink whether or not they want the leadership role. You must start with positive assumptions if you want to improve the culture of your team.

You're Not Going to Get the Golden Ticket

Very few leaders get a perfect team. Many leaders are promoted into new leadership roles because hospitals recognize a lack of leadership in a particular area of the hospital. The role never previously existed, and now management is throwing a leader into the role in hopes of repairing a damaged team.

Some leaders find their way into their role because another leader has left. Often, the departure of the prior manager or supervisor was because they were frustrated with either their own leadership or the hospital team. The prior manager left saying, "Good riddance," and ran out of the hospital as fast as they could. Now you are in charge of controlling the dumpster fire.

Very few leaders find themselves being handed a team that is cohesive and functioning well. Furthermore, very few are given any coaching by the prior manager before taking over the new team.

I can never understand why leaders seem surprised that they are now responsible for improving a dysfunctional, toxic team. Many were part of that toxic, dysfunctional team before moving into a manager or supervisor role.

As much as leaders complain about coaching, it is the job of any leader to coach an individual to become a great employee, including addressing personal life issues. While it is not your job to coach their personal life, you need to coach them on how to manage their personal life and still be an amazing veterinary professional. I will dive into how to navigate some of these more difficult conversations in more detail later in the book.

Stop Your Toxic Traits

Many leaders are toxic, and they don't even know it. The best-selling book *What Got You Here Won't Get You There* by authors Marshall Goldsmith and Mark Reiter discuss 20 traits that hold leaders back from being their best selves (2007).

1. Winning Too Much: You must be right and win at all costs.
2. Adding Too Much Value: You know stuff, cool, but that doesn't mean you need to add two cents to every discussion.
3. Passing Judgment: You rate others and feel they all need to meet your standards.
4. Making Destructive Comments: We will address this in more detail later in the book. Just know there is no room for sarcasm and cutting remarks in leadership.

5. Starting With "No," "But," and "However": Stop using negative qualifiers, which really means, "I'm right" and "You're wrong."

6. Telling the World How Smart We Are: You're in a leadership role. Stop trying to prove or show everyone you are smart.

7. Speaking When Angry: Don't use emotional volatility as a management tool.

8. Negativity or "Let Me Explain Why That Won't Work": Don't be the leader where everything is centered on negativity, what may go wrong, or how it may fail.

9. Withholding Information: Don't be an information hoarder where you try to maintain an advantage over others.

10. Failing to Give Proper Recognition: Leaders must acknowledge others frequently.

11. Claiming Credit We Don't Deserve: Your team will stop trusting you if you don't give credit where it's due.

12. Making Excuses: Owning up to our mistakes is a trait of a great leader. Making excuses is not.

13. Clinging to the Past: Leaders blame the past to deflect away from themselves. Pasts may shape, but they do not define.

14. Playing Favorites: Leaders often fail to see they are being unfair.

15. Refusing to Express Regret: Many leaders believe apologizing is a sign of weakness when it's actually a strength.

16. Not Listening: This shows complete disrespect to your team.

17. Failing to Express Gratitude: Leaders need to say thank you.

18. Punishing the Messenger: We call this referred aggression in cats where you bite the person who is providing the message of, "The team is struggling."

19. Passing the Buck: "It's not my fault because…". The need to blame everyone else.

20. An Excessive Need to Be "Me": Using the excuse, "It's just who I am as a person," is never a good trait as a leader.
   (Goldsmith, 2007)

Throughout the book, we will discuss some of these negative leadership traits. The first step is looking at yourself and seeing if any of them resonate with you. I know I've done my fair share of many of these throughout my leadership career. Catch yourself in the moment when one of these traits sneaks up on you. Then, stop yourself and pivot back to healthier behaviors. These traits are only meant to hinder you from being successful as a leader.

Setting up for Successful Change in the Team

I want to ensure you are set up for success as a leader. I know firsthand the failure of not having the basics set up in the hospital to be a successful leader. It can feel like you're the only one who is trying to make a difference which can lead to frustration, heartache, anger, and eventually resentment. You blame yourself for not being able to improve the team's culture when in reality, you simply lack the tools, organization, and resources necessary to be able to make the change.

Make sure your hospital has a good organizational structure, career paths for the team, salary ranges, and the right people in leadership roles. Refer to my first book, where it lays the foundation for you to be successful as a leader. Even the most experienced leaders will fail if put in adverse conditions in which they cannot be successful. Trying to change a negative team or individual to a positive one is hard enough but attempting to do so without being set up for success will surely fail.

Steps to Changing the Team

1) Start with Assuming Good Intention
2) Take Full Ownership
3) Get the Facts and Seek the Truth
4) Set New Behavior Standards
5) Elevate the Superstars
6) Embrace Polite, Kind, & Honest Conversations
7) Continue to Celebrate & Work for the Wins
8) Grow New Leaders
9) Keep Learning & Be Kind to Yourself
10) Make Tough Decisions When Needed

Each of these topics will be touched upon in this chapter, but some require a more in-depth explanation. I will be expanding on these in future chapters, including communication skills which will span over three chapters. But, for now, we will brush over each of these important concepts. Together they are the meat and bones of successful change management in our hospitals.

Assume Good Intention

As a leader, you need to assume good intention of your team. They are not purposely trying to ruin the hospital with negativity, but it certainly does seem like it at times to any leader. Before you can focus on a more positive assumption of your team, you must be aware of your negative thoughts about them. You need to assume good intention.

Your team is not happy being unhappy. In fact, they are often quite miserable. This misery transfers into their personal life. We see it manifest into marital issues, disconnection from children, and broken friendships. All veterinary professionals want to work in a unicorn hospital. You know, the one where everyone is happy, all pets are saved from disease and injury while clients shower the veterinary staff with praise and admiration. While that seems like a stretch, your team wants to work in a healthy workplace environment. Your team is miserable with being so negative all the time, and they may not even realize their home life is suffering because of it.

If you honestly believe your team is happy being miserable and trying to ruin the hospital on purpose, then I hate to be the one to tell you that you are part of the problem. Only when you assume good intention will you be able to listen, learn, and gain value from your team. Once you can recognize that your team wants to change and needs your help doing so, you will be in a better position to help cultivate that change.

Take Full Ownership

You, as a leader, must be committed to the change. You may be looking just to change one person's toxic trait that is damaging both them and the team, or you may be looking to change a group. It's one thing to assume good intention, but the team will continue to fail unless you take full ownership of the team's well-being.

Too often, leaders feel their responsibility is only to improve the medicine of the team, ensure everyone shows up to work on time, and clients are happy. It's all of those things and more.

Don't think of the team's struggles as burdens but rather challenges that will help you grow as a leader. Take full ownership of the goal of improving a particular team or an individual employee rather than just picking out the easy pieces or the ones you know you will succeed with. When you take full ownership of every aspect of the team, you will be more successful as a leader.

Get the Facts and Seek the Truth

Even if you suspect why a particular individual is negative or a team is toxic, pretend like you don't know anything. Get others' perspectives. Ask questions, listen, be curious, and welcome feedback.

If you are working to improve a team's culture, you must ask the question, "As a leader, what can I improve upon?" Chapter Six will discuss this further because it is the starting point for developing polite, kind, and honest (PKH) conversations.

As leaders, we must recognize and take ownership that sometimes, we may have created a certain level of negativity or toxicity within our hospitals. Leaders are not perfect. When receiving the criticism, stay neutral. Listen without judgment to seek to understand what others' grievances are. Don't respond except to thank them for their honesty.

Getting facts and seeking the truth can be hard for many leaders. It's hard for individuals to hear concerns and criticism and even harder if it's directly about leadership. Unless leaders can be open to hearing from their employees, things will remain unchanged.

Set New Behavior Standards

It is a leader's job to set the bar. Where you elect to set that bar is entirely up to you. However, if you set the bar and then adjust it for those underperforming, it is unfair to those doing good work. Over time, those that are doing good work will see that the bar has been lowered, and they will adjust their good work to mediocre or even fair to meet the new lowered bar standards. After all, if other employees can get away with subpar standards, then why can't they?

Imagine being the best player on a soccer team. Every time you did something great, your coach ignored you. Meanwhile, those struggling had the coach's full attention. As the All-Star player you would eventually start looking for someone who appreciates your superstar quality. This is the same in your hospital.

If you have adjusted the bar for negative behaviors of certain individuals, then the bar will need to be reset. Informing the entire team of the new standards and expectations is important.

When working to improve behaviors, you will need to coach individuals towards correcting actions or behavior. Any manager, supervisor, or director must ensure that everything is documented. This is not just to prevent legal issues down the road but also so the leader can remember what course of action was taken to help develop this individual.

The caveat to setting a bar is that you need to hold people accountable. Stop providing excuses for those that are failing to meet the standards and constantly going below the bar. Be careful where you set the bar. I have seen leaders set a bar too high, resulting in the team failing to meet the high standards. The bar should be set in a fair and reasonable place.

Elevate the Superstars

Too often, managers and supervisors focus on those that are struggling and underperforming. They spend countless hours counseling and coaching those that are toxic and causing dysfunction to the team. Instead, leaders need to focus on amplifying the voices of the superstars. These individuals excel in their position, have ideas, and bring value to the hospital and team.

The Ladders is a job site that helps connect employers with qualified candidates and is dedicated to creating education about how to be a great manager and teammate. In a 2018 Ladders article, a poignant quote slapped me in the face and was one of those a-ha moments. "This is the unforeseen consequence of weak performers: they poison your company's culture and demotivate your more foundational players (Paley, 2015)." Isn't that the truth?

I am not saying that we shouldn't try to help the underperformers or coach those with toxic traits, but we can offer only so much coaching and support as a leader. It may be that this individual would be better suited to a different practice or role. Perhaps they would be more successful in a different profession. Everyone excels at something. Our job is to help our player realize their full potential in whatever that may be. However, when we spend most of our time putting out fires and hosting long coaching sessions with individuals who do not improve, we lose focus of our superstars. If we find ourselves trying to micromanage all the issues, we do a disservice to the exceptional people.

When we elevate our superstars and develop their leadership skills, they are more likely to generate new ideas that increase business or productivity in our hospital. They are also more likely to recommend other great new hires. When we keep our superstars happy, they stay motivated and enthusiastic, which is infectious to the rest of the team. Never forget that one of your main jobs as a leader is to grow future leaders. We all want a team of unicorns.

Embrace Polite, Kind, & Honest (PKH) Conversations

This is the backbone of changing a toxic team or individual. This concept will be fully discussed in Chapter Six. My success as a leader was largely because of my ability to have polite, kind, and honest conversations. While it came naturally to me, I recognize that it may not for others. The polite and kind part usually happens, but the honest part of the conversation is often the hardest part.

Change starts when we assume good intention and see that our team is not purposefully trying to sabotage the hospital. We must then accept that it is our responsibility to improve an individual or team and seek to discover why the negativity is occurring. Next, we commit ourselves to setting a bar that we feel is both fair and obtainable to the team in terms of excellence that we are looking for within our hospital. We elevate our superstars, so the team realizes what behavior we desire. Then, for our underperformers and those with negative traits, we need to dive into the PKH conversations with them individually. This is probably the hardest part of changing an individual or team's culture, but it is one of the most important.

PKH is a skill that must be learned and practiced in order for someone to become fluent in it. It's much like learning a certain surgery or how to perform a dental prophy. It takes time to get comfortable and excel at it. We will start introducing this concept in Chapter Six, complete with a step-by-step of how to introduce it to your team. If you get an opportunity to attend a workshop / continuing education seminar or have the ability to hire a consultant to work one-on-one with the team, it is an even better way to learn this skill.

Continue to Celebrate and Work for the Wins

Too often, a leader lays down a foundation to improve hospital culture. The work that the leader has done was time-consuming and thoughtful. The whole team is excited about becoming more positive. The leader sits back in their chair, grabs a drink, and is happy the hard work is over. Six months later, the team is just as miserable. What happened?

The leader forgot to continue to celebrate the wins. Too many hospitals have a big meeting that focuses on how the leadership and team are committed to changing the culture. The problem is, that's where the conversation ends. Change does not occur overnight. While there is no set time that most employees accept change, most references suggest it takes at least six months to see if the change sticks. The change might take years if the entire team was on the struggle bus. That's right, years of constant gentle pressure in moving the needle of change and rewarding when it inches forward.

As a leader, you will need to work for the change while constantly and consistently celebrating the wins. Talk is one thing, but the relentless pursuit of change is another. Checking in and making sure the change is being worked on is important. No one is handed a win. You have to work for it, which makes the celebration so much sweeter.

I Was Handed a Team with 60% Turnover

Many years ago, a team was thrust upon me. I had not sought out a leadership role, but one was assigned to me. I was terrified to lead this team. Some of its best superstars had walked out in a blaze of glory from the hospital. Two completely left the veterinary profession altogether, citing that the hospital's dysfunction finally drove them to leave their true passion. The rest of the team that left went to work for competitor hospitals. Out of 15 employees, nine quit in four months. This left six full-time and several part-time team members to fill the hours of a 24/7 emergency hospital.

Those that remained in the hospital were pretty upset that I was now their manager. No one consulted with them. My transition into the manager role was dropped on them like a hot pile of dog poop. In my first team meeting, I took the most polite, kind, and honest approach anyone could take. I told them I had no idea what I was doing. It was quite true. I had no idea how I was going to lead this particular team. I told them I would need their support if we were going to become a happier team. I told them that I cared about all of them and didn't want to lose another member. Thankfully, they believed me to be sincere.

Talk about having my work cut out for me when it came to working for the wins. I would need to put in a lot of work over many years to improve the team.

A few truly toxic individuals were still on the team, but the vast majority, while unhappy, wanted to become a more positive and cohesive team. In the first few months of my new role, I did everything I just described.

I assumed good intention and believed the team to be caring and kind at its core. I took full ownership of the issues and dedicated myself to resolving them by finding out why the team was unhappy. I mapped out where I wanted to see the team go and set a bar that I wanted to obtain. I rallied my superstars around me, constantly thanked them for their support, and asked for their opinions and ideas. I had one PKH conversation after another.

It took a good two years to turn the team around and get them to where I had set the bar years prior. Thus, expecting a change to occur from a week with a consulting company or an hour-long continuing education (CE) webinar on team development is unrealistic. If it is done right, it is one of the most rewarding highlights of any manager's career, but doing it right takes time.

Grow New Leaders

Leadership skills are not for you to hoard. The best leaders start to cultivate and grow new leaders. Who wouldn't want a team of amazing superstar leaders? Never fear. Your job is secure if you're doing a great job of growing your team into potential leaders.

Once we start down the path of creating change within an individual or team, our focus must shift to growing them into the leader we know they are. I can hear some of you saying, "Amy, not all people are leaders." As I have mentioned previously, everyone excels at something.

There is something that every single person on your team does better than you. While I do not believe every person can lead others, I do believe that everyone is a leader in something. And yes, I'll go so far as to say it's possible that individual may excel in something outside of a veterinary hospital. Sometimes we grow individuals by having them find their passions and talent and that means some of those individuals were never meant to work in veterinary medicine.

As a leader, your job is to figure out what they excel in and what they are passionate about. Then, once we get them in a mindset where they want to be more positive and contribute better to the hospital, we need to continue to improve them by tailoring our coaching. Great leaders know how to grow leaders.

Keep Learning & Be Kind to Yourself

As you work to improve an individual or a team, you need to not forget about yourself. Keeping yourself educated with new leadership skills is important to ensuring that you can be the best leader for the team. Don't assume all the answers are in one book. I certainly hope you think this is a good book, but you shouldn't stop reading after this. I'd be upset with you if this was the last book you read on leadership. Be active in leadership groups you find via social media, private companies, or other websites.

There will be times when you will get stuck trying to make a change. It could be that a particular employee is not making any improvement, and you have tried everything. The team was doing better but now has resorted to their old ways of gossiping and bullying. Reach out to others in a similar role and ask for suggestions. Listen to a podcast focused on the leadership topic you are struggling with. It's important that you recognize you don't have all the answers to solve a particular issue, and that's okay.

Most importantly, make sure you are kind to yourself throughout this process. You will feel defeated at times. There will be moments where you feel like there has not been any progress.

During National Veterinary Technician Week (celebrated in the United States) one year, I saw the most disheartening social media post from a veterinary technician manager. She had used some of her own money to put together hand-painted bags for each of the 14-member team she was responsible for. She spent countless hours creating the bags. She then filled them with thoughtful gifts and trinkets meant to make them feel special. She was proud of her work, and she did it because she genuinely cared about each member on her team. She wanted them to feel special during the week.

She meticulously laid out the bags on the break room table so that when people walked in, they would see them. She hung up balloons and a big banner that said thank you. Her office was only a few feet from the break room. She decided she would let the team find the bags all on their own.

Shortly after she sat down, she heard a team member find the bags. She was thrilled! That team member called out to other team members. "Hey, everyone, come here!" She strained towards the room to hear their excitement but heard none. Instead, she heard team members saying, "I would've rather have gotten money. Is this all we're getting? They think we are worth a bag of crap?" She was heartbroken. She beat herself up. She took to social media to see what she had done wrong.

Whenever I think of that post, my heart breaks for that particular technician manager. She didn't do anything wrong. Her team was not in a place to accept her kindness. It was quite obvious to me and other managers who consoled her that her team had bigger issues. They were unable to appreciate her hard work because they were drowning in their own negativity.

As a leader, you will have moments like this. Be kind to yourself. Surround yourself with those who support you and who will lift you up when you feel like you are drowning. So long as you are taking forward steps towards helping an individual or team, then that's all you can do. It is up to them to want to change. You cannot force them to. Some individuals are too angry and bitter to help. That is the tough reality of being a leader.

When you feel beaten up and destroyed, remember the truth. You are working hard. You are a good leader. You are working towards improvement. You must be kind and help yourself, or you will be ineffective to the team.

Make Tough Decisions When Needed

The decision to terminate an employee should be one of the hardest and most thought-out decisions any leader makes. But, unfortunately, it is part of being a leader. One day you will likely play a role in terminating an employee. Whether you are a supervisor or manager, your views and recommendations will directly impact the terminated employee as well as the team.

Chapter Sixteen will go into more detail about when to consider letting someone go, suggestions on how to let someone go, and what impact it will have on you as a leader. With any luck, utilizing the recommendations in this book will help keep terminations minimal throughout your career.

Leadership has a responsibility to help any toxic team member, or an entire team, to work towards a happier workplace environment. That responsibility requires the leader to create change, which can seem like a daunting task. This chapter sought to break down, at a high level, the key ingredients needed to create that change. Subsequent chapters will dive into these topics in more detail to provide a systematic approach to tackling your toxic team.

Chapter Four

#Winning

We have already talked about setting a bar. For example, you might set a bar for the skill level of veterinary technicians/nurses. You might set another bar level for how clients are treated. You might set the bar for how much each veterinarian needs to gross in a year. But how does one set the bar for the type of culture and climate you want in your hospital? Ultimately, all veterinary hospitals want to be financially prosperous and perceived as successful places of employment by veterinary professionals. Therefore, the culture you are trying to obtain is one of #winning.

A culture of winning happens when people embrace the hospital that they are working in. They brag to their friends and family about the medicine they are performing and the pet lives they are saving. They become fiercely protective of their hospital team and talk about it as if it is their family because it is. The team respects each other's opinions and differences and values everything that each one brings to the table. It's not to say that it's always sunshine and rainbows, but it is the vast majority of the time.

Before we dive into the nuances of how to change a toxic team member or an entire team, I think it's important to realize what we are all striving for. We want the unicorn hospital that our employees enjoy coming to and others want to work for. We want that culture of #winning.

Stop Leading & Start Coaching

The best leaders coach each of their team members to become great. When we think about what a coach does, they groom each player to be the best they can be in that role. They want them to be a leader of that particular position or skill set. They don't tell them to simply "do the best you can." Instead, they expect the individual they are coaching to be great so the team will win. That is what every manager and supervisor should strive for in each of their employees.

Coaching and sports psychology go hand in hand. An article that sought to create a framework for linking the two found that coaches performed better when they focused on their athletes' mental mindset (Gee, 2010). Another study by the Canadian Olympic Committee found that a strong coach and athlete relationship was the most significant contributor to having athletes win or have their best performance at the 2008 Olympics in Beijing (Hanson, 2020). Countless studies have proven the same. Coaches have the ability to elevate their athletes to levels of winning time and time again simply by building the relationship and then the skill set.

Ultimately, building a better relationship between a coach and an athlete occurs through conversations, observing the player, trusting, and learning about each other. The deeper the coach's relationship with the athlete, the more likely they will be successful. We can see this correlation in our veterinary teams. A great leader's ability to elevate and coach a team to success and greatness cannot be underestimated. Leaders who develop healthy and trusting relationships with each team member are more likely to succeed.

Too often, leaders have a predetermined path for their employees. They have their eyes set on a particular team member, grooming them to be the newest supervisor. Excellent coaches ensure that they never push their players into positions they do not want or are not ready for.

Excellent coaches provide an equal amount of coaching time to the underperformers because they know that the entire team must be at its best in order to win. What does it take to be an excellent coach? How can we groom employees into greatness?

Great coaches focus on eight key steps to develop an athlete. These steps are important to understand so you can direct a team or individual to #winning. When you want to turn that cranky team upside down, you must address each of these steps to make effective change.

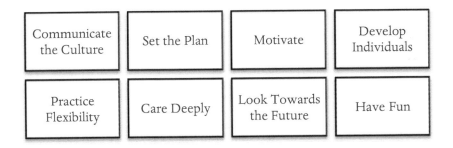

Communicate the Culture	Set the Plan	Motivate	Develop Individuals
Practice Flexibility	Care Deeply	Look Towards the Future	Have Fun

Communicate the Culture

How you decide to communicate the ideal culture is of equal importance to you executing it. If you fail to communicate it appropriately, you might as well kiss your vision goodbye. You want each player on your team to see what you see. They need to visualize the win. Amazing coaches are excellent at this. Scientific data supports that visualization of being successful is the very thing that earns the win.

Let's take the example of the 2021 United States National Football League (NFL) Super Bowl championship game. Tom Brady left the New England Patriots (being a New Englander, my soul is still crushed) and joined the Tampa Bay Buccaneers. Before Brady joined, Tampa Bay was one of the worst teams in the league. The chances of one player making a difference seemed impossible. Yet, from the moment Tom Brady joined Tampa Bay, all he talked about was how they would win the Super Bowl. He communicated his vision to his team, the media, and the coaches. Many laughed. Countless critics said Brady had made the worst decision of his career. It didn't matter that few believed Brady in his claim that Tampa Bay would win the Super Bowl. The only thing that mattered was that his team believed it. Tom Brady took one of the worst teams in NFL history and won the Super Bowl that year simply because he had a vision. That's how powerful a winning mindset is.

In our hospitals, this translates to winning with a positive culture versus losing to a negative one. Too often, a team member or the entire team feels that no change could occur. The hospital is simply going to remain a terrible place of employment. It doesn't matter what is tried. It's going to remain in the suck-state forever.

What is the vision you want for your hospital? What do you see it becoming? The most common vision we will be communicating to our team is one they want desperately for themselves. Our vision is for our team to be the best and work in the best workplace environment. You will want to paint a picture that taps into what your team is aspiring for.

Creating a mission, vision, and values for your hospital is important. A mission is the core purpose of your hospital. "We strive to offer our community the best and least expensive veterinary care." That is an example of a clear mission. Everything the hospital does should be centered around that mission. Are you still offering the least expensive services if you decide to increase prices? If not, you are going against the mission you set for your hospital. Missions are clear, concise, and not too lengthy. In one sentence, you should be able to communicate what your hospital stands for. This mission sets the tone for the culture. For example, Apple's current mission statement, which has changed over the years, is, "to bring the best personal computing products and support to students, educators, designers, scientists, engineers, businesspersons, and consumers in over 140 countries around the world." Everything they do is centered on that mission and you get a sense of who Apple is and what its business stands for.

The vision is a description of what you want to achieve in the future. It is what the company wants for themselves in the future and is the thing they strive for. Garmin's vision is, "We will be the global leader in every market we serve, and our products will be sought after for their compelling design, superior quality, and best value." Wow. Talk about ambition. Visions are fun to write, but they also need to be realistic. You can't write a vision of, "We will be the first veterinary hospital on the moon servicing the space pets of tomorrow," unless you have a rough outline of how you are getting to the moon. The vision you have for your veterinary hospital should evoke a sense of pride in employees and clients.

The last part of identifying who you are as a hospital is to create your values. What is important to your hospital? What values do you hold close? These values help you achieve your vision and ensure your mission stays on target. Amazon has several values, "Customer obsession rather than competitor focus, passion for invention, commitment to operational excellence, and long-term thinking. Amazon strives to be Earth's most customer-centric company, Earth's best employer, and Earth's safest place to work." Talk about values designed to create an impactful and healthy culture.

All three, the mission, vision, and values, are part of the culture. They create a feeling within your hospital. Think about certain brands and how they feel for you. What about Subaru? How does it feel? Most every car commercial is centered around nature, the outdoors, and how a Subaru can connect you with the environment. When you think of Lexus, you don't have that same feeling. That feeling of the outdoors is the culture Subaru wants you to feel. In everything they do, they tie it back to their culture so they provide consistent messaging.

I have owned Swatch watches since the 1980s, and I still wear them to this day. To me, they are fun, whimsical, and unique. All their ads are centered around fun, colors, and whimsy. If I think of Rolex, I think of wealth, business and seriousness. I'd much rather own something fun that makes me smile or laugh. Swatch culture resonates with me better.

There are many blogs, articles, and chapters centered around the art of writing the perfect mission, vision, and value statements. I've sat in plenty of meetings that dragged on because team members were arguing over one word here or there. Mission, vision, and value statements are important. I'd encourage every hospital to complete theirs but spending days or weeks on them takes the fun out of what they were meant to be: improving the culture. Remember that mission, vision, and values can be modified at any time, so even though the team says, "we're done," you can revisit them in a year and see if anything needs a tweak or two.

After identifying who you are as a hospital, it's time to make it fun. Can your employees be called something other than employees? This brings people a sense of unity, like sports teams' experience. Players on a team are called Ravens, Phillies, and Bruins. They are a Bruin. They are a Raven. I once knew a veterinary hospital called Robin Animal Hospital. The team nicknamed themselves the "birds." When the manager arrived each day, they would say, "Morning birdies." Cute. The team loved it and took pride in it as it was part of their culture.

Is there a way to incorporate fun into your culture so people can feel what it means to be part of your hospital team? Can you start each day off with positivity where a different team member shares a special moment that ties back to the hospital's values? For example, if one value is respect, a team member may tell a quick story during the morning moment by recounting, "I watched an angry client yell at Avery yesterday. I was proud of her because she was respectful and kind despite the client's behavior." What a way to start the day.

Can we get the team together for five minutes in the middle of the day and have another magical moment discussed that is centered around our culture? What about the end of the day? My brain thought about calling it a happy-ending moment, but I'll leave that idea for you to decide if you want to run with it or not. Tee-hee. ☺

Too often there is a mission, vision, and values plastered on a wall. It is left there and eventually forgotten. In everything you do, you need to remind your team of what makes the hospital special.

Why don't more veterinary hospitals provide employees with logoed items? It's great advertising for your employees to walk around in a t-shirt with the hospital's name on them, but it also gives them a sense of pride. I worked for two different hospitals. One provided me with only scrubs and a sweatshirt. The other provided me with t-shirts, jackets, fleeces, and more. The clothes were comfortable, and as such, I wore them outside my house a lot. Frequently strangers would come up to me and say, "You work at XXX veterinary hospital? I love that place," or "Can you tell me about XXX veterinary hospital?" Once I had a 30-minute conversation with a grocery clerk about what emergency veterinary medicine was.

All of these small things end up with employees feeling a certain way about the veterinary hospital. When they say to their friends, "Today is random act of kindness day, so I need to get there early so I can decorate someone's locker," you know that hospital's culture is something special.

Communicating who you are to your team is important. If your mission, vision, and values are consistently backed up by action, your team members will begin to believe it. You must get them to believe they work at the best veterinary clinic. Communicate your vision, make it fun, and the team will put in the hard work and see the victory.

Set the Plan

We have now communicated our vision to an employee or team. We are excited about the future; they know we care about them. Time to set the plan.

Take the example of a burned-out employee. We remember when that employee joined the hospital two years ago and was excited to be part of the team. They were motivated and enthusiastic. We want to get them back to that state of emotional well-being and joy. Having a conversation with them that reminds them of how they used to enjoy working at the hospital is powerful. Like Tom Brady, paint a picture of winning. "You have valid reasons for being burned-out. The hospital is working on improving many of the concerns you and the team have. Now my mission is to focus on you. My vision is to have you return to your excited self. The one where you love practicing medicine again. I know together we can make that happen." Now we need to set the plan.

Coaches do this all the time. They see a goal, talk to the team about the goal, and set a plan in motion. However, if the team or individual has not bought into the vision, you can throw out the plan. In response to the above statement, if the employee replies with, "I don't think I'll ever be excited about veterinary medicine again," you, as the leader, need to get them to believe they can. Unfortunately, even if you are the best leader, your employee may not buy in. It is up to the employee to get excited, see the vision, and want to work to obtain it.

Before meeting with any team or individual, we must figure out the best plan to obtain our vision. We can't simply go to an employee and ask them to fix themselves if we don't have a clear plan for how to do so. Asking them to stop with the negativity is pretty obscure and too broad. How does one stop the negativity? What does that even mean? Unfortunately, this is how most managers set a plan. They identify an issue and tell the employee or team what they want fixed by saying, "Don't do XYZ."

When dealing with toxic traits and teams, we need to play a more active role in helping that person or team obtain the desired outcome we are hoping for. We can't just say, "I need you to stop gossiping," and walk away. This will result in a continuation of the gossip and the leader saying to themselves, "I told them to stop, so why didn't they?" The answer lies in the failure to create a plan. You need to provide tools and resources to help them improve. A coach doesn't say to a pitcher, "I need you to throw the ball faster." Instead, they show the pitcher how to stand, build muscle mass, wind up better and throw with more force. Why is your teammate gossiping? Dive into that question, and you'll likely find an answer you can develop a plan around.

As a leader looking to make changes, you need to develop a plan. Next, record that plan so you can track whether or not it is effective. For example, if an employee was struggling with client communication and you sent them for a weekend workshop, was it effective in changing their behavior? Are there any more client complaints lodged against that particular employee? How does the employee feel about their newfound communication skills? Are they more comfortable and less stressed when talking to clients? You will need to set a plan as well as monitor for improvement and change.

I'm often asked, "What are the plans to fix this particular issue?" No one set plan will fix a certain issue because each person is unique. In future chapters, I will discuss common toxic situations and ways to manage them that will help you develop your own plan for your gossiper, bully, or other toxic team members you may be struggling with.

Let's revisit our burned-out employee. We decide to send them to a half-day wellness continuing education seminar. We also want them to focus on their well-being at work by eating lunch, sitting down at times, and going home on time as much as possible. Now we will need to run the plan by them. What do they think of our ideas? A conversation about what they think is important. Even better, ask them what things they believe may help reduce their burnout.

Sometimes employees are so angry about their burnout that their answers are unproductive. Rather than focus on themselves and their needs, they are focused on how the hospital is to blame for their burnout. They may say, "We just need more staff," or "if I actually got to sit down to eat lunch, I wouldn't be so burned-out." When employees blame the employer, the initial reaction is for the employer to become defensive. "I'm trying to get more staff. We have eight job ads out!" Don't get defensive. Instead, do a deeper dive into their concerns and see if you can pull out action items.

"I know you are frustrated, and I'd like to help you become less so. I appreciate you sharing some areas you believe the hospital can improve upon. I want to focus on your well-being. Let's talk about why you don't get to eat lunch, and then tell me about some things you enjoy doing at home that make you smile." Asking employees about their suggestions to fix a frustration will gain better buy-in.

Plans are important because they allow for accountability and for you to check back in to see if the plan is effective or not. If we just tell our burned-out employee, "Maybe you should relax more," we will be left with a burned-out employee. If they agree to a wellness workshop, a commitment to take breaks, and stay off work email when at home, then we can check in and see if those action items are making an impact. I find the lack of any plan on a manager's part to be one of the big reasons why the toxicity remains unchanged in most hospitals.

Motivate

Motivation is the internal characteristic that drives all aspects of our behavior. How motivated are we to perform a certain behavior? How motivated are we to feel and interact with others? How motivated are we to perform our jobs to the best of our ability? There has been much research into motivation. If employers could figure out how to motivate every employee to be their best, they would have nothing but unicorns on their team.

In a workplace environment, employees may be motivated to perform a job to avoid punishment or seek reward. Athletes are typically paid a good salary with the sole purpose of winning games, so it's a strong motivator to do so. Failure to win may result in removal from the team. A 2020 study looked at elite athletes and what traits caused them to be motivated. The most important motivating trait was that the athletes had a high self-belief in their ability to succeed (Wpengine, 2020). They believed they were winners. Self-affirmation is the key to making any individual believe that they can win. Mohammed Ali is quoted as saying, "I figured that if I said it enough, I would convince the world that I really was the greatest." He believed himself to be a winner, motivated himself to be the best, and convinced an entire world that he was the greatest of all times. Self-belief is just as important in an athlete as in our veterinary teams. Does your team believe they are a unicorn hospital?

If your team believes that happiness while working at the veterinary hospital can happen, they are more likely to be motivated to achieve that happiness. If your team walks around saying, "this place sucks," and "nothing will ever change," then they will be right. Change will never happen. Motivation and self-belief go hand in hand.

Suppose an individual believes they will remain miserable and burned-out. In that case, they are less motivated to cope with stress and even less motivated to talk to leadership about changes they feel should be made. What if an individual believes it is possible to get themselves or the team out of burnout? In that case, they will be motivated to speak to leadership about their concerns and find ways to set boundaries for themselves.

Motivation should occur through rewards and praise. Remember that praise should always occur publicly, and criticism should be in private. While you could offer praise privately, it holds more weight if you do it in front of the entire team. The individual will be more motivated to continue their good performance if they are praised publicly. For example, if the hospital team has noticed that there has been a marked decrease in gossip, they could be rewarded with a party to celebrate the milestone. Offering a "good job" to individuals in private will hardly hold the same value as having a party celebrating the win.

The reality is that many individuals are not comfortable with praising others. It comes off as awkward or insincere. Try getting comfortable with praise by offering random acts of praise to a stranger. For example, compliment the cashier at the food store checkout and watch how they immediately smile because you made their day with one compliment. If you have a wonderful waiter at a restaurant, turn to them and say, "Thanks for being awesome at your job." People who are sincerely complimented and praised are more motivated. Sometimes during a bad workday, one compliment can carry you on and even make it feel like it was an okay day in the end. Praising is the foundation to motivation.

In his best-selling book *How to Win Friends and Influence People*, Dale Carnegie (1936) writes, "Appreciation is the legal tender in which all souls enjoy." Think of praise as a way to pay into your teams' Emotional Bank Account (EBA) as an incentive to remain motivated. Think about the burned-out employee. They have bought into your vision of them one day being happy at work. You had a meeting with them and the team and outlined a plan. They are ready for the change.

One month, three months, and six months go by, and you finally check in with them. Yet, they are still burned-out. Why? Ask yourself, "Did I motivate and encourage them through the process by praising their efforts and celebrating progress?" Likely not. It's been six months, and you haven't even bothered to check in once.

For me, when I was really struggling to motivate and encourage change in a team, I would become over-the-top with my praise. Take the burned-out employee example. If I saw that employee sitting down and eating food, I'd peek into the break room and exclaim loudly, "I'm so happy you are taking a break! Eat that food and enjoy it!" Then I'd walk away, leaving them speechless that their manager came in like a cheerleader, acted like a fool, and left. The reality is that the employee will likely repeat that behavior because they knew it made you happy.

When the employee or team is not motivated to improve, no improvement will occur. As a leader, you must figure out what motivates that individual and then offer it to them as a reward for a job well done.

Develop Individuals

The best coaches not only focus on the team as a whole but on each individual player on the team. Imagine how easy a manager's job would be if every player on the team were a unicorn. It would be pretty amazing. This is why leaders must take the time to develop individuals to get the best team as a whole because that's how unicorns are created.

Having short conversations with each member on your team is the key to getting to know them and their career goals. You may see something in them that they don't see in themselves. Plenty of coaches have moved a player from offense to defense. At first, the player may be resentful. They thought they were best suited for offense. Usually, the player realizes they are more comfortable playing defense over time. And yes, sometimes the coach gets it wrong, and the player moves back to offense. When this happens, you must own your mistake and be honest in your error to your team member.

Too often, leaders of toxic teams only see the team as a whole. They forget that there are individuals on the team who are still managing to do an amazing job despite adversity. "My team is so negative," or "They all gossip," is what I hear from leaders frequently. While I am a fan of addressing larger group issues as a group, leaders must follow up with each person individually, or some individuals will fail to make the change. Thus, they will be stuck in the toxicity.

Not developing individuals is where many leaders fail. They have a big meeting about how everyone is burned-out, negative, or inefficient.

They share a vision, and maybe a few buy into that goal. Perhaps a few individuals in the meeting get excited about the change. The leader may spend the first month praising the team as a group, but they never stop to develop each person individually. Those few people who had bought in quickly get pulled back into the toxicity and forget about the plan. If you are tackling a large team or hospital issue, remember you will still need to coach individually, or your plan will fail.

You Cannot Work Overnights

One of the superstars on my team was a dedicated overnight veterinary technician. She had been with the hospital for as long as I had. She had always worked overnights. She was a leader every single night she worked. Her performance reviews were always stellar. If I could've cloned her, I would have.

There was only one problem. She was not suited for overnights. Her body hated working overnights. Yet, she insisted that she wanted to remain on overnights. For anyone who has worked in a hospital where overnight shifts are available, you probably can relate to her love of working overnights. There are fewer human beings in the building. A certain amount of corny fun takes place on any given overnight shift. The team usually grows an exceptional bond together. It is them against the world.

When I suggested that she needed to move to day shifts, she gave me a flat-out no response. In fact, the first couple of times I broached the subject, she told me she would quit.

Year after year, we would meet for her annual development meeting, and I would explain why I felt she was not suited to work the overnight shift. My reasons seemed very obvious. She usually was admitted to the hospital at least twice a year with pneumonia. She admitted to falling asleep at the wheel at stop lights.

In between pneumonia hospitalizations, she developed more illnesses than almost the entire team combined. She lived her life getting over one cold virus just to get another. I was concerned about her health and well-being. I also knew that she could develop into a leader for the entire hospital if she would just get off overnights.

At some point during the third year, I saw her in the hallway coming off an overnight shift. She was coughing and suffering from yet another cold. As I passed her by, I said, "Let me know when you want to come off of overnights." To my amazement, she said, "I think it's time for a discussion about that."

She wanted to wean herself into the dayshift, so we started with her toggling back and forth from overnights to days. The effects on the health of her body were almost immediate. She stopped getting sick.

After a few short months, she joined the day crew full time. It's been years since she moved to the dayshift. She hasn't been hospitalized once with pneumonia since then. She does sometimes work overnight shifts, but only one here or there. She also has moved into a supervisor role and has truly embraced being a leader for both the day and the night shift.

A leader develops individuals not because they want to do what's best for the hospital, but because they genuinely care about the individual. It's not easy to find someone willing to take on overnight shifts. In fact, most hospitals would never ask an employee to move from a night to a day shift because they are near impossible to fill. A good leader develops the individual regardless of what is easier for the team or themselves. The best leaders genuinely care deeply about each employee.

Over my career, I have encouraged great performers to leave my hospital, pursue their passions, and even pursue other hospitals. I encouraged one of my best veterinary technicians to return to school to become a registered nurse. I joked that she was going to the dark side of medicine, the human medicine side. I made sure her schedule was one so that she could work part-time in the hospital and attend school, even though it was difficult to blend the schedule into our structure at the time. I have never regretted making difficult accommodations because, in the end, it was what was best for the individual but also created a better team environment. Having the team see that a leader helps their team members builds a culture of respect and trust. In allowing that employee to remain part-time, I kept an amazing veterinary technician on staff for as long as possible. No leader should want to stifle an individual because it's easier to fill the schedule a certain way. Developing the individual will always be what's best for the hospital and team.

Practice Flexibility

The best leaders have the ability to be flexible in how they develop or coach an individual or team. Yes, you have created a plan that will hopefully get you to your vision of where you see this particular individual or team. However, all plans should be looked at like a marathon. Slow and steady will make the change. Strap in for four months or even four years to make a difference, depending on how toxic an individual or team is. Many leaders think one webinar, outside consultant, or conversation will fix everything. Instead, I want you to think in terms of years if your team is extremely toxic. Years. That is the reality of the timeline in many hospitals. It will take patience, constant gentle pressure, and flexibility on your part for the change to happen.

Leaders must be flexible and bend if an unforeseen opportunity or crisis makes itself known. Be ready to adjust your plan. Despite your conversations with the team and your best thought-out plan, you might hit a roadblock. The gossiping started back, and the team is walking around again like, "This place sucks." Don't panic. Figure out where the speed bump is and adjust the plan. If you have made some forward progress, it's not all lost. There was only some small backsliding. Hold a meeting, talk to the team, and align them back to the vision you all spoke about. Revisit the plan together. You may find out that something in the plan needs to be tweaked, or perhaps a new concern has popped up.

Let's check in with our burned-out employee. You adjusted their schedule. They resonated with the well-being seminar you sent them to and have been finding ways to transition their negative thoughts to positive ones. It's been going great for months. However, this week you see they are coming in late again, and a veterinarian has expressed concern over their negative attitude.

"Great! All my work was in vain," you think.

What you don't realize is that their child is home sick, and their spouse is on the verge of losing their job. This week is a bad week for them due to outside factors. Be flexible. Have a conversation with them and talk about what new adjustments need to occur in the plan to get them back on track.

"I could use a few days off," they reply.

They were too afraid to ask for help, like most veterinary professionals are. The guilt of saying they needed help, and the fear of judgment often causes many to not ask for what they need during the most important times.

Perhaps a colleague of yours suggests an outside consulting company that specializes in changing team climate. If you are a rigid steel rod, you will hold fast and steady to the course you have already set yourself. However, if you practice flexibility, you may take that idea to the owner or hospital administrator. While it had not been considered before, it may be an option to consider now. Realize that changing a toxic individual or team requires flexibility, even if you have been down that path before.

Care Deeply

To be the best leader, you must care deeply not only for the team but also for the individuals. It goes beyond compassion. Compassion is caring. To care deeply, you must be empathetic. Empathy is the ability to place yourself in another's shoes and truly feel what they are feeling. It is the ability to understand where the other individual is coming from. Even if you have a team member who is a bully on the team, your understanding of why they are doing what they are doing will allow you to care about helping them stop their bullying behavior. Recognizing that they didn't set out to be a bully is key to caring about every single person on your team. The more demanding the work is, the more empathetic the leader must be.

In my first few jobs as a supervisor and manager, I did not understand what it meant to care deeply about my team. I cared about them, mainly because I knew my job depended on their success. It was not until many manager roles later that I learned what it meant to care deeply. Only then did I feel myself being fiercely protective over the success of each one of them.

One day I sat across from an employee whose toxic trait was to blame everyone. She was telling me about why she had been late yet again. But, of course, it was not her fault. She was late more than an hour into her shift, causing the overnight veterinary technician to work

14 hours. She said she felt remorse, but this was not the first time she had been late an hour or more to her shift.

It was not her fault because her husband had turned off her alarm this time. He worked overnight shifts and had gotten home early, around 4:00 in the morning. He attempted to set a second alarm and inadvertently shut off hers. She managed to wake up on her own but was 30 minutes late. She needed to rush around to get the children ready for school, and because they had missed the bus, she had to drive them.

At that moment, I was no longer upset with this employee. Instead, I felt bad that my life was less complex than hers. I could feel her anxiety about running around in the morning and what it must've been like to deal with two small children, a husband you're trying not to wake up, and two dogs you're trying to feed. I imagine the loneliness and the chaos that she must have felt. I knew the dread she experienced coming into work late and having to deal with me. At that moment, I thanked her for her honesty and told her I valued her as part of the team.

I still wrote up the infraction but didn't make much of it. It was important to document that this was a behavioral pattern but also to find a solution. I bought her a separate alarm clock with my own money. She placed it on the bureau across the bedroom so that it could not be snoozed, and so that no one would change the time on it. To shut it off, she had to get out of bed. Shockingly that did work. She was so grateful for me, a leader, caring about her that it was the last time she was so late. She remarked that other managers didn't seem to care about her personal life, but she knew I did. As I write this, I realize alarm clocks are a bit outdated, but this was in the early 2000s when every household still used them. That said, even in the year 2022, if someone were struggling to get up on time with their cell phone alarm, I would still encourage them to buy a separate old-school alarm clock and place it across the room. Having to physically get out of bed to shut off the alarm makes it nearly impossible to have an excuse as to why you couldn't make it to work on time.

Caring deeply for an individual rewards both yourself but also makes the other person a better teammate. For every individual that you care about deeply, they will give you so much more in return.

Look Towards the Future

I have already alluded to the importance of this. Not everyone can move into a manager or supervisor role. However, they all can become leaders. Excellent coaches determine what position they can play and put them in that role. See the individuals on your team for what they can become. A good coach looks beyond the years of contribution that a team member may make to the hospital. You should always ask yourself, "Are they a better teammate than when they first joined?" If the answer is no, then we need to figure out what we aren't doing to help them improve.

Jimmy Johnson, the former head coach of the United States football team, the Dallas Cowboys, used to say, "Treat a person as he is, and he will remain as he is. Treat a person as if he were where he could be and should be, and he will become what he could be and should be." If you do not treat every employee as if they can become a leader in some aspect of your hospital, they will become stagnant, bored, resentful, and eventually leave the hospital. Worse yet, they may stay and become toxic.

I once had a part-time employee who worked for me for about a year in the emergency department. She talked to me about her love of internal medicine repeatedly. In return, I talked about how to become a veterinary technician specialist (VTS) and how I thought I could see her obtaining hers one day. She was concerned it would be too much work to obtain her VTS credentials. She thought it was silly that the internal medicine academy required applicants to work in the internal medicine department for a minimum of three years full-time before applying. At the time, she was a credentialed veterinary technician of more than 15 years but had never worked a day in internal medicine. She was very smart and a talented technician with excellent skills.

She wanted to be given more responsibility at my hospital and asked to be scheduled for better emergency shifts. She had been working a lot of swing and weekend shifts. She talked to me about how she might even come on board full-time if she was provided a more senior position.

It would've been easy to provide her with some better shifts and allow her some more responsibility. To anyone else, it might have been silly not to fulfill her demands. After all, most emergency departments are short-staffed. She was a real rock star as a veterinary technician. She could command the floor, take on critical cases, and offer exceptional nursing care. The problem was her passion wasn't in emergency medicine.

I felt strongly that she needed to start pursuing her VTS in internal medicine. I saw her gravitating towards internal medicine cases when she worked emergency shifts. It wasn't fair to stifle her goals. So I pulled her aside and had a firm heart-to-heart with her.

"Listen," I said. "You are too good to settle for something you don't really want. You have some hard decisions to make. You should apply to a hospital that has a full-time internal medicine position for you. And in four to five years from now, you can let me know that you earned your VTS."

I recently booked that employee to speak at my state association's yearly veterinary technician conference. She is a VTS in internal medicine and the manager at an exceptionally large specialty hospital. She is a prominent speaker and an amazing leader. As her manager, I was responsible for giving her a shove because I could see what she could become. Having her settle may have helped out the hospital, but it would not have helped her obtain her passion.

Great leaders look to the future for an employee's goals and paths. It's powerful when employees know a leader is looking out for and cares about their future. Find out what they see for themselves and share your vision for them as well. They may not have even realized you saw them as a potential supervisor, but the constant gossiping was the only thing holding them back. Telling them that you need the gossip to stop is one thing. However, telling them that you need the gossip to stop because you see them as a supervisor in the future will motivate them to focus on the mission and purpose of your vision for themselves.

Have Fun

Having fun while decreasing the toxicity is imperative to the success of creating a happier team. How is any leader supposed to have fun when working to decrease the toxicity level in the hospital? Simple. Enjoy the pain. You know that one friend you have that enjoys running marathons or hiking mountains? They manage through the discomfort and sweat for that one reward: a view at the top or crossing the finish line. The crazy thing is, they enjoy the pain. That's why they keep signing up for more marathons or hiking more mountains. Your toxic team or employee is a similar challenge. Enjoy the pain. Embrace the challenge and celebrate each step along the way. It's going to hurt, but the end reward is worth the pain.

If you do not enjoy the change you are trying to implement in the hospital, no one else will either. You must celebrate the wins as they pop up. Don't wait to have fun until the job is over. The more fun, the faster the change will occur. Change occurs quicker when teams recognize it's more fun to be positive than negative.

When faced with a sick pet, we look at what diagnostics we could perform and what treatments may be applied to improve the patient's health. In veterinary medicine, we enjoy helping the pet and celebrating the wins of making a sick pet better. Is that not the same when it comes to a toxic team? Think of the individual or team as a sick or injured pet. What aspects are broken? What diagnostics need to be performed? What treatments need to be applied to heal the team or person? When things start improving, celebrate those wins with all those involved. Be sure to have fun along the way, or the journey to the top won't be as sweet.

Chapter Five

Trust & Communication

Good communication is one of the most important traits you must master to enact change. If you do not have the ability to communicate to your employees in a way that shows you care, respect them, and advocate for them, they will not trust you. The *Merriam-Webster Dictionary* defines trust as an "assured reliance on the character, ability, strength, or truth of someone or something." Another definition is "one in which confidence is placed." When you look at the definition of trust, it's pretty heavy.

You know how it feels to trust in someone or something. Trust feels like someone has our back. Trust feels like support. Trust feels like vulnerable communication at times when it matters the most. Trust feels like sharing my views openly with others and not being judged harshly. Trust is the very tool that supports effective communication. The two go hand in hand. Building trust allows you to have better communication skills. When you have to coach someone who trusts you, communication comes more freely.

Brené Brown is a social worker and research professor who has spent over two decades studying leadership skills. She is the author of five *New York Times* Bestsellers, including *Dare to Lead* (2018). She discusses the importance of trust as a leader and introduces the acronym BRAVING, a good tool to remember seven important elements of trust in a leader. Leaders must make sure all these traits are present in order for their team to trust them.

Seven Elements of Trust: BRAVING
Brené Brown's *Dare to Lead*

Boundaries: As a leader, you must respect your team's boundaries, and they yours. If you are not sure if an employee has a boundary, ask. If it's important for a team member to be home to tuck their kids in every night, we need to respect that boundary and try our best to make it happen most nights.

Reliability: You need to do what you say you'll do. Be aware of your limitations so you don't over promise. Deliver to your team or they will stop trusting you.

Accountability: Own your mistakes, apologize, and make amends. You don't have to be perfect as a leader, but your team will never trust you if you don't own your mistakes.

Vault: You cannot share information or experiences that are not yours to share. Teams need to trust that what they tell their leader stays with their leader. Do not void the confidence of an individual by unlocking your vault.

Integrity: You practice your values rather than professing them and you maintain your integrity at all times.

Nonjudgement: You will not place judgement on your team. This is similar to assuming good intention of your team.

Generosity: You are generous to every member of your team in your intention, words, and actions.
(Brown, 2018)

It takes a brave leader to be able to embody all of these traits. If you're struggling with trust with an individual or team, ask yourself, "Am I missing an element?" Each one of the BRAVING elements requires you to be genuine and vulnerable as a leader. It's not easy to hold yourself accountable. It's hard to check in with each team member to see what boundaries are important to them. If any elements are missing, your team will lack trust in you as a leader, making communication much more difficult.

For example, perhaps a member of your team felt you judged them too harshly compared to others. Perhaps you cursed at a colleague and lost your integrity for a moment. As a result, this colleague may not trust you as much, and communication may struggle.

I love the quote (author unknown), "Trust is a fragile thing. Easy to break, easy to lose, and one of the hardest things to ever get back." That is most certainly the truth. So, when you struggle with trust, look over the BRAVING acronym and figure out which of the seven elements is missing to complete the trusting communication needed to be an effective leader.

Developing Trust in a Team

Just as important as leaders developing trust between themselves and their team, the team must trust each other. I can assure you that when teams are toxic, there is little to no trust to be found. I cannot overemphasize the importance of trust. Trust is your unicorn, the light to get you out of the darkness. It is the thing that will turn dysfunction to function and negativity to positivity.

Several key components are needed to build trust within a team. First, they genuinely believe that every team member is striving towards the same goal, and they assume good intention of each other. Second, they know they have each other's back, even if things get heated.

Trust in a team is when team members know their fellow coworkers care deeply for them. We see this kind of care in families. Many families fight like cats and dogs but have each other's back when things get tough. They know that they are all striving towards the same thing and their bond of being a family is what supports them through the tough times. Having team members that care deeply for each other helps to increase the trust.

Trust needs to be built in a non-threatening way. A great way to do this is by hosting team builders, in which people get to learn about each other. Patrick Lencioni (2012), the author of *The Advantage*, advocates that for teams to get to know each other, they should first start with a personal but non-threatening question. He likes to ask three questions that every team member needs to answer.

1) Where were you born?
2) How many siblings do you have?
3) What was the most difficult thing for you as a child?

The third one sounds deeply personal, and it is for a good reason. How someone was brought up and the trauma that might have occurred will impact them as adults. The team should know they can share as much or as little information as possible. For some, losing a childhood toy might be all they are willing to share. For others, they may talk about how they were physically abused. Regardless, a level of vulnerability happens with each team member when it's their turn. That team member chooses what they are or are not willing to share. The teammates listening to the answers are most often supportive.

People are generally surprised that they do not know these facts about their colleagues. Team builders like this leave them with a newfound respect for each other. Think about those you work with. Do you know how many siblings they have? Do you know where they grew up? Maybe you do know for some, but I gather for many more you do not.

Team members must grow together both personally and professionally. Complete trust comes from a vulnerability cultivated by leadership through dedication and hard work. When there is trust, they rely on each other to fill the gaps that need to be filled without exploiting the bad things of each other. There is no shame or manipulation in a team member struggling or making a mistake. Instead, there is support and kindness. Trust is the thing that makes teamwork possible. A great thing about the upcoming chapter on polite, kind, and honest (PKH) communication is that when we teach it to our teams, they will eventually develop an entire culture around it, and trust will naturally occur.

Communication is Hard

Many veterinary employees were driven to work in veterinary medicine because they more strongly connect with animals than people. Working in a team is difficult. The one thing that we all need to learn when we enter the workforce is how to communicate with different types of people. Just like learning how to take a radiograph or perform an ovariohysterectomy, people need to learn how to communicate with each other since there are various and often daunting numbers of personality traits in the world.

You probably have no problem communicating with a dog or cat. To me, conversations between myself and my veterinary pet patients flow easily. I could talk to pets all day. They never disagree with me. Most days, I'm grateful they can't talk back, but there are a few times I'd like to hear what they have to say.

It's important that veterinary professionals can communicate to their pet patients with ease, but when you are in a leadership role, that's not going to cut it. You need to be able to communicate with your team and teach them how to communicate with each other. Most individuals promoted into a leadership role achieved that role because of their ability to practice medicine rather than leadership or communication skills. Veterinary medicine skills and knowledge are not the same as leadership skills.

Communication between people still bucks science and data. How science says a communication should have gone, is not how it actually goes many times. There will never be a perfect way to address every person or situation. However, there are some techniques and skills that leaders should learn so they can be more effective communicators. This book merely scratches the surface of communication, so I would encourage you to grab hold of any training offered around communication skills. The better your communication skills, the more trust your team will have in you.

The Make-up of Communication

Albert Mehrabian (1971), a professor of psychology at the University of California, developed the "7-38-55 Rule" when describing the relationship between words and nonverbal communication. His rule was based on two studies he conducted in 1967 that focused on the relationship between body language and verbal communication. While his rule has been argued over the years, it is still considered one of the most accurate ways to describe the relationship between verbal and nonverbal cues when communicating.

His rule pulled in three elements: words, tone, and facial expression. He argued that for effective and meaningful communication in which the individual could understand the emotion and intent behind it, these three items needed to help support each other. Otherwise, if the person said they were sad, but their facial expression showed laughter, different signals would be given to the receiver. We see this frequently when an individual verbalizes, "I don't have a problem with you," but then looks away and rolls their eyes. Talk about mixed signals. Communication is complicated because it contains three elements (words, tone, facial expression) that must agree, and how the receiver interprets those elements is entirely up to them.

The tone of one's voice and facial expression account for 93% of the meaning of the words that are being said. The tone accounts for 38%. The facial expression accounts for 55%, and the words themselves account for only 7% of the actual meaning and emotion behind the statement being made. This explains why when I tell my dogs they are naughty and bad, but I say it in a fun and loving manner, they wag their tails and jump all over me with happiness.

When we are aware of the factors that play into the statements we are trying to make to our team, we can see the complexity that may arise. Should we not be completely focused when we are communicating, we may give off the wrong vibe of what we are trying to say. I am guilty of this. Sometimes I might be talking to a team member, but my brain is thinking about something else. They may walk away from me, thinking that I just didn't care about what they were saying. I verbally said, "I'm so sorry that happened to you. You're right. This needs to be dealt with. Thank you so much for coming to me." Unfortunately, my eyes kept looking away and focusing on other things, and I kept fidgeting in my chair as if this individual was an annoyance.

The first step to better communication is paying attention to the person talking to you. Really pay attention to them. Put your cell phone away. It's better not even to have it on your body. If you are in front of a computer, turn your body away from it and turn off the monitor. Truly connect with that person and look at them while they are speaking.

I once had an important meeting with my boss. She had previously canceled five times before. It was now an urgent matter that she and I speak. Only 20 minutes into the meeting, someone walked by the office and poked their head in. My boss stopped speaking to me and started having a fun, non-important conversation with this other individual. She must have sensed my death stares because five minutes later, she said to the individual, "Amy and I are trying to have a pretty important meeting. I kept canceling on her, and just to ensure we're not interrupted, I put my cell phone on silent and face down." She picked up her phone to demonstrate the motion of putting her phone face down.

The other employee apologized, "Sorry! I had no idea you were meeting. We'll catch up later," and she left. My boss held onto her phone and had not quite put it face down. She looked at the screen. "Oh my gosh, Amy! I forgot about a leadership call I have right now! I have to run. We'll talk later." She gathered her things and left the room promptly, leaving me speechless. The meeting was about my job and whether or not the team would consider me for a newly created role. I quit shortly after that meeting. She was surprised when I gave my notice. While she told me how valued I was, her actions said something entirely different. Her actions conveyed a "you don't matter" main course combined with an "I don't care if you quit" side dish. She did care that I quit, at least in the words she expressed to me, but the damage was already done. I didn't trust her because she never was present for me to rely on as a manager.

If you fail to pay attention to a team member or team while they are communicating with you, they will lose trust in you because they will think you don't care about them. So be fully engaged when someone is speaking to you, especially over a concern they have.

☺😣☹ Different Facial Expressions ☺😵☹

It's hard to write about facial expressions when visually, you cannot see me making facial expressions. What does confusion look like? How about anger? Do most people have the same facial expressions for certain emotions? Luckily, the answer is yes. Most people have the same facial expressions for anger, happiness, or confusion regardless of what culture, race, sex, or religion they identify with. Depending on the individual's background, the expression may be more obvious in some cultures than others. According to Susan Cain (2013), author of the best-selling book about introverts, *Quiet,* Asian cultures are often more reserved. When they experience anger, they will still show angry facial expressions, but they may display it in a more subtle way.

Dr. Ekman was the first psychologist to study ways of measuring nonverbal behavior. He published his first research paper in 1957, which is still valid today when identifying universal facial expressions. He found that human beings are capable of making more than 10,000 facial expressions, but only 3,000 are relevant to emotion. Ten thousand facial expressions! No wonder why we have such difficulty communicating with each other. Here's a list of eight universal facial expressions and the nuances that are paired with them. While we can't be together to do this exercise, I want you to read the description and then attempt to make that same face.

Disgust

The face looks like you smelled something bad. Pretend like you smell something bad right now. You will lift your upper lip. You will wrinkle your nose and squint your eyes. You may or may not lift your lip high enough to expose your front teeth. People make this face when they taste or smell something bad, but also when they are disgusted by a situation or event. For example, when you are watching a movie and are disgusted by a scene that grosses you out or upsets you, you will make the same face. In our veterinary hospitals, we see this expression when a new hire is not working out, and the team feels they are disastrous. If you walk up to someone on the team and ask, "How is that new hire doing?" they might make a disgusted facial expression.

Anger

Pull your eyebrows in and wrinkle the part of your forehead right above your nose between the eyebrows. Usually, there are two vertical lines between your eyebrows. Tense your lips and harden them. You might have even started feeling slightly irritated if you did it correctly. This is called the facial feedback hypothesis, in which your facial expressions have learned how to produce an emotional response. Our face and our emotions go hand-in-hand.

Sadness

This is a hard expression to fake, so if someone shows you a facial expression of sadness, it is often genuine. First, turn the corners of your mouth down into a frown. Next, puff out your lower lip just a bit. Some people can even make the lower lip quiver. Lastly, bring your eyebrows together just a little bit. Your eyebrows will come down just a little so that your eyes are not fully open. People who are sad will not have wide eyes but ones where the eyelids are slightly lowered.

Happiness

True happiness is beyond a smile. The telltale sign of true happiness is where the cheekbones become engaged. Pull your cheeks up to the corners of your eyes. Try to think of something funny and laugh about it right now. You will feel your cheek muscles being pulled up to the corner of your eyes, along with a big smile. When people try to fake being happy, they fail to pull the cheeks up to the corner of the eyes.

Fear

Think about your eyes and eyebrows jumping because they are scared. Your eyes will open wide, and your eyebrows will crinkle inwards just a bit. Most of the time, your mouth will open, even if it's just a little bit. Think about what happens when you gasp out of fear. Look around the room when you are talking to your team and have just notified them that a schedule change is happening. Their eyes will be wide, and their eyebrows will be flat and pulled in slightly. They are afraid of the new schedule and what that means.

Surprise

This is like the fear expression. It is almost identical, except that your lower jaw and lip will be pulled down, and your eyebrows will be pulled up. Think of how to make your face as long as possible. This is considered the longest expression because the eyebrows are pulled up, and the jaw is pulled down. Sometimes the mouth is open in an "O" shape. The eyes are also open wide in this expression.

Contempt

This is an emotion where the individual will have a one-sided smirk with their lip. Any type of asymmetry with the face means contempt, disdain, or hatred in some sort of way. Think about how you look when you are sarcastic, and this is that type of facial expression.

Confusion

Usually, for this emotion, one eyebrow is higher than the other. The nose becomes wrinkled, and there is a crease between the eyebrows. One corner of the mouth is usually raised just a little bit, opposite of the eyebrow that is raised. Many individuals will look up and away as if they are thinking about what was just said. When you are talking to a team member who says they understand, look at what their face is doing. If one eyebrow is raised and they are looking into their own head, they probably don't understand and need a little more clarification.

Look at Their Eyes

When you communicate with someone, you should look at their face and eyes while they are speaking with you. Maintain a soft gaze so that you are not staring at them to intimidate them but rather just calmly focused on what they are saying. This conveys you are listening intently.

When someone is speaking to somebody, they will often look directly at their face to see how the information is being received. Too much blinking usually represents nervousness. Try not to move your eyebrows, as they will give away your inner emotions as the individual is speaking.

What to Do with Your Body

Should you cross your legs? Where should you put your hands? Should your body position change based on the other person's emotions? What to do with one's posture and body can be a difficult but important decision when communicating.

Open Posture: This means that you are open to receiving information. This is a posture that conveys friendliness and willingness.

- Hands down or on your lap
- Relaxed shoulders
- Head in a neutral position but gently moving
- Soft, slow movements

Closed Posture: This posture conveys that you are closed off and struggling with the information you are receiving. This conveys hostility, unfriendliness, and anxiety.

- Hunched forward
- Closed arms and/or legs
- Clenched fists
- Rigid in seated or standing position

Should I Flap My Hands Around?

Yes, you can use your hands to tell a story. But be sure not to overdo it. I am an individual who uses my hands a lot and, at times, too much. Anyone who has seen me lecture will attest to this. It can be said that I may flap my hands around like a crazed lunatic on a stage at times. I have purposely tried to restrain my hands when I lecture, but they seem to have a mind of their own. I have been known to fling a laser pointer off the stage. If you get a chance to see me speak in person, you should consider wearing a hard hat.

One of the best ways to use your hands is to utilize movement between changes in a scene or emotion you are trying to convey. Start at a neutral position. As you start the conversation, you may move your hands a little to convey a poignant part of the story. If your hands start taking off in flight, try to be aware and ground them back down to earth.

Much like universal facial expressions, there are universal hand gestures that can be used to convey emotion. Here are some of the more common ones:

- Pleading (hands together)
- Anger (clenched)
- Sadness (holding yourself)
- Concern (touching face)
- Contempt (soft clench)
- Happiness (open hands)

Movement

The movement of your body can convey flexibility, sadness, anxiety, command, or anger. Just be aware of what your body is doing. Much like my hands, my body is usually also flailing about. I'm a naturally fidgety person, so when I talk to a team member who is having a serious conversation with me, I make it a point to sit still in a neutral position. Here are some other main movements and what they convey:

- Moving Forward: Conveys dominance, assertiveness
- Moving Away: Conveys avoidance, submission, end of conversation
- Fidgeting: Conveys anxiety, fear (flight or fight)
- Frozen: Conveys fear, anger

Tone of Voice

Once you master your facial expressions, body, and hand position, the tone of your voice is next. Unfortunately, it is also one of the most difficult things to improve. Years of your voice having certain tones for certain emotional communication makes it difficult to change.

Sometimes I come off sounding aggressive, particularly when I become passionate about a particular topic. In my mind, I have a passion for why something should be done a particular way. It's not to say I believe it should be "my way or the highway," but I'm passionate and hope others buy-in to my vision. Unfortunately, my passion causes the tone of my voice to sound excited, and it increases in volume. The increase in volume with the matter-of-fact excitement comes off as aggressive as if I'm pushing only my agenda onto the project.

My tone and behavior often betray my words. Those who know me are aware my tone is my passion. They know if they say, "Amy, what do you think about XYZ," I would respond, "I hadn't thought about that. Tell me more about that idea." My tone betrays me, causing people to believe I would respond with, "I think it should be done my way!"

Tone of voice is largely centered around the pitch of your voice. Be slow and methodical with how you say something. However, if you are too slow in speaking, it will come across as strange or like you have a problem with receiving the information. Try to hear what you sound like. Try recording yourself talking to a friend. As you speak, make sure you listen to what you are saying.

Touch

I'm just going to say it. There is good touching and bad touching. As I write this book, there is a hypervigilance centered around touching in the workplace environment, and for good reasons. Inappropriate touching of any kind in which another feels unsafe, insecure, intimidated, threatened, or harassed cannot be tolerated.

The unfortunate consequence of those who cross the line is that many employers now believe and even state that no touching is permitted in the workplace. While that is arguably the safest thing to say, touching is one of the most powerful tools in communication, but it's rarely used because of the fear associated with how the person receiving the touch will perceive it. While it is safest to suggest no touching should ever occur, I also feel we are missing out on a powerful communication skill that can be used in some of the most needed times.

Let me also preface by saying I am not a fan of people touching me. Although I do hug, I'm not a hugger. I will only hug my close friends and family. I must know the individual very well to offer a hug or comfortably receive one.

There are four main categories of touch: friendship, professional, social, and intimacy. The rule for professional touching should be on a shoulder or arm and be brief. Touches in a workplace environment should never be rubbing or grabbing. A gentle touch on a shoulder or arm can go a long way to stronger communication.

I Touched a Client

Besides not hugging or touching strangers, I also try never to cry in front of anyone. I'm just not a fan of displaying emotions. Let me correct that statement. I'm not a fan of displaying sad, depressed, stressful, or even fearful emotions. Should happiness come my way, everyone will know. I never have an issue with displaying happiness to anyone and everyone, but I like to keep the rest of those other emotions in check.

I worked with a veterinary technician who was overly emotional almost every day. She experienced high highs and low lows. Everyone working with her knew exactly how she felt. She did not hold back. If she was sad, there were lots of tears. If she was anxious, she sometimes suffered panic attacks. If she was angry, her face got red, and everyone had to watch out. But, when she was happy, she lit up the room.

It sounds like a lot to deal with, but the team adored her. She was the best teammate to everyone who worked at the hospital. She understood everybody's emotional state and helped support them when they struggled. If you were not a hugger, she knew that, and she didn't bother to hug you. But, if you were a hugger, she would give you the longest and the best hugs ever. She had this innate sense of how to handle everyone else's emotions.

While many felt she had no grasp of her own emotions, she actually had high emotional intelligence. She knew exactly why she was sad and why she was happy. She even knew when she might be overreacting. She was the first person to call herself out on her emotions.

This veterinary technician received more accolades from clients than everyone else combined. She received gifts from clients, countless cards, phone calls, emails, and reviews, all showering her with praise and thanking her for being amazing. Clients would request her to be their veterinary technician. She made every client feel special and unique. No matter how demanding, angry, or upset a client was, she had the amazing ability to calm them down and connect with them on an emotional level.

I couldn't figure out how she could calm clients down so easily until I saw her one day with a grieving client. The client had just received bad news that their five-year-old dog had lymphoma. It simply was not fair. She went in to take a deposit for treatment. The doctor had already told the client about the terrible diagnosis. She needed to secure payment so we could move forward with treatment for the dog.

I walked by the room and heard sobbing. As I got closer, I slowed down so I could peek in on my way to the lab. I saw this veterinary technician sitting on the bench next to the client. Her hand was placed gently on this client's shoulder. The client turned to her and quietly said, "Thank you."

She had offered a gentle hand on the shoulder to someone who was suffering. That technician had made an exceptionally powerful connection by doing something so simple, a gentle touch of kindness. She was sitting next to the client, paying attention to her, touched her shoulder briefly, and provided genuine empathy to the client, who needed to be cared about more than ever.

Some months later, I brought a cat into our bereavement room so the client could be with their beloved pet in its final moments. I could have easily handed the cat to the client, said I was sorry, and walked out of the room, but I saw the client was all by herself. She held back tears and tried to mutter a happy, "Hello, Peanut," to her cat. She told him that she was there and loved him very dearly.

I could have just walked away, but after I handed Peanut to his mother, I saw a look of sheer loneliness on her face. Something possessed me to sit next to her on the couch, and I quickly put my hand on her shoulder, took it away, and told her I was sorry. I said to her that I could tell she loved him to the moon and back and that I would be thinking of her. I knew Peanut was lucky to have such a wonderful owner who loved him for his entire life. She looked at me and quietly said, "Thank you."

We often forget how to connect to each other as human beings. For many of us, there is general fear of being near and connecting to other people. A quick brief touch reconnects us in an immensely powerful way. It could be a gentle touch on the shoulder to tell a colleague that they did an amazing job through a difficult situation. It could be a gentle hand touching a forearm quickly to say that you are sorry for a loss. For those uncomfortable with the idea of touching as a form of communication, I encourage you to step out of your comfort zone when an opportunity presents itself. It will be incredibly impactful for both you and the receiver.

Practice Your New Communication Skills

Practice with a friend by playing a game. It sounds corny, but it's pretty fun. You will need to record the session. I promise that you will both end up laughing at numerous points. Have your friend role-play three separate roles. In the first role, they will play a client who is angry about something. In the second role, they will play a member of your team who has an issue with another team member and has come to you to talk about it. In the last scenario, they will play your boss and inform you of your recent poor performance.

In the first two roles, you are the receiver of the other person's emotions. Therefore, you must maintain a neutral facial expression when listening. For example, you may nod your head and tell them how you are sorry they are struggling or angry. In the last role, your friend will be the receiver of your emotions.

It's going to get silly because role-playing usually is. However, it's meant to teach you how to remain neutral during stressful times. In Chapter Ten, I will discuss how to respond to conflict. This exercise is meant to teach you how to control your body language, movements, and tone of voice.

By recording this exercise, you can go back and listen to the tone of your voice. Ask your friend if you looked neutral as they were yelling at you or talking to you about a serious problem they had. Did you look as if you cared about them? Did you seem like you were actively listening and paying attention to them? Could they read your emotions and facial expressions, or were you truly neutral?

The last role-playing scenario is where you receive criticism and want to take the time to digest that news to figure out the next steps. Are you able to take criticism and keep your emotions fairly neutral?

We certainly don't want you to have a deadpan stare when your friend communicates with you. Ideally, they should tell you that you looked like you were engaged, listening, and genuinely cared about what they were saying. When we can master our facial expressions and body language, the words coming out of our mouths will be conveyed better. Focusing on those items before you focus on the actual words will allow you to be a more efficient communicator, no matter the situation.

Chapter Six

Polite, Kind, & Honest Conversation (PKH)

Throughout my many management roles, I have tried many different communication styles. However, I finally landed on what I believe to be the best communication style for most of life's communications: polite, kind, and honest (PKH).

It's a bold statement to make. How is it possible that one communication style could be that good? Every human being communicates a little bit differently. At times, men and women communicate very differently. Different cultures and ethnicities communicate differently as well. The family environment in which one was raised will also affect how an individual communicates. Yet, I will stand by this statement time and time again. Most people would like to be communicated to by another individual utilizing PKH communication.

I wish that 15 years ago, when I discovered this technique, I was smart enough to create an edgy title and publish a book that would be a national bestseller. Kim Scott did just that. I need to give credit where credit is due because Scott was the vanguard of creating a movement toward this type of communication. She wrote *Radical Candor – Be a Kick-Ass Leader and Empower Your Team*. She has since revised her bestseller and released a new addition in 2019. It's a fantastic book, and I would encourage you to pick it up or listen to it on an audiobook. The technique described is what the absolute best leaders have been doing for years. I like Scott's book because it's down-to-earth and honest. She doesn't sugarcoat or try to use big words to impress readers. Instead, she delivers her material in a practical way that is applicable in any industry.

While I could go on and on about how much I love Scott's book, what I don't love is the title. I dislike the words radical and candor. Funny enough, the author agreed. At the beginning of her new edition she pushes to instead use the term "compassionate candor." She reasons that the terms radical and candor have permitted many leaders to be cruel because they are being too honest. Is it radical to say to an employee, "You suck?" It's also quite candid. The title of her book may permit some individuals to be rude, which is not what was intended.

When people ask me what my communication style is to my employees or team, I have always replied that I strive to have a polite, kind, and honest communication style. No one has ever questioned what that means because there is no room for misinterpretation using those words.

Starting with politeness is key. That opens the door to allow the listener to understand you are attempting to be kind. If we miss being polite, kindness will likely not be received. This will, in turn, cause our listener to shut off and not receive what we are trying to communicate. From there, I need to be honest with them.

I want the individual to know that I am sincere and truthful. I don't just need to be frank. I need to be sincere and free of deceit, aka honest. There are two ways to be honest. The first is to be blunt and rude. Just put it out there without caring about how the receiver processes the information. The second way is to be honest but ensure we take into consideration the other person's feelings. We don't want to lie to them and it's important they hear what we need to say. Taking the polite and kind path will allow you to be honest while keeping the relationship as intact as possible.

What is PKH?

It sounds so simple. If you can manage to be polite, kind, and honest in any communication, you will likely be successful. It is a great communication style to choose in almost every situation because it's how everyone wants to communicate. Think about how you would like someone to speak to you. How do you want your boss to talk to you? How about a friend? Your answer is likely the same as everyone else's. People want to talk to someone who is polite, cares about them, and tells them the truth. While this is the style of how we want to be communicated to, it's not so easy. If this communication style was easy to do, more leaders would be doing it. In fact, more people would be doing it.

This form of communication consists of caring deeply on a personal level, but only after developing a mutual trust between the individuals having a conversation. I want to break down each component so that you can understand the power of PKH and how to implement it in your daily life.

It Starts with Trust & Mutual Respect

While I will say that this is one of the best ways to communicate, I will also say you need to proceed with caution. You need to learn how to perfect this communication style for it to work best. While you may be great at delivering PKH communication, the receiver may not be used to this style, and it may fall flat. Practice, practice, practice.

I'm not suggesting that you are honest with every person you meet. If you are, it's a good bet that it will probably result in you getting punched in the face at some point. Honesty will get you more places in life than lying, but only if it comes from kindness, and only if the receiver of the honesty feels that kindness. If we are honest with individuals we have not yet built a relationship with; it may not land well. You must have a relationship built around trust in order for this to be the most effective.

When you need to challenge someone on your team and have not yet built up the trust to be able to communicate honestly, using this communication style may be a struggle. If the two individuals don't have mutual respect for each other, this style can come across as abrasive. Mutual respect and trust are needed for healthy conversations. If you don't show that you care deeply about the individual you are trying to challenge, you will come off as a jerk. If you don't respect the other individual, you won't listen or react well. All components must come together simultaneously to make PKH communication effective.

If you think you came off as polite, kind, and honest, but the receiver feels like you were direct and rude, you have failed. As a leader, how you communicate is only as good as how the person receives the communication. There are two reasons this communication style will fail you:

1) You missed being either polite, kind, or honest.
2) The receiver did not trust you enough to assume you came from a place of kindness or honesty.

Polite

What does the word polite entail? I choose to use it because, by definition, it is "having or showing behavior that is respectful and considerate of other people" (Merriam-Webster.com, 2022). These two traits are necessary to develop trust, arguably the most important trait to have as a leader.

Steps to Being Polite

1) Assume good intention. Polite individuals do not judge others.

2) Don't make it about you. Too often, I find the leaders try to share personal stories with their teammates in an effort to relate to them. It's not about you.

3) Don't gossip or spread rumors. If a member of your team comes to you to complain about someone else, just listen. Above all else don't agree or add to it with more gossip and rumors.

4) Don't push your own opinions onto someone. It's rude and will make the other person defensive. "I think you should," should be banned from your language unless someone says to you, "What do you think I should do?"

5) Be sure you use your please and thank-yous. Showing your gratitude for someone who is expressing their emotions when it may be difficult for them is the polite thing to do.

6) Learn how to listen and be sure not to interrupt. Pay attention to what is being said.

7) Have the ability to apologize and acknowledge you were wrong. You need to learn to take criticism graciously.

8) Care about the individual you are having a conversation with. Think about that individual more than you think about yourself. Be empathetic.

9) Have good manners. When you walk into the room smile, greet everyone appropriately, and thank them for their time. Praise others when praise is due.

10) Keep negativity, nasty comments, and rude thoughts to yourself and only share with people in your inner, trusted circle. If in a heated argument, you can stand your ground, but do not add in emotions or unkind remarks.

I know I have lost a little bit of trust in certain individuals because I failed to use the polite element of PKH. I came across as disrespectful and inconsiderate. Always start from a place of politeness.

Being polite maintains stability in the conversation. If you give politeness, you are more likely to receive it in return. On the other hand, if you come in with a lot of emotion and try to win an argument, the other individual will likely follow your lead.

Of course, these things are easier said than done. The reason why it's so hard to utilize these ten tips on how to maintain politeness is because of emotions. If someone is criticizing you, most likely, you get defensive. It is common nature to want to defend yourself. Most defensive people will snap back using the word "you." "You are…, you need…, you caused…, you are too…." Minimize, if not remove, the word "you" from the conversation so it is not seen as attacking someone.

Along the same lines, remember that over-personalization can be an issue. When you center everything around yourself, you take on a defensive posture. "I need…, I want…, I think…." Remember, the conversation has two sides, and it's not all about you.

Another trick I have found that has increased my politeness in conversations is to think about a sentence that I am struggling to make polite before I actually say it. Generally, it's a good rule to slow down your speech to allow your brain time to think about sentence structure. Unfortunately, this is exceptionally difficult for me. I am an extremely fast talker. Whenever I am lecturing at a conference, I give a disclaimer to the audience that they need to strap in for a fast-paced lecture. I started this disclaimer more than a decade ago after countless conference reviews stated that "she is knowledgeable and engaging but talks too fast." Despite trying to slow down my speaking style, I have learned that it is just part of who I am.

That said, there is a difference when I am lecturing to an audience versus when I am trying to communicate to a team member about a difficult situation. When I'm lecturing, people have come to my lecture to listen to me, not communicate with me. I'm educating them on a subject, so most of the conversation is one-sided. When I am communicating with another person, I not only have to listen, but I also have to give a response in return. I have done my best to take pauses and slow down when I'm trying to communicate. This allows me to think before I speak, which I can assure you is necessary.

If I find myself wanting to say something that is clearly not polite and borderline inappropriate, I will pause. There is no shame in saying to the other person, "Let me just think about how I want to say this." This gives you time to formulate a polite response in your head. If you fail to be respectful and considerate, the very definition of what polite is, you can throw the rest of the conversation in the trash. You will never get any buy-in to what you are trying to communicate.

Kind

Show that you care immediately when you are also polite. Being polite is going to occur over the entire course of the conversation. Being kind also needs to happen for the entirety of the communication. For example, let's say that you have a veterinary technician struggling to calculate drug doses. They are struggling with their math calculations and keep coming up with wrong doses. The good news is that they know they are not strong in their math skills. As a result, they frequently have a coworker double-check them or ask them to do the math. Unfortunately, this puts an extra burden on those asked to help this individual time and again. You must address this teammate regarding how they need to sharpen their math skills and why it's important.

Scenario One:

"You keep making mistakes with your drug calculations. Everyone keeps having to double-check you, and frequently it's wrong. Unfortunately, you could end up killing a patient one day if you don't get any better. I have some material and quizzes I'm going to need you to do so that you can get better with your drug calculations."

Scenario Two:

"I am so frustrated. I know you love your patients and are a good technician, but you keep messing up the drug doses. Everyone is worried you will end up killing a patient by accident. I can't have you continue to make these mistakes, so I have some material and quizzes that I need you to do so you can get better with your drug calculations."

Scenario Three:

"The team can see that you love being a veterinary technician. You care about your patients. However, if you cannot do accurate math calculations correctly, you could cause irreversible harm to a pet or even death. I have put together some material and quizzes to help you improve your medical math skills, and one of our veterinarians mentioned they would be willing to help teach you a few tricks."

When we review scenario one, it is honest but lacks politeness and kindness. It starts by confronting the individual using the words, "you keep." Yes, it's an accurate statement, but it will not be received well because it lacks both the P and K of PKH communication.

In scenario two, it starts with emotion. The individual knows exactly how frustrated you are. The second sentence is one of kindness. However, it lacks a certain level of being polite. The last sentence that starts with, "I can't have you continuing," is all about you. This suggests that this person's poor math skills are a personal attack on you. Look at scenario two again and read all the "I" statements. "I can't have you" or "I need you to do so." Instead, make sure that they understand the impact it has on the hospital, team, the veterinary care of a patient, or the client's care.

Scenario three starts with both polite and kind sentences. It's also truthful. As a leader, you know that your team member went into this industry because they love veterinary medicine and want to help pets. As a leader, you are saying I can see that you care. The third sentence is one of honesty. It needs to be direct, so the receiver is clear with the issue. The last sentence says, "The team cares about you, and we all want to help."

In all three scenarios, you managed to develop a solution to the problem. However, unless you show that you care, you will come off as aggressive, and they will never receive your criticism or solution.

You should care deeply about how your team member will receive the information you are about to give them. You want to make sure that you do your best not to offend. Certainly, it gets the best buy-in from the individual receiving the criticism if you do not offend them. But it goes beyond just trying to get them to buy into wanting to improve or agree with you. Your heart and mind should get upset if they perceive you as cruel or inconsiderate. You should want them to know you care because you do.

Honest

There is such a thing as being too honest. It's called being a jerk. You can't just simply go up to anyone you want and provide them with honest feedback. Individuals who walk around providing honesty to anyone they want to are often seen as exceptionally arrogant. They pride themselves on their honesty and often tell people, "People don't like what I have to say, but at least I'm honest," or "I tell it like it is." Often the direct candor of brutal honesty comes from a place of malice or authoritarianism. People who are too honest continue to do so because most other individuals are afraid to speak up. However, when an individual forgets about being polite and kind, the honesty turns to blunt candor, damaging the relationship and destroying trust.

My suggestion of slowing down and thinking about what you will say will help you organize sentences in a way that incorporates all three of these components. When you start with kindness, it's much easier to follow up with honesty that is not cruel. When you start off being polite, it's much more likely they will believe your kindness. Whenever you face a tough conversation and wonder how it could have gone better, write down a few PKH statements you wish you had made. Here are a few examples to get you started.

Examples of PKH Statements

Statement That Was Made	PKH Statement
If you are late again, I'm going to write you up.	I care about you as a team member, but it's not fair to the rest of the team when you are consistently late. I'm going to need to write you up because you've received numerous warnings. Let's talk about how to help break the cycle of being late.
I heard that you have been doing a lot of gossiping, and I need you to stop. It's upsetting everyone. This is not the kind of culture that we want in our hospital.	You have some fantastic technician skills, and we enjoy having you here. Unfortunately, I have heard that you have been doing a lot of gossiping, which is disrupting the team. I want to hear from you. Is there something you are upset or concerned about?

Statement That Was Made	PKH Statement
I need you to stop being so negative. It's bringing the entire team down.	I'm concerned about you because you are a valued team member. You seem to be in a negative space lately. Do you mind talking to me about what's bothering you?
You can't yell at clients! We keep getting bad reviews because of you. You're going to need to knock it off.	I see how much you care about your team members and the pets that come into the hospital. However, you appear to be very frustrated with clients lately, and we need to address why. What's going on?

I am going to let you in on a little secret. The statements on the left are statements that I personally have made in my career to those I have managed. Unfortunately, like most, I have failed time and time again to convey kindness to the individual I'm providing the criticism to. Instead, I have just been candid and brutally honest.

Being brutally honest isn't something to brag about. By definition, brutal is "savagely violent" or "punishingly hard or uncomfortable." (Merriam-Webster.com, 2022) When you see the word brutal defined, you realize that it's probably not the best method of communication. Yet, I know countless leaders and even individuals who brag about their ability to be brutally honest. They state they love writing people up. They will say the person receiving the criticism needs to learn how to take it better. They don't see they are the problem. Rather, the other person is. In the end, being brutally honest will cause the other individual to shut down. In some individuals, it may cause them to become defensive, and in others, it may cause them to be self-loathing. It is hard to move forward with correcting any issues if the person has completely shut down and stopped listening.

In the revised PKH statements listed earlier, you can still manage to get your point across while not being cruel. You will still need to create corrective action and directives to help coach and improve the individual. The more you become comfortable with this style of communication, the more empathetic a leader you will become.

A leader who comes from a place of kindness and honesty takes no pride in corrective action against a team member. I always felt a sense of sadness that I had to write someone up over an issue. When I wrote them up, I wanted them to understand that I cared about them and took no pleasure in the corrective action.

In order for those on your team to receive criticism or communication from you, they have to know that you care about them. Furthermore, they have to believe that you are holding their best interest at all times. The honest statement will land well if they believe and trust that you care and want the best for them.

Trust Before PKH Conversations

Trust, Trust, Trust. Are you sick of me saying it? Remember that you won't have PKH conversations if the individual receiving the communication does not trust you. If they do not trust you, they could think the honesty is rude or manipulative. The reality is it may take years to build a trusting relationship with every individual member of your team.

In my first book, I wrote about ways to develop a trusting relationship with every member of your team. For many of us, we are put into leadership roles in which the team is highly toxic prior to us obtaining that role. Often trust is broken because a manager or supervisor is part of that toxicity or even the driver behind it. It's okay if you realize that you may be the issue. When leaders admit to failure and apologize for their mistakes, the team learns to trust them even faster.

I once was talking to a manager, and she started crying. "It's my fault. I've been burned-out. I've hated coming to work. I expected them to work through their breaks, and I micromanaged them. I did all the toxic things you were just describing."

I responded, "That's okay. They know you are human. Let's talk about how to get you back on track to being the manager you want to be." Remember that it will take time for the team to learn to trust you again if you were part of the toxic culture. Building trust starts with honesty and listening to them.

I Just Listened to Them

I was thrown into one of my leadership roles on the eve of Thanksgiving. The role was more or less handed to me in a last-ditch effort to decrease the high turnover of veterinary staff. I had built a trusting relationship by working on the floor with the team for more than a year. However, the owner passed over more senior veterinary technicians and handed me the role. I worried the team would not be supportive of me. What made me so special to get this role over others? Would they just quit? Would they yell at me? I really had no idea how they would react when they learned.

I did what I thought I would want if I were in their position. I would want someone to listen to me. I would certainly not expect any new leader to be able to fix all of the hospital and team issues overnight. I would expect any new leader to listen and care about me.

I took the time to meet with every single member of my team individually. It was not easy. It was very time-consuming. All I wanted from my first meeting with each of them was to listen. I wanted to hear from their perspective why they felt turnover was so high, why they personally stayed, and what changes they would like to see made. For some, this conversation took more than an hour. For others, it was done in 20 minutes. In total, I had about 26 hours of individual meetings.

I took copious notes. I made sure that I was humble and respectful of whatever they threw my way. I also wanted to ensure they knew I appreciated their time and valued them as a team member. Lastly, I asked for their help.

It seemed so natural and innate to me to have these lengthy conversations rather than just start trying to fix things without input from the team. Luckily, my Spidey sense was right. What I was not consciously aware I was doing was building up trust between myself and the team. I was building up their emotional bank accounts (EBA) by depositing kindness into each of them. One of the most common things I heard at the end of every conversation was that they felt it was wonderful someone had just listened, and for the first time, they felt hopeful that things might change. Without them knowing it, they were depositing right back into my EBA by paying kindness into mine.

The best way to ruin the trust I built up in those conversations would have been to do nothing afterward. I immediately held a group meeting and laid out the concerns they had presented to me in the individual meetings. I was honest with them that some of the areas that needed to be improved upon were daunting. However, I was committed to making the majority of the changes they wanted because they were in the team's best interest.

Some of their concerns were that they felt underappreciated and micromanaged. Nobody liked the level of gossip currently running rampant throughout the hospital. Several felt like they were pulling more weight than others. A few had pay concerns. A few more had concerns with the relationship between departments. Every single one of these concerns was valid.

Over the years, I committed to addressing each of these separately. As more concerns popped up, I added them to my list and tackled them accordingly. As a result, my trust was strengthened with my team from the first time I spoke to them because they saw my commitment to developing a happier team environment.

Confession:
I Destroyed a Relationship With a College Because of Bad Communication

While I always strive to utilize PKH communication, there have been some failures. I once single-handedly destroyed a relationship with an accredited veterinary technician college program because I forgot the polite part of PKH.

Many veterinary hospitals host veterinary technician students who are required to perform externships to learn the skills required by the college in order to graduate. The hospital I managed had a high number of students that would rotate through at any given time. We welcomed students because approximately 35 to 40% would result in a hire after they graduated. Like almost every veterinary hospital worldwide, our veterinary hospital struggled with staffing. Hiring a credentialed veterinary technician out of college helped fill some of our staffing shortages.

I had developed what I thought was a solid student externship program for the hospital. Students could come in and stay in either one department or rotate through a few specialties. They were provided a packet of information that included a timesheet to log in and out of their shifts, a code of conduct, a bag, a pair of hemostats, and their schedule. When students would come in for their shifts, they were assigned to a senior veterinary technician. They knew they had to treat their externship shift like a job. It was a well-run, organized program I was proud of.

Our students were expected to perform their skills with a senior veterinary technician who would double-check their work. All medication doses needed to be double-checked by a veterinarian or a senior veterinary technician who would then watch them administer the drug. Physical exam findings were also double-checked. This was a great way for students to utilize their skills to the fullest while also ensuring patient safety. The senior veterinary technician was aware that the student fell under their responsibility and care. We would never blame the student for any mistake made because they were still learning. Instead, the veterinary technician would coach and mentor that student if a mistake occurred.

At one point, we had three students rotating through our hospital while the hospital was also experiencing an exceptionally high caseload. As a result, it was difficult for the team to actively teach students as well as perform their jobs. I could see it was causing stress to some staff because they wanted to be there for the students but struggled to balance their regular duties. However, I figured they were managing well enough. Even though I had heard some grumbles, I trusted my team to find the balance between educating students and their normal day-to-day responsibilities.

I came in to work an overnight shift and heard the team making fun of one student. Luckily, no other students were present at the time. The comments were, "How could she not know that? What is the school even teaching her? If she doesn't know, she should probably start back in semester one." They were pretty harsh, so I inquired about what the issue was.

It was explained to me that a student had written down a heart rate of 60 beats a minute for a cat on a treatment sheet. Four hours later, she wrote down a heart rate of 50 beats a minute. If you are not part of veterinary medicine, then you may not be aware the average heart rate in a hospital setting for a cat is between 180 to 200 beats a minute. The two heart rates the student wrote down would be considered life-threatening emergencies, and the cat would most likely look like it was dying or, at the very least, critical. I looked at the cat patient the student had examined, and it was walking around its cage and seemed fairly healthy. It was impossible that the student could've obtained such a low heart rate, given the healthy appearance of the patient. The student had not counted the heart rates correctly.

After recounting the story to me, they started making fun of the student again. One even called her an idiot and felt sorry for any hospital that she would be employed with in the future. I became angry. I asked who was in charge of the student and why they had not caught this mistake. My concern was that the student went home thinking that a heart rate of 50 beats a minute in a cat was normal. "Shame on us for not helping that student out," I thought. I was so enraged that I walked away from the team, thinking about what I needed to do about the current situation.

In my frustration and anger, I composed an email. It took a straightforward, honest approach and one that was centered around kindness. However, it lacked the polite part of PKH. Here is part of the email I sent to my hospital's entire technician and assistant team that same day.

"I am disappointed today. I learned that a student made a mistake and our team's response was to make fun of that student. We are obligated to educate students to be the best they can be as veterinary professionals. While I agree this student should have learned what a normal cat's heart rate was from school, we must remember that students forget things. Sadly, this student went home thinking that a normal cat's heart rate was 50 to 60 beats a minute. Shame on us.

I have been hearing a lot about how students are a burden to our hospital. Many students who have done externships with us are now valued team members. Students are never a burden, and the fact that many of our team think so makes me sad. Many of us used to be students. We have always prided ourselves in offering the best externship experience for those that rotate through here, but we failed to do so today. I expect better of everyone on my team."

I look back on that email, and I cringe. I cared deeply for the student but forgot to care about my team. I also started off the email by talking about myself and my emotions. "I am disappointed today." Who cares about my emotions when the focus should be on the team and the student? After that first sentence, I lost any semblance of getting the team to understand what I was trying to convey.

This atrocity didn't stop with that email. As I mentioned, we had many wonderful team members that had been students themselves. They were close with some of the students who were rotating through the hospital, and many personally knew the very student that the team was making fun of. In true email-gone-bad-fashion, a few of my employees who knew the students currently in their externship at the hospital forwarded the email. That's right. My employees forwarded three students my email. And guess what? Those students forwarded my email to the entire veterinary technician college class. Did your heart just sink? Mine just did all over again.

Every student in the college veterinary technician program now knew that my staff largely felt students were a burden and that one student had been made fun of. The program director called the hospital and asked to speak to me directly. She wanted to know why my hospital no longer appreciated having student externs. When I took the call, she told me the story of how every student had read my email. I thought I was going to vomit right then and there. I had no idea how I could fix the kerfuffle I had created.

From the student's perspective, they learned that the hospital team was making fun of them. The student who had made the mistake was now the laughingstock of her class and was embarrassed. She didn't even want to attend classes in person. The other students felt unwelcomed at my hospital because of what had happened.

It didn't end there. My hospital team was mad at me for not supporting them sooner when they voiced their concerns that they were struggling to maintain a balance between educating students and their day-to-day responsibilities. They were also upset because the entire school thought poorly of them as a veterinary medical team.

I know what many of you are thinking. "I'd be pissed if my team forwarded one of my emails outside my hospital." Let me be clear. Those thoughts did enter mine, but the reality is if it were a better-worded email, none of this would have happened. It takes a lot of internal analysis within a leader to stop and ask:

- Why would my team forward my email?
- Why did it upset so many people?

I did a lot of apologizing. I also spent hours trying to fix what I had done. Talk about breaking trust. In one email, I destroyed the trust between the college, my hospital, and myself and my team. Unfortunately, sometimes you can't fix everything. The students of the class were really angry, and two out of the three of our students elected to finish out their externships at other hospitals. I did manage to apologize directly to the one student who was the most affected. She accepted my apology, but I knew I had caused her irreversible harm. To this day, I regret it, and I can only hope that she is doing well and is successful in the profession.

Our hospital saw a dramatic decrease in the number of student externs that wanted to come to our facility. Unfortunately, it took two years to recover from that email to get back to the number of students we were hosting before the email.

My own team was angry with me and for good reason. I had failed them. I kept thinking they could handle the increased caseload and the students. They had been vocal, but I didn't see a way to solve the problem, so I figured they would just work it out. When they failed, I threw them all under the bus, and an entire school found out about it. They were so angry with me that they forwarded my email. I failed them as a leader, and they did the very thing every leader fears. They took matters into their own hands. While it was uncool what they did, I could hardly blame them. It was out of character for my team to react that way. Ultimately, I had to recognize my failure.

To date, this was one of the biggest blunders of my entire career in a management role. Even though it's been more than 15 years, it was an exceptionally difficult story to recount for this book. However, I think it's an important story because of the many lessons learned.

My biggest lesson is that I am eternally grateful that my team trusted me before my mistake. Even though the email centered around the student's best interests, they knew deep down that I was upset because I wanted them to be the best they could be. They saw that I was passionate about elevating them to a higher standard than they had portrayed that day. They also accepted the humility and sincere apology I offered them countless times. It would've been a completely different story if I had not had their trust before my email. That said, I still lost some trust from my team.

Did I go after the individuals who forwarded my email to the students? No. I was smart enough to recognize that would only cause my relationship with them to become even more broken. I did acknowledge it by saying, "While I would have preferred you not to have forwarded the email, I understand why you did it. I didn't support your hard work and wasn't there when you needed me. I didn't listen to your concerns and blamed you when you failed."

Another very, very, very (not a typo) large lesson learned was that you do not criticize in public because it's not polite to do so. By emailing an entire team about an error or criticism, you are doing so in public. It will never be well received. Before sending out any email that offers any sort of criticism, stop. Have someone else review the email. Don't send it out the same day, even if you think the email needs to go out because it's an "emergency." Emergency is in bunny-ear quotes because rarely, if ever, is sending out an email an emergency.

If you're going to send out an email with any criticism, get a second person to look at it and send it out the next day after you've had time to rethink it. There is nothing that is an emergency that needs to be sent in an email on the same day. Always remember this valuable rule: criticize in private and praise in public. If I had remembered this golden rule of leadership, I would have saved a few pages of storytelling in this book.

The point of this humble and humiliating story is to drive home the point that it is important you share your mistakes with your team. It will allow them to see that you are human and build trust between you and them in times when you need it most. My team never expected me to be perfect, but they did expect me to apologize when I made mistakes. This story illustrates the vulnerable honesty that all leaders need to give in order to have the most effective communication with their team.

The Leader Is the Problem

Some of you reading this book are the problem. Maybe you just realized it, or maybe you have yet to realize it, but without question, some of you are the toxic member of the hospital. Many hospital leaders find themselves burned out at some point. The result of this is that they become disconnected from their team, and they become toxic. The team then loses trust in that leader. Sometimes, the leader has an eye-opening experience where they realize that they have broken their team's trust and are not sure how to get it back.

The good news is you can regain the trust of your team. The bad news is, it's going to take time. First, you must be honest with your team that you recognize you are the toxic individual. Call out your toxic traits. Perhaps you are absent, micromanage, set the bar so high that it is impossible to ever reach it, or maybe you are angry all the time. Whatever it is, acknowledge how you recognize that you need to be better and ask the team for their support as you work toward improving your leadership skills. It's not easy to have such a conversation. Start that conversation with someone who supports you before talking to the whole team about it.

I have coached a few leaders who recognized that they caused some dysfunction in the team and wanted to make amends. After working on a plan to improve themselves, they had to meet with the team and ask for forgiveness and support. These meetings are often emotionally draining for the leader who needs to expose their soul to regain the trust of their team. That said, every time a leader does this, it transforms the team. The team sees a humility and a rawness in their manager that has been previously hidden. They see their manager's vulnerability and often support them in moving forward.

Every person knows what it feels like to make a mistake. However, a mistake is made okay when others support you in getting through it. When leaders apologize for their toxicity and less-than-ideal leadership style, the team often rallies around them to help support that leader. When leaders have such honest and raw conversations with their team, I have found that they become closer than before the toxicity started.

In short, a leader goes from being toxic to being trusted by apologizing and asking for support from the team in their new transformation. Trust isn't going to occur overnight, but through honest conversation, the team will learn to trust all over again.

Chapter Seven

Starting to Change the Culture

Creating a different culture takes time. The steps toward this should not be rushed. It's about developing trust and respect within the team. Minimally, the process below will take six to nine months, and for most, it will average about 12 to 18 months. This might seem like forever but remember that it took years for the toxicity to occur. A year of working to improve the hospital is not that long when it's been years of toxicity.

The five steps listed below are the start of change, but hardly all you need to do. Each step is described in detail. The rest of the book will provide you with other solutions and ideas to continue improving your hospital's culture. When you decide to move forward with change, you must write a complete project plan for every item you wish to change. Too often, leaders do one little thing here and there, which results in no real change. I call this the "one yoga class method." The thought is, "If we bring in a yoga instructor, then the team will see we care about them, and all will be fixed." Real change requires hours of planning, follow-through on implementation, and re-evaluation of the plan throughout the process. Because it is a lengthy process, you can find a shortened step-by-step outline in the book's Appendix One to refer to.

- Step One: Admit There's an Issue at a Meeting
- Step Two: Tackle a Few Concerns
- Step Three: Receive & Share Feedback About Yourself
- Step Four: Teach the Team to Give & Receive Compliments
- Step Five: Bring in the Honesty (addressed in the next chapter)

STEP ONE:
Admit There's an Issue at a Meeting

Before you dive into trying to create a change, you must first have the team acknowledge there's even an issue. If teams can't agree there's a problem, then why would they ever agree to change? Unfortunately, this step often gets missed by leadership, resulting in poor buy-in. In order to change the culture, you have to change the conversation. You have to start with admitting there's an issue.

There are several ways leaders can help their teams realize that they are struggling with toxicity and negativity. Unfortunately, most leaders fail at this crucial step because they have a meeting and start by saying, "There has been a lot of negativity and gossip lately. We need to figure out how to stop it and be more positive." Don't tell your team what is wrong. Instead, listen to them and have them tell you.

You can have your team admit there is an issue in two ways. Both ways start with a meeting centered around leadership listening to the issues from the team. That's right, just listening. No input, no arguing. "We will have a full team meeting on XXX date to discuss concerns within the hospital." The team is now prepared to discuss issues and will know what the meeting is about.

The meeting should be scheduled for only one hour, not any longer, or it will become unproductive. You will want to start by expressing your concern that you are worried there is a lot of negativity in the team and that you genuinely want to get to the root of the issue. This is where you can talk about your goals to the team in general terms. Instead of blaming the team for the issues (there's too much gossip, you are all so negative), present larger goals. The goals should be broad-reaching, such as "I'd like to see less burnout" or "I'd like this hospital to be a place where people love working."

Whatever your goals are, you must come from a place of caring deeply about the team. Your main concern is about the team's health and well-being. You should genuinely want to help them. Practice what you will say to the team before the meeting. Once your team hears you care and want to help, they will be more likely to participate in the meeting. Here's an example of how to kick off the meeting.

"I have some concerns about the team and hospital. Several of you have come to me and expressed your concerns about how you are worried about the team's culture. I care deeply for the hospital and, most importantly, you. I know we all want this hospital to be a place people enjoy working in. Today's meeting is so I can listen to your concerns. I'm not going to try to solve anything today. Instead, I want to listen to your concerns, think about them, and come back to you with the next steps. I know it will be difficult for you to be honest with your concerns, but I cannot improve issues if I am unaware of them. My main objective is to make this a great hospital that you are all happy working at."

So how do we get the team to open up? It sounds nice in theory, but in reality, teams will lie and say, "everything is okay," or sugarcoat what is truly happening in the hospitals. You will need to ask, "What are one to two things that need to be changed for you or the team to be happier at work?"

I know what many of you are thinking, "That's a nightmare of a question to ask!" But, how else will you know if you don't ask? Too often, leaders would rather just fix the things they believe need to be fixed rather than go to the source and work with them on the concerns. I didn't say this would be easy. However, if teams are going to embrace PKH communication in an effort to start to change the culture, then leaders need to get comfortable with honesty.

Method One: Hybrid Method in a Meeting

- This is a fact-finding meeting, not a bitching and complaining session.
- You set the rules of the meeting upfront.
  - Everyone is provided 3 minutes to discuss their concerns (maybe less if the team is large).
  - Only the person who is speaking is allowed to speak.
  - Yelling or inappropriate language will not be tolerated. If that occurs, the individual will need to excuse themselves or be excused until they can come back to the meeting and act professionally.
  - Individuals are asked to stick to the facts of what is wrong rather than hearsay or gossip.
  - Ask the question, "What are one to two things that need to be changed for you or the team to be happier at work?"
- Leaders will not speak but instead listen.
- Go around the room and ensure everyone has time to talk. If the team is large, the meeting should be split to keep it under an hour.
- The meeting is to gain insight into the concerns of the employees.
- Employees are encouraged to be honest but also professional.
- The meeting will not last longer than one hour.
- Individuals who do not wish to speak may write down their concerns on provided paper or email them to their manager.
- Concerns not voiced must be submitted by 8:00 am the following morning so leadership can start evaluating and discussing the concerns submitted after the meeting.

This hybrid model gives those who wish to speak a chance to do so, but there is also the option for those who would rather submit concerns privately. The cons are that emotions may escalate for both leaders and employees. It's hard to listen to one criticism after another without leaders saying, "But you are wrong," or "We are working on that." Sometimes the meeting can spiral out of control, and leaders may feel ganged up on by the employees. This method also does not allow for any anonymous reporting. Even those who email or write down their thoughts should be expected to attach their name to their concern.

Method Two: Silent Conversation in a Meeting

- You will host your regular meeting with routine agenda items. However, the first agenda item will be the concern of the team's culture and climate.
- Pass out sheets of paper where the top reads, "What are one to two things that need to be changed for you or the team to be happier working here?"
  - Name: (this can be omitted if you think your team will respond better to it being anonymous)
  - Area for the employee to write concerns.
- State that all team members must contribute. Give them 10 minutes to complete their thoughts. Have them turn in their paper. Resume the regular meeting.

The pro of this method is that it allows reporting to be either anonymous or not. It does not take an entire meeting to do and will result in less heated emotions. You will continue with your regular meeting after explaining to them what you and the leadership team will do with the information provided. The con is that no one has an actual voice. It does not allow for any reduction in emotions, which can be beneficial. The act of allowing someone to express their concerns is more impactful and meaningful than only having individuals write down their thoughts. Those who get to use their voice feel heard and cared for. That said, if you know your team will struggle with communicating professionally, this may be the preferred method to obtain the information needed to identify the issues.

Method Three: Engagement Survey with Meeting After

Leadership must first convey their commitment to change and inform the team that they will be sent an engagement survey that will be anonymous. I prefer this communication to be done in person to allow the team to ask a few questions. I also prefer the survey to be anonymous because it usually allows for greater participation. Employees should have the option of providing their names if they so choose. For an example of an engagement survey, take a look at Appendix One in the back, which breaks down these steps in a simplified step-by-step process.

Leadership will send out the survey and set a time in which it should be completed, usually two to three weeks. From there, the leadership will compile the data and provides detailed responses at an in-person meeting. If you fail to provide any information, you will lose the team. You need to be as transparent as possible with the data. Be sure to show the good, the bad, and the ugly.

Remember that when filtering data, it should be filtered around PKH communication. Therefore, if an employee attacked another employee in the survey, that information is not shared, but perhaps the general concern is. "Ally is lazy and never helps to clean" is different than "Ensure all team members contribute to cleaning." Tailor to ensure the same message without it being cruel. After reviewing the information as a leadership team, move on to step two.

After You Have the Information

First, thank the team. This is critical to the process. It doesn't matter if they cited your poor leadership skills as a reason for their negative behavior. You should be grateful they were honest. Be sure to thank your team.

Next, inform them when you will next follow up. I would suggest no more than three weeks, preferably two. The momentum will be lost if it's closer to a month, two months, or even longer. The team will assume it's not a priority. They just shared important information with you about why they are so negative. As a leader, you must prioritize that information and not sit on it for weeks. The team needs to feel like there will be action; otherwise, the meeting was all in vain.

Take time to review all the information with the other hospital leaders. This process should take a couple of hours. Identify common concerns to tackle first. Next, choose two, no more than three concerns that you commit to improving first. Then, create a plan centered around each of these concerns.

For example, if the team has identified being short-staffed as a concern, it's important leadership develops a plan around this. Perhaps leadership does not feel the team is short-staffed. It is important to provide a list of why they feel this way to the team. If the hospital has been trying to hire for some time with little success, consider hosting a brainstorming session. Instead of providing a new hire bonus, can we offer a finder's fee to current employees? Would that cause our team to work hard to find staff for the hospital? Write down the plan, include a timeline and goals, and be ready to share an abbreviated version with the team at the next meeting.

Here's what I have found every single time I've done this: communication issues are always identified. It may be between departments, teams, individuals, or in the form of gossiping, attitudes, or even yelling. Regardless, communication will be listed as one of the main concerns. In fact, I will bet that most of the issues listed are communication-based. I would recommend starting with improving communication as one of the items to work on. Communication will be an ongoing plan to work on throughout the year.

In developing your plan, I would recommend introducing PKH, but this should not be your only communication plan. You should consider educating the team on conflict resolution, client communication, communication skills after the loss of a pet, and more. Teams should learn better ways to communicate throughout the year, not just in one meeting.

STEP TWO:
Tackle a Few Concerns

Hold your second meeting. Review the trends in the concerns that were brought up and discuss which 2-3 issues the leadership team will work to improve first. Since one of the concerns the leadership has chosen to work on is communication, ask the team if they would like to improve communication issues. The answer will be yes. We can introduce PKH communication during this meeting which I would strongly recommend as one of the items leadership tackles right away.

While many of the concerns discussed at the first meeting were centered around communication, many others were not. These likely include pay, being short-staffed, high patient counts, lack of benefits, poor medical practices, or hazards in the workplace. As a leader, you must address these issues as well. While we want to introduce PKH as a concept, you must acknowledge the other concerns. You do not have to have all the answers, but a timeline of how the other concerns will be handled must be presented. Remember, acknowledge all the concerns the leadership team is committed to improving, but let the team know that the first two will be communication and whatever else the team chooses.

This second meeting is where you will share your plans with the team. In the communication improvement plan, you will share with your team how you want everyone to learn PKH communication and whatever other communication skill you wish to teach them. Be sure to share the plans for the other one to two concerns the leadership team has decided to tackle for the next few months.

Run through the plans and then leave a minimum of 20 minutes during the one-hour meeting for open discussion and questions. List the common concerns, then acknowledge and thank them for their honesty. Next, inform the team that you and the other leaders are working to fix the other concerns, but you will focus on improving communication as a team. This is where you can now directly impact the team's culture by improving the toxicity through bettering communication.

Let me be clear. Should you drop the ball on all other concerns, you can forget about changing the culture of your team. I know what many of you are thinking, "I can't just give everyone a raise, and they are citing that as an issue of their unhappiness." It is always reasonable for a leader to reply to this concern with, "Many of you cited salary as a cause of your unhappiness. We are taking this seriously and will be doing an in-depth analysis of veterinary salaries in the area and looking at our payroll budget. It is always valuable for a hospital to dive into payroll and adjust where possible. That said, this will take time, and I'm not going to make promises that payroll will change. However, I appreciate you bringing it up, and as we progress with our analysis, we will keep you informed."

From there, leadership should analyze salaries, profit and loss statements, payroll budgets, and other metrics. Why not? This type of practice is called good business, and your team should know you heard them and the steps that will be taken to address their concerns. Maybe you will find nothing needs to be changed, or maybe you will alter your payroll drastically. As an aside, good businesses analyze their payroll at least once a year. While I am focusing on communication to help change the toxicity within your team, do not mistake this as the only thing you need to focus on as a leader.

Starting the Conversation Around PKH

It seems obvious by the sheer definition of the words polite, kind, and honest as to what that type of communication style this should be, but it is harder than it seems. First, explain what PKH is to your team and its benefits.

Benefits of PKH Communication

- Increases trust between team members.
- Helps share ideas without fear of ostracization.
- Builds respect.
- Decreases bullying in the workplace.
- Decreases the fear of what others think when mistakes occur.
- Increases honesty between teams.
- Creates a more professional work environment.
- Decreases negativity.
- Creates a more supportive culture.
- Breaks down the divide between departments and teams.
- Decreases gossiping.
- Increases psychological safety (discussed in Chapter Eighteen).

Once you've highlighted the benefits address any concerns. Get them excited about this "new form of communication." It's not really a new form of communication, but when getting teams on board with a new method of anything, explaining that it is new often creates excitement. They feel like they are part of a movement. It will be better received than saying, "This is how you should have been communicating this entire time rather than treating each other like garbage." Sure, that's what you want to say, but don't. You'll lose them.

Explain that the entire team will embark on the same journey towards improving their communication using a new communication style. You will get better buy-in when you point out the issues they cited that were centered around communication are being worked on through learning about PKH together as a team.

If you have individuals who feel like this is just hogwash and some new fad of communicating, ask them questions that will get you a yes response.

- "Do you want to share ideas and not worry about people making fun of your idea behind your back because they provide honest answers upfront?"
- "If you make a medical mistake, would you like your team's support and kindness?"
- "Would you like to be able to provide criticism to a team member without them thinking you are rude?"
- "Would you like others to talk to you in a kind manner while also being honest?"

Research has shown that when selling something, even if it's selling an idea, getting naysayers to say yes to questions that only have a yes response will get better buy-in (Carnegie, 1936). Call it a life hack when dealing with change management, but I find "yes only" questions highly effective in getting others on the path to agreement.

I know some of the responses that people will follow up with on the questions I provided above, as I have been the person to provide snarky responses to some of them. Let's take the example, "Do you want to share ideas and not worry about people making fun of your idea behind your back because they provide you honest answers upfront?"

A snarky response would be, "Yes, but I don't care what anyone thinks." In your head, you are thinking, "Cool story, bro, but the majority of other people do care." As a leader, you must accept that a certain number of "I think everything sucks" team members will never agree that anything new is worth trying. You will present them with an amazing plan to help change something they were concerned with, and they will poo-poo all over it. These individuals are most likely the brutally honest people on your team who are causing some toxicity.

Don't engage with these naysayers. There is no point. They believe they know what is best, nothing will change, and the hospital will fail.

Here's the thing about the snarks and naysayers of the world. If you ignore them, they will eventually go away. If most of the team is committed to developing a culture of kindness and honesty, your few negative individuals will either come around or leave. What the dark clouds hate is light in the form of kindness. They would rather surround themselves with thunderstorms and darkness.

Focus on those dedicated to developing a positive culture and climate. Give your energy to them, and you will elevate them even more. I often think of the image of the vampire seeing the light of day. When the bloodsucking vampire is surrounded by too much daylight, it has to retreat back to its coffin, or it risks being disintegrated by the light. Don't let the few vampire team members suck the life out of the entire team. Just ignore them because the daylight in the form of positivity will eventually eliminate them.

By the end of this meeting, you have created excitement about the two or three items the team will work to improve. Be sure to discuss the next steps towards tackling these plans.

STEP THREE: Receive & Share Feedback About Yourself

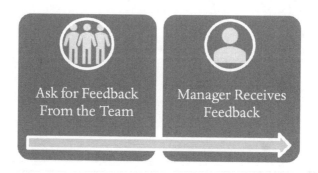

For many of you, looking at this graphic brings shutters down your spine. I'm sure many of you thought you could just start dishing out honest criticism to everyone on your team. You were hoping to tell the team what it is, walk away, and let the magic happen, right? Sorry, changing a toxic team takes much more work, as I've mentioned. Unfortunately, there is no magical unicorn that will come to save your hospital.

PKH does not work if you cannot learn how to accept feedback. You need to know how the receiver will feel when you provide feedback. When you request feedback from a team member or your team, it shows that you know that you are open to being vulnerable and needing self-improvement. You need to want and appreciate the feedback. During your first meeting, you may have received some feedback directed at yourself. The good news is the first meeting sets you up for this part of the process. Changing a team's culture starts with you wanting to be the best leader you can be.

Remember that you are in a leadership role, and people are uncomfortable criticizing you. Even if you were best friends with everyone on your team before taking a leadership role, you are now their manager. Here's the even harder part. You will need to reward them for their honesty if you want to get the truth out of them. If you interrupt or criticize them, you might as well give up receiving feedback from your team.

There are various ways of getting your team to open up and provide you with feedback. Soliciting feedback, especially if it's criticism, needs to happen more than just once. It has been suggested that the best leaders gain the trust of their team by soliciting guidance daily (Scott, 2019). That seems like a lot, but not if you structure your day by asking your team for feedback such as, "How could I help the team with XYZ?" or "Is there something I could be doing differently to help you better?"

After introducing the concept of PKH communication, let them know that you will be speaking with each of them individually to connect with them. After your second meeting, you will want to schedule one-on-one sessions with each team member. These meetings focus on building your relationship with them, asking about their career goals, and having them provide feedback on yourself as a leader. During the meeting, ask a few of these questions:

- What is one thing that I could improve upon to help you be more successful?
- What are you getting from me that you want more of?
- What are you getting from me that you want less of?
- What could I do to improve as a leader for you or the team?

These are some tough questions, and listening to the answers will be even tougher. The toughest situation is when you are faced with someone you know is not being honest. These are the individuals who say to you, "You're amazing. There's nothing I would want to be changed."

How do you pull the honesty out of them? It's important you realize they are not honest with you because they don't trust how you will react. They worry that you will be upset, angry, or self-loathing. For many, not being completely honest is because they don't want to hurt your feelings. Many people justify not being honest because the things you may need to improve upon are "really" not that big of a deal. But they are a big deal! You do want to know about areas that could be improved upon.

To get someone to open up to you, make a joke. Suggest that the reason why they can think of nothing that you need to improve upon is because you're already perfect. Point out a flaw that you know exists. For me, I would point out that, at times, I interrupt people. Most of the time, once you point out a flaw, that person will agree with you. They may even say something to the effect of, "Yes, you do sometimes interrupt people." Encourage them by responding with, "Great! See, there is something I can work on. What else? I know there are other things I can improve upon." This technique permits others to offer feedback. By openly acknowledging something you can improve upon, you give permission to your employees to do the same for you.

Your team will only be honest with you if they feel you will not retaliate against them. If you have become visibly upset with an employee in the past for providing criticism to you, it's going to be exceptionally difficult for them to overcome this fear. As a leader, all you can do is continue to praise them for providing feedback and never become angry, defensive, or criticize back.

If your team struggles to open up to you directly, start with an anonymous survey. Ask some tough questions where they can provide feedback to you. Writing down thoughts is often easier than directly saying it to the individual. An anonymous survey may help to reduce anxiety about providing feedback for those that may be introverted or nervous. The only time you should take this route is because the one-on-one meetings didn't produce results. You want to hear their feedback, and despite your best efforts to meet individually, it didn't go as planned. The 1:1 meetings are important in building relationships.

Now, Share the Feedback

That's right, after you receive the feedback, you are going to share it with the entire team. If you cannot show your team your vulnerability, then a culture of PKH communication will never happen, and the team's culture will not improve. The team needs to see a commitment from you that you want to change before they believe their leader is invested in changing the hospital.

Leading by example is important. Act how you want them to act. You want them to reflect and make changes within themselves and the team. For that to happen, you need to commit to changing the way you lead.

To share the feedback you received from the team, have a meeting with them to share some areas of improvement you're going to commit to working on. For example, perhaps you heard from your team that they felt you lacked consistent communication, were a little harsh at times, or wished you came in on time. During this meeting, acknowledge the feedback. "In speaking with all of you, I understand you wish I would come in on time. I'm sorry about not being here when I said I would be. I will post my schedule on my door and hold myself accountable for being on time. I want to make sure you know when I'm available."

Imagine a meeting where a leader thanked the team for their feedback and laid out their performance plan to improve themselves. Imagine how powerful of a meeting it would be. When leaders can fully embrace that kind of honesty and accept that their team's critiques are only meant to help improve their leadership abilities, it opens the door to an influx of trust and kindness from the entire team.

Prepare them at the end of this meeting that the next step is for them to learn how to receive healthy criticism. Recognize that it's not easy. Consider a book club requiring them to read a book centered on developing their communication skills. This will help strengthen the team's communication skills and prepare them for the next step.

Don't forget you are still working through your plan on the two to three items the leadership committed to changing. How are the plans going? Share that with the team so they can see and hear about the improvements.

Some Leaders Can't Handle Criticism

There are many leaders who say they welcome criticism, but very few who actually do. I once was in a role where my manager did not handle any criticism well. This individual didn't have the skillset to be a manager, but sadly they felt like they knew it all. As the problems compounded, I tried to express my concerns using a PKH approach.

I expressed my concerns about the disorganization, poor communication skills, and lack of review of my work. My manager often went to meetings with his boss saying, "I don't understand what's going on with this project," which reflected poorly back on me. Unfortunately, my manager was not understanding my concerns. They didn't recognize they needed to improve their leadership skills.

It wasn't until my manager circumvented me and met with my employee behind my back for a project I was managing when I finally got upset. My manager's reasoning was that I was busy at that moment, and they just wanted to talk about my project with my employee.

There was no emergency to meet. It could have waited until I was available. Even my employee was confused why I wasn't at the meeting and more confused when my manager started making decisions about the project they had little understanding of. The decisions made would have caused issues with the project.

Despite expressing my concerns to my manager, they were not grasping why I was upset. I had to fix countless issues my manager caused by circumventing me.

No matter my approach, my boss truly felt it was okay to leave me out of the conversation and make decisions without me. This was a clear example of why circumventing should not occur because it leaves the person being circumvented upset. The conversation came to a head when my manager told me I was in the wrong. I was just an employee and if they, the boss, wanted to get involved at any point they were allowed to do so.

I asked if they didn't trust me or if I was not meeting their expectations. The answer was, "No, why would you feel that way?" I explained that when a manager circumvents an employee and starts doing the work it is because they feel the work isn't being done to their liking. "Your work is great," my manager replied. I kept trying to have them understand why I was upset. "You have no reason to be upset with me," my boss said. That's when I resorted to calling them a micromanager.

My manager's fist clenched, lips tightened, and they asked me to take it back. I said I would not. The reality is they were not allowing me the full autonomy to do my job. Instead of reflecting on the feedback they stayed focused on their anger. As a leader, when your employee provides criticism the first response should be to take a look inward, not get angry.

The example just listed was one of many times the team and I struggled with our manager. When we provided negative feedback, they would get visibly upset and defensive.

Only you know how you accept criticism. If you become defensive or angry, you need to realize those feelings will distance you from your employees. Your employees should be allowed to express their feelings about you as a manager. It's how they feel. Asking them to take it back only shows you are uncomfortable with criticism. This will result in your employees providing you with fake or no feedback.

One of the greatest strengths of a leader is to be okay with hearing criticism from their employees. The unicorn strength of that is welcoming and accepting criticism. When leaders welcome criticism, they improve their leadership skills and develop the relationship with their employees even further. Conversely, when they dismiss it, become angry, or ask an employee to "take it back," they destroy trust and distance themselves.

Step Four:
Teach the Team to Give & Receive Compliments

The team is nowhere near ready to sit together as a team and discuss each other's strengths and weaknesses. That will cause complete chaos and distrust in the team. Team members who are burned-out or negative often have forgotten the art of praising each other. Instead, they assume the worst of each other. As a result, praise is few and far between from their teammates.

We need to start the team off by trusting each other to provide and accept praise. While this skill seems simple enough, many toxic teams have lost the ability to provide praise to each other. If they can't even praise each other, how will they be expected to receive or provide criticism when necessary?

There are many ways to teach your teams about handing out and receiving compliments. Simply ordering your team to just praise each other is probably not going to land well. Instead, take on a praise challenge, which can be done in one of two ways.

Have a meeting. I know what many of you are thinking. "Another freaking meeting, Amy?!" Yes, another meeting. Do you think you will get a team that believes in one mission and vision if you never meet with them? Remember, change is slow. As I have said and will continue to repeat, there is no magic fix. Think turtle. Correction, think tortoise, which is slower moving than the turtle. Slow changes and you will see results. Fast changes and you will see none.

If you require them to read a book focused on communication, provide them two months to finish it. Reading a book will only make this step easier. If you did not require material, you can likely hold this meeting a month after the last one.

As people come into the meeting, hand them a slip of paper with a team member's name written on it. Ensure that each person has a different team member, so there should be no duplicates, and they aren't given their name. It's also best to ensure that people who are comfortable with each other do not get each other's names. The less familiar they are with each other, so long as they work together from time to time, the better.

Request that they write a specific personality trait that they value and appreciate in that individual. It needs to be a personality trait, not a medical skill or knowledge. After about 5 minutes, have them turn in the pieces of paper back to you. If they seem like they are struggling, give them some examples.

"John knows how to make people laugh."

"Darnell is kind to all team members."

"Tina is so calm around upset owners."

"Courtney is a good listener."

You will now read each personality praise, announcing who it is for. After reading the compliment, the person who wrote it needs to acknowledge they provided the praise. Often, during this exercise, the receiver of this praise is surprised about who wrote it. They are genuinely touched by that individual's kind comment about them. The receiver will usually say, "thank you."

Having them write down the praise on a piece of paper is less threatening than complimenting directly. Verbally providing praise may become awkward or not land well. Because you, the manager/supervisor, are reading the compliments, you will ensure that they are read positively to make the intended impact. You will remove face-to-face awkwardness by being the middleman.

Other ideas to help encourage specific praise between members of the team include:

- Kudos/Appreciation Board: These boards are great because they allow for praise to be given similarly as described above. Team members can begin to trust that each person has their best interest at heart. I'm not a fan of anonymous boards. Ensure your team knows that when they pay a compliment, they need to sign off on it. There is no shame in praising, so make sure the one who praises announces themselves.

- Check a Box When You Have Paid Someone a Compliment: Challenge your team to give everyone a compliment or praise who works at the hospital during a specific time (usually two weeks). Hold them accountable by having a checkbox system. Every time they pay a compliment or praise to someone, they will check the box next to that person's name. Once someone has complimented or praised every employee in the hospital, they are rewarded in some way. Think outside the box with an extra PTO day or a generous gift card to a spa.

You're On Your Way to a Happier Team

By utilizing these four steps, you are well on your way to having a happier team. You have listened to your team's issues and started plans to improve the culture. You have shown that you want to be the best leader by collecting feedback and sharing a plan with your team for your own personal growth. This has started to improve the trust between your team and you. Lastly, you have started teaching your team the importance of praise and compliments. In turn, this will help build trust between team members.

But what about how to manage criticism? That's the fifth and final step in this process, but to be prepared for it, teams need to know how to manage the polite and kind part of communication. The entire setup and prep work for coaching a team through more difficult conversations take six to seven months. While you have made progress, you still have a way to go. Remember, it's a marathon, not a sprint. Runners take years before they attempt to complete a marathon. The training and dedication you're putting forth to lay the foundation for the most difficult piece of changing the culture is important. Throughout all this, you are analyzing your plans to make improvements, revisiting those that may not be making the impact you want, and keeping the team informed along the way.

Chapter Eight

Managing Criticism

At this point, you have introduced the PKH concept to the team and had them practice being polite and kind to each other. You have also started working on one or two more concerns the team had discussed. How do we move from giving praise to managing more difficult conversations? How do we coach our team to manage criticism and conflict?

Bring in the Honesty

Steve Jobs used to say, "Your work is shit" (Holland, 2020). Harsh, right? While Steve Jobs had many wonderful attributes, including being considered a pioneering leader, he scared the living crap out of many of his employees. He was too honest. His statement was meant to shock the individual into realizing that it was not their best work and that they could do better. His direct statement only landed well if he had a trusting relationship with that individual. I would say, don't be that honest. We don't need the crap scared out of our employees.

How do we start bringing in honesty? If it's not a concept we previously had in our team, we need to baby-step in. We can't go right for the jugular or the Steve Jobs approach. Instead, we need to start with a gentle, honest approach.

At this point, your team has already provided you with feedback and criticism. They have learned to embrace compliments from each other. There are many ways to introduce honesty into the team. Most of the time, when we try to be honest, we soften the blow by using empathetic statements. "We no longer can tolerate you yelling at the staff," turns into "We know you have a lot going on, and it's been very busy at the hospital. Clients are more demanding than ever, and we know you've been putting in longer hours. It's hard right now, but we can't have you yelling at the staff. Everyone seems on edge." Do you see what happened there? You ruined your honest statement with too much empathy.

Adding in too much empathy damages the relationship or communication with someone else to a point where the message is lost. When we use too much empathy in a conversation, we soften and may even completely change the context of what we were going to say. I am guilty of this, and most of you are as well.

Let's use the example again with the veterinary technician struggling to calculate drug doses. For many of us, we would approach this conversation like this.

"I want to talk to you about something. You're doing a great job. The team appreciates you. I have heard that you sometimes don't calculate the right drug dose. Math can be difficult. I don't like it either. It was my least favorite subject in school."

What point were you trying to get across to your employee? If it was that math was hard, you accomplished that. In an effort not to upset someone, you ruined the important honest part of the conversation with empathy. For many employees, when they hear a conversation like this from their manager, they walk away thinking it's not a big deal. After all, they were told they were doing a great job. The team likes them. The manager can relate to the difficulty of math. Unfortunately, we fell victim by injecting too much empathy like many others. Our empathy got in the way of the message.

If we inject too much empathy when providing feedback, we do a disservice to that individual. Fast-forward three months from now when this employee continues to struggle with math. Now their manager is threatening their job, and they can't understand why. The worst is when employees are terminated and truly don't understand what went wrong. The manager will say things such as, "I explained to them countless times that they needed to improve their drug calculations." The problem was the delivery fell flat. Too much empathy muddles the water and adds confusion to what you are trying to say. You need to still be kind, and you can add in empathy because you want to make sure the other individual knows you truly care about them but make sure that you are honest and clear.

Another mistake many managers make is to sandwich criticism between two compliments. Nobody wants a criticism sandwich. Managers do this to soften the blow. They pay a compliment, make a criticism, feel bad about it, and soften the blow by paying another compliment. It's a systematic approach: Compliment-Criticism-Compliment.

Use the following formula for constructing your honest feedback so that it lands well and is effective.

1) Be polite above all else.
2) Ensure the individual knows you care deeply by adding kindness.
3) Provide feedback (the criticism, which is still polite and kind).
4) Offer help to find a solution.

Now that the leadership team has started to work on a few of the concerns, they should start to coach the team on accepting and providing constructive criticism.

Ways We Manage Criticism

There are three ways that people handle criticism. They can either acknowledge it, ignore it, or attack it. Sometimes when we think we know how the person will respond, we end up being surprised. We thought they would acknowledge the criticism, but instead, they attacked back. There are no individuals who love and embrace all criticism. It's uncomfortable for the individual giving and the person receiving. Recognizing which of the three ways the individual has chosen to manage the criticism will allow you to respond in a more productive manner.

Acknowledge It

Generally, most people that accept criticism will say, "Thank you for letting me know." Praise the individual. Thank them for handling the criticism well and acknowledge it was hard. "First, I want to thank you for handling that so well. I was worried about how you would receive it, but I wanted to be honest with you." You showed that you cared and acknowledged that it wasn't easy for them, either. Now it's time to devise a next-step plan for the feedback you just provided.

Ignore It

The individual may go silent or even change the subject. It may be difficult to tell whether or not they heard the criticism. They often dismiss what was just said to them by saying, "Sure, I'll work on it." When you continue the conversation, you may get an abrupt, "I said I'd work on it." People who are trying to ignore the criticism will often use phrases such as:

- "I guess I will."
- "Okay then."
- "News to me."
- "Got it."
- "Whatever."

The difference between someone who has accepted and acknowledged the criticism is that they will talk through what the solution could be and want more details. The person ending the conversation, because they are trying to ignore it, will not want any more information and will not work to find a solution. They were done with the conversation right after you provided the feedback.

With this individual, you must continue to try to show them that you care deeply about them and want the best for them. Most of the time, the person who is ignoring the feedback is doing so because they are hurt or feeling dejected. It's acceptable to offer a few more kind accolades so they know that you do have their best interest at heart.

For example, "You have so much knowledge that I want people to feel comfortable going to you to ask questions. People are worried about your reaction, so they are not utilizing your knowledge." Continue to show that you are coming from a place of kindness. Hopefully, the person who is ignoring the feedback will come around to accepting it.

That said, some individuals will not want to discuss or work towards any solution during this meeting. That's okay. You can allow them to think about it. One of my favorite techniques when providing feedback to someone who didn't want to talk about it was that I would table it for later. "I recognize this may be a lot to process. I understand that feedback is hard. How about we stop talking about this today? I want you to take time to think about it, and next week, let's pick back up and work on some solutions together. What are your thoughts on that?" Providing them time to process what you said on their own terms may help them accept the criticism.

Attack It

The employee may either subtly or quite aggressively attack the statement you just made. As a coping mechanism, many people laugh at criticism. They try to laugh it off as if the accusation cannot be true. For example, the employee may laugh and say, "Are you serious? People think I'm abrasive and hard to talk to?! That's ridiculous!" Often someone who attacks criticism wants to know exactly who and how many people said it. They think if they can figure out who has made this claim, they can confront that person and tell them exactly why they are wrong, or they can discredit the person by telling their manager why that person is wrong.

Many individuals who attack the criticism may even say they don't care about what anyone thinks. "It's ridiculous they think I'm hard to talk to. What do I care?!" Yet, they do care because they are visibly upset by what was said. You must handle this upset individual gently. If you return the attack, the behavior will only get worse. If you tell them their reaction is inappropriate, they will escalate.

The first thing that you should do is to remind them of the PKH style of communication. "I can see that you are upset by what I just said. I know it wasn't easy to hear, but I also know that you would want to be aware. I could not have said anything to you, but we're working on improving our team right now, and part of that is working through concerns with polite, kind, and honest conversations like these."

You can try to make it relatable so they can hopefully see the other side. "As you know, I just received a lot of feedback from all of you. It wasn't easy. Some of it was pretty harsh. I understand how you are upset by this, but ultimately, it's important for us to realize that we all have some areas we need to improve upon."

Regardless of your kindness and explanation, only they can accept the criticism. For many, no matter how you try to rephrase or relate to this individual, they will not be able to look past the fact that everyone else is wrong and they are right. Keep bringing it back to the original statement and why they need to improve upon it. "I want to make sure everyone on the team is comfortable going to you because you are a wealth of knowledge. While this is hard to digest, I'm hoping we can work together to find ways for this to improve."

Lastly, if all else fails, you can point out that they are disagreeing with the criticism instead of wanting to improve themselves to be a better team member.

"I hear you continuing to disagree with what I said. Whether you think you are approachable or not, your team members do not feel the same way. I am trying to help and support you because I care about you. I want to ensure that every member of the team feels comfortable going to each other because, in this hospital, that is what's best for our patients and the team. I know you disagree, but I'd like to figure out a way to move you past the disagreement and into accepting so we can work together to help find a solution."

If that technique fails, the final thing is to offer them time to think about what was said. "I know that criticism is tough. Let's stop here and think about our conversation today. I'd like to schedule another meeting in X number of days from now to speak again. I hope you know that I care about you. I want you to be the best team member you can be because you have amazing skill and knowledge as a veterinarian / veterinary technician / client service representative."

At this point, you have tried everything. It is up to the person to accept the criticism and decide if they want to improve or not. Be sure to document all of these conversations, including whether or not they appear willing to improve. Make notations of what specifically is being done to coach the individual.

Learning to Embrace Criticism

There are two different methods to start coaching individuals with accepting and even embracing criticism. These methods are meant to get you thinking about ways to introduce this topic to the team. Some hospitals like to do both of these methods, as they are both beneficial in their own way.

Method One: Start by Having 1:1 Sessions

Communicate with the team that you will be holding follow-up career growth meetings with each individual. I like the term "career growth" rather than performance meeting, as it tends to create less worry. Developing someone's career means their skills, knowledge, as well as their behavior. When you come from a supporting place, the follow-up discussion of anything that needs to be improved upon will land better.

Set each meeting to be no more than 60 minutes. You could consider sending them a survey ahead of time that asks some questions such as:

- What goals do you want to obtain for yourself in the next six months?
- Where do you see yourself in your career five years from now?
- What strengths do you bring to the team?
- What are some areas for improvement?
- How do you feel your overall communication skills are?
- How do you feel you do when managing difficult conversations?
- Do you feel like you have a good work-life balance?
- On average, how stressed do you feel at your job?

Getting the survey back before you meet allows you to spend more time discussing ways to help this individual. The goal of this meeting is to provide some gentle feedback on one or two things they can improve upon to be a better team member or a veterinary professional. If you elect to ask the individual the questions at the meeting rather than a survey ahead of time, I would encourage you to ask each employee the same questions. Try to spend the first 20 minutes listening when you ask questions. Too often, managers ask a question and then try to solve all the issues right there. The first half of the meeting should be a fact-finding mission only.

Make sure if you find something to critique, you use the formula listed above. Too often, managers use 1:1 meetings to "tell them everything they have done wrong," which leaves the employee feeling overwhelmed. Employees learn to dread meetings with their managers.

Receiving feedback can be difficult. After you have collected the information, you should decide on one to two items you want to work through. Don't decide to try to work on everything. For example, if the employee comes in late, gossips, lacks anesthesia skills, and struggles with client communication, don't provide all that feedback. It would be overwhelming. Instead, narrow it down to no more than two items that you want to focus on.

"Thank you so much for sharing your goals and thoughts. I want to talk to you about something you mentioned you'd like to work on." You are offering to help.

"You mentioned that you sometimes struggle with certain team members." Now provide the feedback.

"You can be short with your coworkers and come off as abrasive and uncaring at times." Don't pay another compliment. Let them take a moment to digest what you just said. You can acknowledge that it was difficult to hear.

"I know that was difficult to hear. How do you feel about it?" You should follow up with why and how it can be improved upon. "I'd like to figure out a way to work on this together so that the team feels comfortable going to you for help or their thoughts. First, I want to hear from you about this, and from there, we can discuss a plan."

Remember, this is where the employee will decide whether they want to accept, ignore, or attack the feedback you provided. They may not be in a place to accept it. You may spend some time trying to coach them through the feedback, or you may put a pause on the meeting and resume once everyone has had time to digest the information. Putting a pause on the meeting allows you to think, "Is there another approach I can try."

Method Two: Group Meeting to Practice

I like when leaders embrace both method one and method two. Method one focuses on the employee receiving honest feedback from the manager in a private setting. Method two focuses on hearing feedback from their colleagues with you as a mediator to ensure it goes well. It doesn't matter if you do method one or two first. Together they help the team understand the new communication style. Remember, don't rush things! It is better to have completed method one, wait a month, and then move on to method two or vice versa. Changing culture and climate is not a race.

During a group meeting, you will repeat the exercise in which they are given a piece of paper with one of their teammates' names written down. However, instead of writing a compliment focused on their behavior, they will write a polite, kind, and honest criticism. To help them out, make sure that the piece of paper looks something like this:

Team Member Name_____

Polite & Kind Remark About Member_____

Feedback for Improvement_____

_____

Give them an example to review ahead of time so they have some guidelines.

Team Member Name: <u>Megan Vetear</u>
Polite & Kind Remark About Member: <u>Excellent when handling dogs.</u>
Feedback for Improvement: <u>She can be loud around cats & scares them.</u>

You may have a few team members who refuse to complete the exercise. Remind them of why it's important they get comfortable with giving and receiving criticism. If the team is hesitant, members likely do not trust each other. If this is the case, you can leave the exercise anonymous. This would leave the receiver of the feedback not knowing who wrote it, which will cause many "who said that about me" thoughts. I would prefer the team to own their feedback because it shows vulnerability on both sides and teaches them how to communicate better while someone is there to facilitate the session.

You will be the one reading back the comments so that you can screen for anything inappropriate. If a comment is exceptionally rude, don't repeat it in front of the entire group, or be sure to soften the blow with better wording. For example, if someone writes, "You are the worst veterinary technician I have ever worked with," you should not say that aloud to the entire group. Instead, figure out who wrote that statement and address them after the meeting. That employee missed the mark when it came to how to deliver PKH communication. Then, on the fly, you can soften the blow and say, "Some of your medical skills need to be improved upon." I find that often people are never so cruel because they know they will be receiving criticism in return and that their manager is there reading the comments.

For the person receiving the criticism, they need to acknowledge and thank the individual for it. If it were anonymously read, they could say, "Thank you to whoever mentioned that sometimes I could be loud when working around cat patients." As a leader, you need to praise both the giver and the receiver. Acknowledge how uncomfortable it is, but also acknowledge how important it is. "I am so proud of everyone on my team because this is not easy. Other teams ignore issues and go around talking about each other behind their backs. I'm so proud that we all want to improve our communication so that we can become an even stronger team." Remind them that when working together, criticism and feedback happens in private. The exercise was done together to coach the team. Real feedback should not occur in a group setting.

You are the mediator of this session. How it goes is dependent on you. First, you must build the team up and get them excited about this. Then, you need to reward their behavior and coach them when it's difficult. Finally, you need to ensure that every person is kind and polite.

If there were a comment made that someone took exceptionally hard, it would be important for you to acknowledge it and meet with them after the meeting. "I can see you are struggling with what Erin mentioned. Let's meet after this meeting to discuss this further. I think it's important for you and Erin to discuss the concerns in more detail."

If the session went well but was full of hesitation and you're unsure if the team has bought into having honest and kind conversations, talk to the team about their hesitation. Having multiple coaching sessions in which the team has you as a mediator to help ensure statements are made using PKH communication skills will help them when they are working together in real time.

Lead by Example

Getting a team to communicate using PKH does not occur overnight. How long it takes is dependent on the team's culture before implementation. If the team previously had a healthy level of trust and respect for each other, they will likely embrace PKH and quickly increase their communication skills. On the other hand, if the team was a toxic level 9,000, it would take a lot of time, multiple conversations, and dedication over the years to improve the communication health of the team. By slowly integrating PKH into your hospital, you will be more successful rather than trying to shock and awe them with it.

Ultimately, the manager or supervisor must lead by example. This is how you should strive to communicate to every employee for almost everything in your hospital. They will follow suit when you become the leader they can trust because you are polite, kind, and honest. By having better communication, the team will increase their respect for you. By increasing the level of respect, it will develop more trust. They will feel psychologically safe around you. Feedback will be able to occur within the team without the all-too-common harassment, berating, or even yelling we see.

No leader is perfect in their communication. You will fail. Be sure to acknowledge when you do. Remember back to my personal story where I destroyed an entire relationship with a college single-handedly. All I could do was apologize and then work to ensure I never made such an egregious error again. If you had 100 productive communications and one that failed in a blaze of glory, it is easier to recover from that one. If you only intermittently utilize good communication techniques, recovering from those train wreck conversations is harder. All leaders steer a conversation into a train from time to time. Strive to get it right most of the time.

Remember that if you are like me, where you may think and speak simultaneously, slow...down. It will only help to protect you from yourself. Getting your team to communicate honestly and kindly is one of the most rewarding accomplishments as a leader. Imagine walking through a treatment area and overhearing a conversation between a veterinary technician and a doctor.

"You are usually so happy, and I enjoy working with you, but today you are negative about everything. What's going on? I'm worry about you."

Did you also get a little heart melt? I did. I love witnessing those conversations. It starts off being polite and kind but then honest. The last part brings it back to concern and caring. It sure beats the typical veterinary technician gossiping about the doctor. "Doctor Schmidt is acting like a total ass today. I'm so sick of it."

Having the veterinary technician address the concern while utilizing kind communication skills will decrease gossip and increase the relationship between them and the veterinarian. They likely will receive a good reply from the doctor because they have a trusting relationship, and the doctor knows the technician is coming from a place of concern and kindness. Here are some examples of heart-melt conversations:

- "You usually handle clients pretty well. What happened with that one? I heard you screaming on the phone. I don't know what happened, but screaming back is never appropriate. What happened because that's not like you?"

- "Do you have a second? I saw you come out of that exam room. You seemed pretty upset, and then you snapped at the front desk. I know they were euthanizing their cat you and you were pretty close with them. Do you want to talk?"

Wouldn't that be great if that's how your team talked to each other? Not to mention that it will improve your life as a leader. Look at how each individual is helping to coach the other person. In both conversations, the person delivering the healthy communication strives to keep a cohesive and happy team climate. They care about their teammate, and they go to them directly with their concerns instead of talking about them behind their backs, or worse…ignoring the issue until it spirals out of control. Essentially these team members are acting like unicorns.

Don't get discouraged when conversations like this take time to develop. Remember that each person has to trust and have a respectful relationship with the other person in order to make the PKH style of communication effective. Without mutual trust and respect, the receiver may snap back, "I'm fine." They don't trust the intent of the person offering kind feedback. However, if you as a leader demonstrate healthy communication through your actions, the professional communication you want will occur naturally.

I Want to Tell My Boss They Suck

I get it. Sometimes the manager is the problem. I'll even go a step further in saying that in many toxic cultures, the main driver of the toxicity is the manager. To the team they have a myriad of obvious flaws. They are unapproachable, a micromanager, dictator, nonexistent, and unappreciative. They may have unrealistic expectations, be uncaring, money-centric, a liar, and play favorites. The list of traits that bad managers have can go on and on. At some point, employees decide they need to talk to their manager about their behavior because people are leaving or are thinking of leaving. Ultimately, one or more employees will attempt to be honest with their boss about the undesirable behavior.

First of all, good luck! If you are not in a position of authority, be cautious when being honest with your manager. If your boss is not familiar with PKH communication, then telling them exactly what you think could end up with you being fired. If you find yourself in a hospital where this communication style is nonexistent, I would encourage you to introduce it to them. Ultimately, it is up to them to embrace something they are unfamiliar with. If they can be introduced to the concept before a conversation occurs, it will make things easier for you. That said, some managers are so shut down from new ideas that even the suggestion of engaging in something new will cause resentment or anger.

If you find yourself in a situation where you need to be honest and provide feedback to your boss, make sure that you are first polite and kind. You can start by obtaining permission from your boss to be honest. "I have something I would like to talk to you about, but I'm nervous about it because it requires me to be honest with you. I know that what I want to talk to you about may hurt your feelings or cause you to be upset. Can I be honest with you?" Remember that the best conversations are those where individuals trust that the communication is delivered from a place of deep caring. While your boss may say, "Of course, you can talk to me about anything," they may not trust that you are coming from a kind place.

Unfortunately, if you have to ask permission to be honest with your boss, there is already distrust. They're probably going to squint their eyes, look at you sideways, and wonder what you're up to. You need to be prepared for any and all responses. I have worked with plenty of veterinary professionals that have reached a breaking point where they are prepared to be fired over an honest conversation. They have had enough and said, "I need to talk to my boss about how they are ruining the team." Be sure you go in with examples and specific information. Too many employees fail to do so. Telling your boss, "You don't appreciate us," is one thing. Telling your boss, "On average, we have all been working an extra shift a week, and you haven't acknowledged our hard work," is another. Now your boss has a clear example of failing to acknowledge the hard work rather than a generalized statement. In a perfect world, the feedback lands well and makes an impact so that change occurs.

I will say this. If you are truly polite, kind, and honest, and it results in you being terminated or retaliation from your manager, it's time to find a new job. Find a new job in which you can have an honest conversation with your boss. The ability to be honest with your boss is important to the success of your career. Bosses should have the humility to recognize that they are not perfect and be humble enough to accept feedback from any member of their team, regardless of the position.

I was truly honored when my team members provided constructive criticism and feedback. I couldn't believe they trusted me enough to tell me exactly what they thought of my leadership skills. I thanked them every time. I couldn't believe I had such an open professional relationship with every single one of my employees. They wanted the best for me, and I wanted the best for them. Do not accept a toxic manager. Life is too short, and veterinary medicine is too stressful to be miserable in a workplace environment. Do your best to communicate with your manager. The reality is only one thing will truly enable any change to happen. Themselves. The manager has to want to change, and no one can make them change. Not even you.

I have seen exceptionally toxic managers do a complete 360. A toxic manager does not become a unicorn overnight. If the manager has acknowledged that they want to improve, then little by little, trust will be built. The team needs to be patient and kind. Over a year or more, the manager will evolve because the team will help to support the evolution.

Differences in Sex, Race, Age & Religion

This was a tough topic for me to dive into because I wanted to do it justice and not offend anyone. I'm not an expert in diversity, equity, and inclusion (DEI). I'm still learning, like many of you. That said, I thought it important to include it because it is critical to a healthy team.

I'm grateful for the woke movement working to educate all of us on how different races, religions, ages, and sexes have been unjustly discriminated against for far too long. It is important to treat everyone equally. When developing teams, we need to be cognizant of some views or opinions that another individual may be experiencing when we have a conversation with them.

While many individuals may exhibit behaviors that are representative of their race, religion, gender, age, etc., it is important to remember that each individual is unique and will have their own behaviors and personality. Do not assume you know what someone else is thinking based on their appearance, religion, or sex.

I need to acknowledge that my view of the world as a white woman from Massachusetts will be different than that of a black man from Idaho. Let's first talk about men and women and how they may struggle to communicate.

A study published in 2017 found that women actively utilized their facial expressions more than men, particularly when it came to positive and happy facial expressions. Conversely, men were found to produce more negative facial expressions and fewer facial expressions overall (McDuff et al., 2017).

A 2014 study published in *Science Magazine* found that two-thirds of men would rather choose to receive electric shocks over trying to analyze their own thoughts. Only one-quarter of women wanted to receive electric shocks (Feltman, 2014). Yes, you read that right—the study concluded that most men would rather get electrically shocked than deal with their feelings.

The Journal of Neuroscience published a 2015 large-scale study of more than 3,000 participants. It concluded that women had stronger facial and motor reactions to emotional images than men. The study also concluded that gender differences in emotion processing were linked to a genetic sex variation in memory and brain activity, respectively (Spalek et al., 2015).

Many other studies conclude that men have the same amount of emotion as women but expressing it through facial and verbal activity is decreased. For men, they see women as overly emotional simply because most women do express their emotions louder. For women, they find most men to be callous and uncaring, which is not true. Men do care but don't express it the same way women do.

While this doesn't pertain to all men and women, I can say that I have struggled with an occasional conversation with a man because of this. I have a lot of emotion in my voice, and when a man on the receiving end of the communication sits emotionless, I immediately think, "he must hate what I am saying." Instead, I need to recognize that how he shows his emotion is different than mine. I've gotten better at asking, "Tell me how you feel about what I just said."

A woman is also more likely to muddle what they were trying to communicate by adding in extraneous compliments or emotion to soften the blow. Men are more direct. They are better at getting to the point, but in doing so, they may leave out emotion and may come across as harsh. A woman receiving feedback from a man may feel like he's bullying her when he's really just being direct in his delivery. By no means does every woman or every man fall into their genetic predisposition. However, science shows that there are genetic differences in how each communicates.

If a man is completely honest with a woman and she starts to cry, then he is less likely to be honest in the future. He may avoid situations because he feels bad about the woman's emotions. Therefore, he does not provide the criticism and feedback she needs to succeed in her position.

In her book *Radical Candor*, Kim Scott tells a story in which a male professor provided negative feedback to a female student. In return, the student wrote a scathing review about how the professor was not fair because she was a woman. The professor took that review to heart and thought hard about his behavior towards female versus male students. He wondered whether or not he was preferential towards the male students. In an effort not to play favoritism, he decreased the amount of feedback he gave to the female students. Unfortunately, his empathy in wanting to help the female students ruined his helping them. He provided little to no feedback. Other female students started telling him they were disappointed he didn't seem to care about them. He had over-corrected rather than asking the female students how they would prefer to receive feedback.

In the 2016 United States Presidential election, many Americans said they would not vote for Hillary Clinton because she sounded shrill and screechy. The speeches she gave were played back in a man's voice to participants of a study. Those participants stated that the man sounded confident and would be somebody they would vote for (Kurtzleben, 2020). Simply by changing the voice to a deeper tone, it changed the context of what was being said.

Michelle Obama (2018) described in her bestselling book *Becoming* how she was asked not to sound angry when giving passionate speeches. She was provided a speech coach who coached her to be more inviting and warm when giving speeches.

Women and men will continue to have differences when communicating because there are true genetic differences between the sexes. It is up to us, the individual listening and receiving the communication, to make sure we are not holding a bias. Play back the conversation in your head and pretend the other sex said those sentences to you. Would you be as offended or upset? Would you find a woman as annoying or emotional if it were a man speaking? Do you think your male employee is a jerk when in reality, he's not going to display his emotions as much as a female? It is important we keep our biases in check at all times.

Your Bias

The other elephants we need to call out in the room are racial, religious, and ethnic differences. Author Kim Scott tells another story about how a tall black man approached her after a communication workshop she held and told her that while her communication style worked well for her (a short white woman), he would be viewed very differently if he tried it. She had to reflect a bit and agreed he was right. A black man providing honest feedback to a white woman will land differently than if a white woman provided that same feedback to a white woman. We need to recognize these differences, biases, and beliefs if we are ever to move past them. It's also important to acknowledge that all of us need an education on how the other person may view the conversation. These uncomfortable things must be discussed.

We also must recognize that all humans, including you, reading this book and myself writing this paragraph, have biases. When we lie to ourselves and say things like, "I don't have any bias against anyone. I treat everyone the same," you are doing yourself and others a disservice. You are lying to yourself, and that becomes dangerous. Here's how I know you have a bias.

Think about a Husky. Do you think that particular breed is brave and stoic? Likely not. Most veterinary professionals believe that Huskies are a wimpy breed of dog. What about German Shepherds? If you thought, "They are also not brave," you are not alone. Now think about Chihuahuas. Did you envision one snapping at you? Now think about an Abyssinian cat. Did you just envision yourself being bitten? Yes, you have certain biases toward your pet patients.

You likely even have biases against clients. In every hospital I've worked at, at some point, an employee will say, "Where is the client from?" Their teammate will reply with the city or town where the client lives. The reply back will be, "Thank goodness. They likely have money to pay for the broken leg." Bias. They assumed that because the client lives in a well-off wealthy town, they can afford pet care.

Where bias becomes an issue is when we treat individuals or pet patients differently. A few studies have concluded that some biases, to some level, are based on truth. For example, there have been studies that have shown that Huskies have a lower tolerance for pain. It does not mean we should withhold pain medication, but rather need to provide it sooner. Certain traits or characteristics of a particular race, religion, age group, or even breed of dog or cat may occur more frequently in that group. That said, even the biases that have some truth are not true for all individuals. For example, I know plenty of cuddly and nice Chihuahuas, even though many more I met wanted to bite me.

Some studies have concluded that Asian individuals are quieter in how they communicate (Cain, 2013). This causes a bias for many to believe that all individuals of Asian descent are quieter. Human bias becomes dangerous when someone treats an individual of Asian descent differently. Even if a bias has been studied and is largely true of a group of individuals, we cannot treat someone differently because of our preconceived bias toward that individual. Acting on a bias is dangerous.

On the flip side of this topic is that we must recognize differences exist. I will see the world differently because of my religion, age, skin color, and where I was brought up. I was walking with a black female colleague and her dogs. A police officer walked toward us, staring. As he approached he said, "Great-looking dogs." We thanked him and continued our walk. She replied, "My heart was beating when he walked towards us because he was staring at us. I was worried he was going to stop us." I replied, "Why would he do that? We're just walking the dogs." That's when I realized my upbringing was quite different. My dad was a firefighter. I was surrounded by police and fire professionals growing up, shaping my view of police officers very differently from hers. Differences do exist, and we need to acknowledge them but not treat people differently because of them.

The first step to ensuring we don't act on our biases is acknowledging we have them. Next, every person has to stop themselves from acting on their bias. I address people's biases between generations in Chapter Thirteen: Blame the Millennials. Talk about a huge bias in which millions of older individuals are biased against younger generations. My challenge to every person reading this is to acknowledge and take ownership of your own biases. Then, focus on working each and every day to not act on your biases. Treat every person and pet you interact with the same, regardless of your past experiences. Ensure you do not discriminate. Together we can break down the walls that divide us all.

The receiver of a conversation has an equal responsibility to that of the individual delivering the message. They must receive the information the same way they would from anyone, regardless of the sex, religion, or race of the individual providing them feedback. Stop and close your eyes whenever you struggle to receive feedback from someone who does not look like you and may have a different background. Now envision if someone of your gender, religion, and race said that to you. Would it land differently? We have to be honest with ourselves that differences exist and that sometimes it is the receiver who's misconstruing the feedback.

If you speak to someone of a different culture, race, religion, or sex that you do not have a trusting relationship with, ask if they are okay if you provide honest feedback. Get permission for an honest conversation to happen and ensure they know you are coming from a place of kindness. Above all else, be polite. Don't forget to ask how the other person feels if you think the conversation isn't landing well. "How is what I'm saying making you feel?"

It is hard to overcome the differences at times. When it comes to communication, asking permission to provide feedback and ensuring that the receiver knows you care deeply and have their best interest is important to it landing well. Learning about others by asking for their feedback can help break down barriers and build trust in communication.

While it's a difficult conversation, I would encourage you to bring in a diversity, equity, and inclusion (DEI) expert to speak with your veterinary team. Everyone on the team should require mandatory training on DEI every year (leaders are not exempt). Opening up the dialogue and stopping bias and discrimination is important. The first step is education and acknowledgment. It is imperative that hospital leaders incorporate DEI education and conversation into their hospitals to promote psychological safety.

You're on Your Way to Change

It wasn't easy and likely took six to seven months, but you are on your way to change! Change never stops! Keep reevaluating your plan. What other items identified by the team should you start tackling? What about another engagement survey? Keep analyzing, asking the team for feedback, and developing plans. Keep the team involved. Initiatives and change are not driven by leadership alone. Focus on the unicorn. For a timeline and a quick summary of these two chapters, be sure to check out Appendix One about how to create a change.

Chapter Nine

Conflict 101

When we think of conflict, we think of an argument between two people, but conflict is much more than that. Employees are conflicted about policies, team members, clients, and even the medicine they practice. Every day countless conflicts happen in your hospital.

As a leader, conflict skills are imperative when trying to change the culture within your hospital. All leaders have rolled out a policy or procedure to which the team did not buy in. Leadership usually spends countless conversations trying to get people to understand their points of view and why the change was important. Utilizing some of these techniques will hopefully set you up for success when you need to coach people to see a different viewpoint or buy into change that needs to happen. These techniques will help you coach through conflict.

The Most Important Fact of Any Conversation

No matter how heated the debate or how upset you get in the conversation, the most important thing you must remember is that no one made you have those emotions.

Only you can control your emotions. This is an important fact that all leaders need to communicate to every member of their team. Whenever we are developing a healthy workplace culture, it's important that the individuals working in the team take personal responsibility for their own emotions. Teaching teams that no one made them yell, break something, become depressed, cry or react in any way is important in developing high emotional intelligence (EQ). All individuals need to recognize that how they react and what they feel is solely their own doing.

Emotional intelligence is considered one of the most important traits when it comes to communication. Some studies suggest that 90% of top performers have high emotional intelligence (Aguilar, 2016).

When people blame others for the cause of their sorrow, frustration, or anger, there can never be any resolution to those feelings. One statement we hear frequently is, "They made me so mad/sad/angry." But, in actuality, that person hasn't made that individual any of those things. A more accurate statement would be, "Their actions of doing XYZ caused me to feel mad/sad/angry."

It is always easier to blame someone else for the cause of why you are feeling the way you are. Most people would rather someone else be the cause of an issue rather than take ownership themselves. I would encourage leaders to educate teams on EQ. You can find literature, seminars, and online videos about how to help develop EQ in individuals.

We cannot persuade others, dominate the conversation, or win an argument until we are the Jedi Masters of our own emotions. Therefore, being responsible for what you say and how you react is the most important fact of any conversation.

What Is Your Conflict Style?

Most experts agree that there are five main conflict styles. Each one offers a different approach to how an individual handles conflict. When you have developed an open and trusting relationship with individuals on your team and are faced with a conflict, you can better understand how they respond if you know your own and their conflict style. Each style of conflict puts a value on how the individual views the relationship between themselves and the other person. Does the individual place a high value on their relationship with the other person, or does it not matter as much compared to winning the argument? It also determines how strong that individual desires to win the conflict. Does the person need to win, or is preserving the relationship a higher priority?

As a leader, you must understand your conflict style. I would also encourage you to have each team member discover which conflict style they tend to gravitate to. Simply reading over the descriptions of the five types of conflict styles will allow some individuals to determine which one they most commonly fall into.

Plenty of online assessments can help you determine which conflict style you use more commonly. If you search for Conflict Management Style Quiz, an assortment of online surveys will pop up. Try one or two and find one that resonates with you. There is also a quiz located at the back of this book in Appendix Four. In most surveys, you may have more than one style you prefer. Most people use a few different styles depending on the type of conflict and who the conflict is with. Most of these surveys are quick, ranging from 10 to 20 questions.

Accommodating

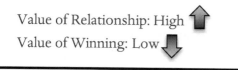

Value of Relationship: High ⬆
Value of Winning: Low ⬇

This style is the opposite of the competing style. There is an element of self-sacrifice that will satisfy the other person. Most people have been in situations in which they are willing to accommodate another individual. For individuals where this is their main style of managing through conflict, this can cause problems. They often are the only ones accommodating all of the time. They may feel like they have lost or even sabotaged themselves. They sacrifice themselves to maintain harmony in the relationship. The large pro of this type of conflict style is that it often ends the conflict quickly because the individual just gives in, keeping the relationship intact.

In some instances, this may be the best type of conflict style to have. For example, I am not passionate about what restaurant I eat at. If I am conversing with a friend about going to dinner and I want Italian food, but they want Chinese, I will likely accommodate their desire for Chinese. In my opinion, it's not worth much of a discussion. I laugh because one of my best friends is also an accommodator. Together we are the worst at making decisions because we want to make sure that the other person is happy. We don't want any conflict between us.

If this is your conflict style, challenge yourself to speak up when it's something you are passionate about. Speak up and get uncomfortable with announcing what you will or will not give up. If you have a conflict with someone you know is an accommodator, stop and get their opinion. Challenge them by encouraging them to speak up. If you manage an accommodator, you must coach this individual not to be so agreeable just to get out of a conflict.

Collaborating

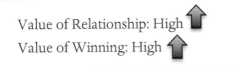

This individual sees a win-win situation. It is a combination of both being assertive and cooperative. Those with a collaborating style attempt to work with others while also pushing their own agenda to find a solution that satisfies everyone, including themselves. The opposite style of this is avoiding.

Negative feelings are typically minimized because both sides get what they want. This tends to foster trust and respect, but the downside to this style is that it can take a long time to find a solution that works for everyone. If the team does not have a great relationship together, then someone may eventually give in to the detriment of their views.

While I have utilized this style and found success with it, I become frustrated if the other individual is more aggressive. It makes me bitter that they are unwilling to collaborate and give a little. But, on the other hand, if I'm the only one willing to give up some of what I was interested in obtaining, it makes me feel like an accommodator. The best outcome is when both individuals are collaborators, which rarely happens.

This conflict style is how many of the best relationships interact in life. One person has a strong opinion about where to go for dinner, and the other has a strong opinion about what movie to see. So they collaborate and choose a different place for dinner that they both agree upon. Then, they work together to review the movie options until they have agreed upon one they are both excited to see. It's a win-win. Everyone is happy in the end. No one wins, and no one loses. It's a true collaboration.

This is a remarkably similar style to compromising. However, compromising is a 50-50 split. In collaborating, it is a win for all involved. No one feels like they have to give anything up. As previously mentioned, this conflict style, while great because it makes everyone feel like they won, can be exceptionally time-consuming. In some situations, it may be impossible to use due to the time factor alone. True collaboration sometimes takes hours, days, or weeks for individuals or teams to develop a true win-win solution that works for all.

Competing

Value of Relationship: Low ⬇
Value of Winning: High ⬆

This individual believes their way is the best, and everyone else needs to agree. They are willing to jeopardize the relationship to get what they want. When working in a team, this individual feels that they have the best interests of the team in mind, which is why they fight so fiercely. What they don't realize is that they are destroying the trust within the team because they are competing for the win.

While this seems like a very harsh conflict style, it can be beneficial. Many leaders are often faced with unpopular decisions that must be made. They have the team's best interest even though the team disagrees with them. The organization would be less fruitful if they couldn't implement tough policies. Many leaders must make decisions that fall solely on them because it is best for the hospital.

I once worked for a hospital that had unlimited vacation time rollover. Some members of the hospital had six months of vacation time saved. They were the type of individuals who rarely took time off. To add to the vacation time surplus, the paid time off (PTO) policy was that anyone over three years accrued five weeks a year. It was an incredible PTO benefit. No one had to worry about vacation time. The problem was that if everyone decided to cash in their vacation time, it would have resulted in a payroll cost of over $1 million.

The hospital owner, practice manager, technician manager, and medical director all met about this situation. As the practice owner, she knew what she needed to do. She needed to start limiting how much vacation time could be rolled over and reduce the amount of vacation time that accrued annually. Having ten employees suddenly decide to take off for six months would have been devastating to the hospital.

The leadership team fought with her and argued against restricting it. They threatened people were going to leave and even sought an employment lawyer to see if what she was about to do was legal. Ultimately, she decided to limit how much could be rolled over. She was the owner and could override the other leaders. She broke some trust with them but knew it was in the hospital's best interest. She gave the employees eight months' notice that only three weeks of PTO were permitted to be rolled over in any year. She essentially created a use-it - or-lose-it policy. She also decreased the maximum number of weeks that could be accrued to only four weeks, and that was for individuals who had been there for at least five years or longer. No one quit, but many were upset and outraged over the perceived injustice.

The disadvantage of this style is that relationships will become broken. No friends will be made using this style of conflict. For individuals in a leadership role, I would recommend not utilizing this conflict resolution style unless absolutely necessary. In the above story, it was necessary to get a handle on the vacation time. Most leaders, at some point, will have to use the competing style of conflict resolution because it is best for the team, but ultimately they will lose trust and even respect of those around them.

If you have a good relationship with your team before you need to make a tough decision, you will be able to recover from it, but it will take some time. Do your best to explain the whys to the team and focus on connecting with individuals who struggle with the decision.

Avoiding

> Value of Relationship: Low ⬇
> Value of Winning: Low ⬇

This individual simply doesn't want to deal with any conflict. They may not care about the conflict at hand, and they also don't care about the relationship. These individuals are unassertive and uncooperative. They simply withdraw to save themselves from the stress and hassle of dealing with a conflict.

The person withdrawing is hoping that the conflict at hand resolves itself. This can be perceived as obstinance by others. That said, there are times when this is a safer conflict style. I have been known to use this style at times.

Think of the last time someone drove up behind you, tailgated you, started flipping you off, and honked their horn. It has happened to every driver at some point. This is a good time to be an avoider. Just pull over. Don't engage. You don't care about the relationship with the other individual, and you shouldn't care about winning. That person is crazy. It's simply not worth it. Avoid conflict by removing yourself from it.

In situations like that, avoiding conflict can save your life or a relationship. However, true avoiders often give up what they really want. This causes their emotions to simmer and escalate over time. Almost everyone has had someone in their life who is an avoider. If you have a teammate who avoids all conflict, challenge them to give their opinion. If you know that you like to avoid all situations that are even remotely uncomfortable, try to step outside of your comfort zone and announce your opinions.

Compromising

> Value of Relationship: Medium ⮕
> Value of Winning: Medium ⮕

This style aims to find a mutually acceptable solution that satisfies both parties while maintaining some assertiveness and cooperativeness. This is similar to collaborating. The difference is that each individual involved in the conflict will have to compromise in some way. People will leave feeling like they did not get what they wanted because instead, they compromised.

Let's review the dinner and movie scenario again. One person has a strong opinion about where to go for dinner, and the other has a strong opinion about what movie to see. Instead of collaborating, the person who doesn't care as much about the movie agrees to see the movie choice the other person wants to. The person who has a strong opinion about the movie agrees to go to the restaurant that the other person wants to go to. They each had to give up a little to compromise to make a decision.

Compromising often occurs faster than collaborating. When things are in a time crunch, this is often how people decide to make decisions. It focuses on saving the relationship by making a decision faster. Each individual involved will be disappointed but happy with the outcome overall. This is the easier way out of many conflicts but leaves each individual slightly dissatisfied.

The reality is, at some point, we have all compromised. And even though we were okay with the compromise at the time, we eventually threw it back into the face of the other person. "I gave up XYZ for this decision! I compromised for you!"

As you can tell, there isn't a perfect style for managing every conflict. You will find one that you lean on more than others but be sure to be open to other styles when they may be more appropriate.

Learn to Listen

If you want to resolve any conflict, then one of the first things that you need to master is the art of listening. I will openly admit that I am not the best at this. It is a skill I have had to work to improve throughout most of my adult life. In my younger years, I didn't recognize that it was a downfall of mine. I prided myself in quickly lambasting others who wanted to argue with me. I'm a fast talker, and throwing verbal jabs is something I excel at. If I just talked over everyone, I thought they would agree. After all, I researched why my way was the best. Surely if I just talked over them, they would see I was right.

The Dalai Lama is an amazing human being. I have had the honor of listening to him lecture on a few occasions. He has mastered the art of listening. He is methodical with every sentence and inspires me to slow down and think. He articulates beautifully what many struggle to. One of my favorite quotes of his is, "When you talk, you are only repeating what you know. But if you listen, you may learn something new." When it comes to my listening skills, my goals are to be a little more like the Dalai Lama.

The owner of the hospital that I worked for was a master of listening. He would sit and reflect after each person spoke at a meeting. When you're not prepared for a long silence, you assume you're doing something wrong. He would average (because I timed him one day) 10-20 seconds of silence between someone ending their conversation and him starting his. While that doesn't seem like a long time, I want you to count out 10 seconds. It's a long time in reality. To fill the silence, I would start yammering on and looking at his facial expression in hopes of figuring out whether or not what I was saying was landing well or not. The second problem was that he was also the master of neutral facial expressions, which I discussed in Chapter Five. Having conversations with him caused me anxiety.

While listening is important, it is possible too much listening can be damaging. When there are long silences and the boss never speaks, it's hard for employees to figure out what the boss wants. This often leaves employees guessing and making decisions without the manager's or leadership's input.

Psychologists have written about how you can use listening and uncomfortable silence as a form of intimidation. It's almost like it's a poker game. When you stop and allow your team to digest what you said, you will likely force them into a reply because of the extended silence. This can sometimes be beneficial. Silence from a manager usually tells an employee, "I am going to need you to share your thoughts or ideas."

Andy Grove, the former CEO at Intel, used to say, "Listen, challenge, and commit." This was an immensely powerful phrase that he used to mean that a strong leader had the humility to listen, the confidence to challenge when necessary, and then the ability to commit to a mutually agreed-upon decision. I love the saying because it's essentially a more eloquent way of saying you know when you need to stop arguing and get on the bus of agreement. All leaders need to know when to stop arguing and get on board with the changes that need to take place. Many leaders will challenge, but few listen, and even fewer get on board with a decision unless it was their decision. Make sure you slow down, listen, and think about what you really want to say. Is it worth winning a petty argument if it took an hour of conversation and jeopardized the relationship? Listen before you react. That's one of the most important things to master when managing conflict.

Stop Trying to Make a Point

I get it. You like to win arguments. So do I, but you will need to stop trying to make your point all the time. The minute you have informed your opponent that they are wrong, you have already lost the battle. Human nature wants to defend or get defensive when someone informs them that they are wrong. It doesn't mean you can't still prove your point, but your approach is important to whether or not you are successful. Too many leaders flat out say, "That's not right," or "You are wrong." Trying to prove a point by being brutally honest instead of using kind communication skills is the fastest way to get the other individual to close their mind to anything you say. The conflict will only get worse.

When dealing with someone confrontational, use questions that will provoke a yes. If they can focus on more yeses, they are less likely to say no.

- Do you want to work in a happy workplace environment? *Yes*
- Do you want to be less angry at work? *Yes*
- Do you want to get along better with your team / doctor? *Yes*
- Do you want to make fewer medical mistakes? *Yes*

Now we can open the conversation to why their gossiping is inappropriate or why their discriminatory, biased behavior needs to stop. If you go into any conversation with, "I'm going to make this person understand why they are wrong," you will never win any argument. Instead, you will get them to shut down. Find common ground you know they can agree with and make it your starting point for a productive conversation.

Yelling Over Email? DON'T!

Sometimes there are tough things that you will need to communicate over email. When you send an email that may contain harshness, make sure you don't send it on the day you wrote it. Instead, try to have someone else read it. Utilize the same approach when communicating with someone. Regarding conflicts, it's always best to wait a day. Have them verbally, not over email. The back and forth over email is surely going to make things worse.

If you must respond to an email centered around a conflicting view, remember to remain professional, polite, kind, and honest. Start with thanking the individual for providing feedback or criticism. It does not matter how out-of-control their email is, assume good intention and don't reply with yelling in return. While I would love to live in a world where everyone had appropriate email etiquette, unfortunately, that will never be the case. Email has become the device in which people are comfortable venting their frustrations and feelings. They do not think of the receiver when they hit send. I am often shocked by veterinary technicians, veterinarians, client service representatives, and even practice managers that send some pretty offensive emails. Here's a great example of one that I just saw come through my inbox a few short weeks ago:

"This is my third attempt to get you to reply. This entire system is stupid. Employees should have the ability to get a faster response. I need to change my payroll deductions for my federal taxes. I need it done now because it should've been done two weeks ago! Can someone get back to me!?"

Wow. That's one angry person. The problem was they failed to email the correct individual or realize they could solve this problem themselves. They took to writing an angry email that went out to an entire region's leadership. The employee had the ability to change their deductions within the system. All they had to do was read the instructions online. No one who received the email could help the individual directly. Instead, all they could do was point them in the right direction of making the change themselves. Not only was it an angry email, but the individual sent it to the wrong group of people. Oops.

Even if you receive an angry or offensive email, it serves no point in responding in an unprofessional manner. If someone has offended you via email, it is always best to deal with that offense in person, as it will land better. Simply replying with another email will not solve the problem and will only make the person even more frustrated and angry. Instead, come from a place of kindness, meet with the person face-to-face, and explain why the email was unprofessional.

8 Golden Rules for Composing an Email

1) Start from a place of kindness and politeness.

2) Thank them for their email, even if their email was harsh. If you do not like the harshness or tone portrayed in the email, address it face-to-face. If the level of unprofessionalism is tolerable (and there is often some level of unprofessionalism in most emails), then thank them for sending their concerns to you. "I genuinely appreciate you bringing your concerns to me. I know that you have the team's best interest in mind."

3) Remember that emails are always judged more harshly. People assume that you are going to retaliate or write something negative. If you want to convey your message, you need to make sure they see kindness. Overdo it with the kindness in the email but not to a point where you lose the message.

4) Deliver the message. Make sure it focuses on the issue at hand and the points you'd like to convey. Leave out feelings or perceptions. Stick with facts.

5) Acknowledge if you think they may be unhappy with your response. "I know this may come as a disappointment to you." This shows you care.

6) Provide them the opportunity to speak to you directly. Acknowledge that receiving or communicating through email is not preferred. "I recognize you may want to talk through a few more questions that you have. It may be easier to do this in person, as sometimes emails can misconstrue the meaning. My door is always open for you."

7) Offer to answer any other questions. One of the lines that I use the most in almost any email is: "If you have any other questions, please feel free to reach out to me directly."

8) Sign off with your name and, if you prefer, your credentials as well. I also like to include a phone number so they can call if they would like to speak more about their concern.

Be consistent in how you sign your name. I know many colleagues or coworkers that casually sign off on their email with just their first name. It bothers me when, in an effort to drive home a point or be more aggressive, they suddenly add in their credentials. Flipping from casual to professional changes the tone of an email, so either always use credentials or do not.

If you want your team to be more professional in emails, you need to be the trendsetter. If you take a casual tone, it gives them a free pass to be casual with their emails. On the other hand, if you maintain a professional, businesslike response, they will likely do the same in return. At the very least, they will know your expectations when communicating via email.

Understanding these basic conflict 101 skills will help you avoid and even diffuse communication issues. Learning how you manage conflict, how to listen better, and how to communicate clearly and conflict-free in emails are important skills, especially for leaders. Preventing conflict is always best. We will address prevention in the next chapter and then follow up with managing and even embracing conflict in the one after that.

Chapter Ten

Strategies to Avoid Conflict

There are things I immediately regret in a heated conversation. Unfortunately, I don't apologize as quickly as I should, and I sometimes make things worse. In fact, I have done almost everything you shouldn't do in a conflict at some point in my life. Learning how to end a conflict with resolve is a skill set every human being must continuously work to improve. Let's start with the things you should never do or say in a conflict unless you want it to become worse or not end with a resolution.

Things You Should NEVER Say Unless You Want to Fight

Unfortunately, even I am not great at following all these rules every time. Sometimes my emotions get the better of me. I just want to get a jab in. I want them to know how angry I am, so I let an insult fly. Most of the time, I regret what came out of my mouth and wish I had never said it.

We've all joked and even dreamed about the day we would quit or retire. In one of my jobs I had visions that on my last day, I would tell off a client, "You are a royal bitch who needs to stop treating the staff so terribly, and you need to shut up and just pay your veterinary bills instead of complaining about it. For f-sakes, you're driving a Lexus!" Then I would turn to my team and exclaim, "I quit! Good luck without me!"

While many of us have joked about doing this from time to time, my advice is don't. Leave the mud-slinging insults at home unless you want to quit and leave the veterinary profession entirely with no hope of ever reentering the profession. Yes, I mean the entire profession.

I have heard too many horror stories of someone telling their boss or hospital exactly what they thought and storming out in a grand fashion. Trust me when I say that the world of veterinary medicine is small and maybe even smaller, thanks to social media. If someone leaves in a blaze of glory on the West Coast of the United States, someone working in a veterinary hospital on the East Coast will hear about it. This makes the individual less hirable. Individuals who fling insults should be talked to immediately. When we are trying to create a better culture in our hospitals, laying down insults just to hurt people is the opposite. Stay away from these statements unless you want to pick a fight:

Statements to Pick a Fight

- "Don't take it personally…"
- "Don't be sad/mad/angry…"
- "No offense but…"
- "Don't get emotional…"
- "Always or Never (You always/never) …"
- "That's Stupid/Ridiculous…"
- "Everyone thinks…"
- "I (You) don't care…"
- "Last week/month/year you said or did…"
- Most statements with the word YOU in it:
  - "You are a…"
  - "You are making this…"
  - "Here you go again…"
  - "You need to calm down…"
  - "You are exaggerating…"

All of the statements above devalue someone else's feelings or attack another individual. When you tell an individual you do not want them to be emotional, you're basically saying, "I can't handle your emotions, so I need you to knock it off."

When you use the word "you," that is essentially pointing a finger at the other person. You are pointing at them and making sure they know that you are accusing them of something.

Make sure that you stick to the timeline you are speaking of. Unfortunately, spouses often violate this rule of conflict management. They start dredging up the past of everything the person ever did to tick them off. For example, a wife blows through a stop sign. The husband turns to his wife and says, "You need to be more careful." His wife turns the criticism into an all-out argument when she says, "Well, you're a terrible driver too! Last month you blew through that red light and almost got us killed. You're always doing stuff like that."

Look at how many of the statements said are on the "how to pick a fight" list. The reality is that the husband has the right to bring up his concern about a blown stop sign. The wife does not have the right to bring up the past history, which has nothing to do with the current conversation. How will his past history stop her from going through another stop sign? Criticism is hard. Unfortunately, for most people, the initial response is to attack and fling insults.

Another good rule is to make sure you don't turn the topic into making it all about yourself. "I definitely understand..." and "I can relate because..." should be removed from all conversations. It's not a competition, and it's not about you. Telling a story from your past has nothing to do with the situation at hand. Too often, the listener jumps in with an "I can relate because..." story. All this does is devalue the feelings, emotions, and story of the individual telling theirs.

The Worst Communication Sins

It's hard to imagine that there are even worse communication sins than the ones already listed. However, these are in a league of their own. If you do any of these, you will destroy 90% of the trust and respect you had with your team or an individual.

> - Cursing
> - Character Attacks
> - Stonewalling
> - Not Accepting the Apology
> - Walking Out/Hanging Up

Cursing

I understand that sometimes things slip out. I am by no means a prude and will let the obscenities fly from time to time. However, in more than 20 years of veterinary medicine, I have maybe cursed 20 times in the hospital. However, in my personal life, my friends will tell you they have lost count.

When I work in a professional medical office, I am cognizant of my behavior, particularly when I am in a leadership role. Leaders should not curse, even if it is not directed at someone. It's unprofessional, and if you accidentally let one fall out of your mouth, immediately apologize. If an obscenity fell out of your mouth and was directly flung at someone, you will need to apologize and keep working to make amends.

I once had a boss tell me that my actions were "not f***-ing okay, Amy." This was after I had already repeatedly apologized for what she saw as a direct assault on her as a leader. The situation arose from a regional manager calling me directly to ask if I could come to one of her hospitals to coach their new leadership. The leadership was struggling, and they could use some guidance. I told the regional manager I would have to check in with my manager but mentioned I thought it would be okay. After all, me going to hospitals for an occasional consult was something I did. It wasn't part of my job per se, but because I could coach teams and leaders effectively, sometimes regional managers would ask for my help. When I informed my boss of the request, she told me the answer was no.

The backstory was that my manager and the regional who came to me directly had significant communication issues. They didn't get along. In fact, my manager complained a lot about the regional manager quite frequently.

My boss was insulted that this individual did not go to her directly and instead went to me. She had expected me not to speak to the regional leader and instead reply with, "I'm sorry, I cannot talk to you at all about this. You will have to speak to my manager."

To add to the confusion of this story, my boss repeated multiple times that she did think I would be able to help the team, but it was the principal of the matter. She was upset with the regional leader for circumventing her and angry with me for having a conversation without her. Because she disliked this individual and felt they had purposefully gone around her, she took it out on me. She explained that she "was going to have to be the bad guy" in declining the request of the regional manager. My actions were "not f***-ing okay."

I felt devalued and humiliated. Those emotions quickly turned to anger and resentment. I never completely trusted her again because I saw an ugly side. It doesn't matter if you think you have the best relationship or not. When a curse is flung at another individual, it will result in a broken relationship. It's difficult to heal a relationship after throwing curse words at someone, and it is up to the person who made the offense to work to build the trust again. My relationship with my boss was never the same.

Character Attacks

We have already discussed a little bit about character attacks, but let's dive into them some more. Unfortunately, many dysfunctional relationships utilize character attacks to win whatever perceived battle that is raging. "You are a liar, the worst person, a terrible human, ugly, and disgusting." The list of attacks goes on and on, and in the workplace environment, we see words thrown around, such as lazy, uncaring, rude, incompetent, and not a team player.

Character attacks are part of bully behavior. When bullied, the other individual can only defend themselves, or they shut down.

- "You are lazy" is different from "you aren't motivated at times."
- "You are not a team player" is different from "you don't seem to want to be part of a team."
- "You are rude to clients" is not the same as "you sometimes act rude to clients."

In all three instances, you see the sentence set up "you are" versus "you act." Describing an action is different from personally assaulting another.

This is something that leaders and teams struggle with at times. Much like teaching teams about destructive versus constructive criticism, which we will review later in the chapter, you can also teach teams about the difference between a character versus a physical attack. Write out ten insults and have the team reconstruct the insults into action statements or feedback. Even better, have them construct the insults into PKH statements. Here's an example of an insult that morphs into a PKH statement.

"You are rude."

↓

"You act rude."

↓

"You are a kind person, but lately, you have been acting rude to members of the team. What's going on?"

We must teach ourselves and our team the difference between attacking personality versus behavior. This is the difference between teams being able to communicate with kindness versus maliciousness.

Stonewalling

This term describes the behavior of an individual who checks out of a conversation. They simply don't say anything. The cliché version of this is a husband who is listening to his wife yell at him, and he goes silent. She finally screams at him, "Don't you have anything to say?!" When he says nothing, she yells at him, "It's clear you don't give two shits about me or this problem!"

From his perspective, he's trying to defuse the situation by simply keeping his opinion to himself. He refuses to communicate through any engagement. Often, an individual who does this is involved in self-reflection or taking the time to digest the situation. The individual who is being stonewalled sees the silent person as being defiant or even obstinate.

If you are in a leadership role and stonewall an employee, they will think you don't care. When they think you don't care, they will lose respect and trust for you. If you are a manager or supervisor who needs time to digest the conflict or think about what to say as a response, you need to communicate your need.

There is no shame in saying, "I need time to think about how to respond to you." You can also try saying, "This is a lot to digest, and I need time to think about it." Make sure that you come from a place of kindness and communicate that you need some time to think about how to respond because you care about the individual, you want to work to find a solution, or you need to think about the role you played in the conflict.

Stonewalling never improves relationships between team members. Instead, it increases distrust and decreases respect. If you find yourself shutting down and wishing the conflict would disappear, make sure you don't stonewall. Catch yourself before you do it. Don't completely shut down. Stay engaged but ask for the time to think and digest. Get the time you need to gather your thoughts and be respectful of someone who requests time to gather theirs.

Not Accepting the Apology

When you provide criticism or feedback because someone has done something wrong, the goal is to ensure that you receive an apology and the behavior is ideally corrected. Too often, I have witnessed or been part of a conflict where one individual apologizes, usually multiple times, but the attacker does not stop. Instead, they drone on and on about the injustice of what happened. The individual already apologized. What else do you hope to get out of them?

Too often, the excuse for continuing the assault is because the attacker does not feel the apology was sincere. Who are you to say whether they were sincere or not? You are not only attacking them but now also calling them a liar. The entire conflict will only get worse from there. The person who apologized loses respect for the other. They start getting frustrated that their apology was not accepted. Ironically, this causes them to strike back.

Accept the apology and say, "Thank you." It was not easy to give. Believe it to be genuine and assume their good intention of giving it. Failure to do so will only result in the fight continuing. No one gets to demand an apology and then be both the judge and juror to decide whether or not the apology was to their liking. That's simply unfair.

Walking Out/Hanging Up

This sin ranks up there with cursing directly at someone. The minute a manager or supervisor walks out/hangs up/closes out of an online chat in the middle of a conversation is the minute they should just stop being a leader. Yes, I feel that strongly about it.

You are in a leadership role. You don't get to walk away because something is unappealing, offensive, or difficult. You don't get to close out of the online chat session because someone has said something you don't like. You don't get to hang up on a call because you feel like your team is attacking you. You are a leader. No matter how bad the situation is, you never get to leave.

I once had a manager who was visibly upset that most of the team voiced concerns that he appeared disconnected in his role. He was not present in the hospital most days. The few times he was present, he did not appear to care about the team or his responsibilities. The team decided to hold a team meeting and bring up their concerns. He became defensive, and when a team member cited a time they needed his help and he was not there for them, he stood up, threw his chair back, and exclaimed, "I don't need to deal with this shit!" Then he left. The problem is that he did need to deal with it because he was in a leadership role. It was the very definition of his job.

You will lose the respect and trust of your team if you ever hang up, close out a virtual meeting, or walk out. I also understand that meetings can become emotional and difficult at times. Emotions run hot. Tears start happening. Many individuals would rather run out of the room and pretend like it's not happening. It is hard to stay in the room and continue dealing with the conflict.

I certainly do not condone a team member for leaving a conversation or meeting due to emotions, but it's different than their manager leaving. That said, we shouldn't force employees to stay in the meeting who cannot or do not want to.

The problem with anyone leaving the meeting or the conversation is that the feelings are still there. Nothing has been resolved. The conflict is still in limbo. I've seen countless managers walk out of meetings as if, suddenly, a unicorn will come in and fix it. However, with no resolution, it means that it will have to be addressed at another time in order for it to be fixed. Otherwise, it just stays broken.

All this said, a leader can leave a meeting if done properly. Excuse yourself if you feel you need to exit a difficult conversation or meeting. Provide a plan for how the conversation will continue in the future. There is a difference between a leader abruptly ending a meeting while maintaining control versus a leader just storming out of a meeting without any control. To maintain control, you first need to acknowledge your feelings and communicate them to the group as to why you want to stop the meeting. Secondly, you need to explain why you must exit. Lastly, you must provide an action plan of how the conversation will continue. Following that formula, you are more likely to maintain the respect and trust of the team. Here's an example of how to exit a meeting:

"As you can tell, I'm pretty upset right now. I can't even think straight, and I'm afraid if we continue with this meeting, I'm going to say or do something that I may regret. I'd like to end here to let us all think about what has been communicated and pick back up tomorrow."

Get control of the meeting because you are the leader. In the rare instance that you feel the need to walk out of a meeting, follow the guidelines. Think heavily about the decision of what the team or individual may think about your departure. Never just walk out, but if you have to end quickly, please use the guidelines provided.

Constructive vs. Destructive Criticism

There are two types of criticism: constructive and destructive. Constructive criticism is the beneficial type of criticism. It comes from a place of kindness though the receiver of the constructive criticism may not feel that way. Constructive criticism does not insult you personally but seeks to help, guide, or improve a situation. It is considered helpful.

Destructive criticism is malicious. The person making the criticism does not offer any type of solution and is instead assaulting you as a person. They are seeking to insult your self-esteem, the job you did, or the values you hold. It's angry, resentful, and hateful.

In a workplace environment, most criticism is meant to be constructive but often is mishandled and becomes destructive. An individual might not go about it in the best way despite their intention of trying to be kind. It's important that we have a bigger conversation with our teams about how constructive criticism is only well-received if the receiver receives it as such. Likewise, we need to have conversations with our teams about not assuming mal intent of the person delivering the criticism.

Before you or any member of your team decides to offer feedback or constructive criticism, ask yourself, "How would I feel if someone provided me this same feedback or criticism?" Running the criticism by someone else before delivering it may help provide insight as to whether it will land well or not.

Because most people believe conflict is bad, they tend to avoid any criticism. Author Patrick Lencioni wrote about conflict in his best-seller The Five Dysfunctions of a Team (2002). The fear of conflict is listed as a team's second dysfunction out of the five. Teams that lack trust between members and the ability to engage in healthy conflict do not openly air their concerns. They end up sharing criticism privately with others in the form of gossip. Healthy conflict is necessary for the team's overall health. Without it, they end up dysfunctional.

Reshaping Destructive to Constructive

How can we coach teams to understand the difference between the two? Having them work through a few mock scenarios is a good way to start. Below are a few examples of destructive criticism to get you started creating some of your own:

- "The surgery techs are so slow. It takes them forever to get into surgery."
- "The practice manager only cares about how much money the hospital makes."
- "The surgeon comes in whenever he wants and makes us late leaving. He doesn't care about us at all."

Technically, all of these comments are valid, and any leader should follow up on the concern. But unfortunately, due to their deconstructive nature, most leaders just tune out these types of comments. Their statements don't come from a place of kindness. Rather they attack the individual. They pounce on a personality or perceived flaw in an individual or group of individuals.

Here's how all of the above statements can be made constructive:

- "The surgery techs are great in their roles but struggle to get into surgery quickly. As a result, they end up staying late almost every day. I thought we could help organize their department better so they can go home on time."

- "I know the practice manager cares about everyone in the building, and her role is to ensure the hospital is profitable, but at times it seems like she doesn't prioritize the team. I'm hoping that we can have a conversation with her that is centered on her focusing back on the team and making them feel valued."

- "The surgeon is talented but comes in late for his shift daily. Unfortunately, this causes the rest of the team to be late. I'm wondering if there's a way that we can speak with him so that he understands it's important to come in on time?"

What a difference rewording makes. The meaning is still the same. The individual who makes the first versus the second statement still wants the best for the team or individual. However, the individual who makes the second statement uses constructive criticism instead of destructive. You can teach this skill to your team by having them rework destructive criticism into constructive criticism. This is a great skill for all team members to have.

Leaders often are frustrated because individuals are constantly going to them and complaining. Unfortunately, leaders often dismiss valid complaints because they are destructive. Leaders often say, "Don't bring me a concern unless you have a solution." I really, REALLY, dislike that comment. What that says to the team is, "I don't want to hear your issues, and you better fix all the problems yourself." As a leader, I always valued when someone came to me with nicely worded constructive criticism. If they did not, I became frustrated like most leaders, but I learned that many times team members voice concerns to their leaders because they are struggling to find the solution. A more appropriate statement from a leader would be, "Please come to me with your concerns. I'm here to help." That's it—that's what a role of a leader actually is. You need to accept destructive criticism and coach for constructive in the future.

Leaders will say that their teams whine and complain all the time. The complaining occurs because teams are unskilled with how to create constructive statements. Leaders need to be skilled in the art of creating constructive statements as well as coaching team members. I always told my teams I was there to help them and appreciated their criticism. When a member on my team would start with a deconstructive comment centered only on the issue, I'd remind them that what I needed to know was:

1) What is the issue?
2) How is it affecting them or the team?
3) How is it impacting the person they had concerns about?

The last part was particularly important. This reminds them to think about the person they had an issue with. I once had a team member complain about a veterinarian they perceived to be short-tempered. I asked, "How is this harming them?" They replied, "I don't think they want to be so angry." This statement brings the criticism back around and centers it nicely on kindness. Essentially this is "help me help you" so you as a leader can productively get the entire picture. We could go on and on about why the veterinarian is a jerk, or we can start to develop reasons for why the issue may be occurring. When your team helps you understand the issue and what they hope will be changed, it allows you to help develop solutions. As a leader, involving teams and individuals in those solutions is key.

What to Say to Stop a Conflict

There are eight golden rules for delivering feedback or handling conflict. These are important so that the conflict can end on a positive note. Yes, ending conflict positively is possible.

8 Golden Rules for Delivering Feedback

- Be Kind
- Be Helpful
- Be Clear
- Be Immediate
- Deliver in Person
- Deliver in Private
- Don't Personalize
- Stay on Topic

Post these on a wall and memorize them. Then, whether or not you need to provide difficult feedback or manage a small conflict, these eight golden rules will help keep the conversation professional and on point.

Ideally, you should never provide criticism in an email, no matter how gentle you think it may be. If you work on Tuesday during the day and need to speak to an employee who starts their week on Friday overnight, it may be difficult to provide feedback immediately. If it is going to require substantial conversation, find a time outside their normal working hours that you can meet. Remember, if you request to meet with an employee, even if it's over the phone, that is still work time and should be compensated. Too often, hourly employees are asked to speak to their manager or others on the phone about a work-related matter on their day off. Be sure to provide compensation if this occurs. Verbal conversations through virtual platforms, phones, or in-person are best for any feedback. Avoid email like the plague it often is.

If it is something quick and not too heavy, you can ask to meet with your team member right before their shift starts. Make sure you give the conversation the time it deserves, so it does not feel rushed. Find out what works for them. "I want to talk to you about something, but I don't get to see you that often. I also don't want to cut into your days off, so let me know when is convenient for you in the next week to talk." Do you see how I put a timeline in there? A timeline is important because too many leaders say things such as, "Let's meet when you have time." This could mean any time. By the time you actually meet, the issue has escalated or been forgotten about.

The last two rules of the golden eight remind you not to personalize the conversation and to always stay on topic. If you can adhere to the eight golden rules, you will have a much better conversation.

Using "I" Statements for Bad

The use of "I" statements is tricky in conversation. I will address the use of them twice in this chapter. In this section, I want to discuss how "I" statements may add fuel to the fire. When "I" statements take an authoritative tone centered around attacking someone else, they will miss the mark most of the time. Most of the use of an "I" statement is centered on tone. "Wellllll (long drawn out), I know that I have the right answer" will not go over as well as "I believe I may have a solution."

In some incidents, "I" statements centered on confronting are necessary and can deliver a powerful message from a leader. However, if the receiver becomes more defensive after you attempt to use a powerful "I" statement, recognize you may have crossed the line. Apologize. Retract the statement and try to explain it again. Remember these "I" statements general rules:

- Feelings are good. ("I feel…")
- Opinions are good when they have been asked for or when it is required to give one. ("I think…")
- Refrain from using "I", "you," and an adjective in the same sentence. ("I think you are lazy.")
- Restrict your use of "I" with a verb when coaching individuals. Sometimes this is unavoidable but remember that it's not only about you. It is about the hospital, the team, and the larger picture. "I need you to" should be replaced with "It would be better for the team if you would."
- If you repeat an "I" statement and it sounds like an attack, it probably was. "I" statements centered around kindness and caring always land better.

Using "I" Statements for Good

Until now, I have stressed that you must leave the emotions out of the conversation. The reality is that all leaders have emotions. In fact, most have the same number of emotions as the individuals they are trying to communicate with. It is not natural for individuals to not express any emotion. In many conflicts, it is healthy to do so. It makes you human and shows that you care. It shows that the other person's words and what they are saying to you impact you emotionally. So how do you express emotions without making it overly emotional? There is a big difference. Expressing emotion is healthy. Being overly emotional is not. The ability to communicate your emotions and feelings to benefit the conversation is an important skill. You are allowed to be angry, but if you are screaming and hysterical, you will lose the conversation because the emotions are now the star of the show. Productively conveying your anger and frustration will be more powerful than if you let it overtake a conversation.

Use "I" statements to express your emotions but use them at moments where they will make an impact. "I feel…," "I think…," and "I am…" are all powerful statements. Acknowledge the feelings you are having through purposeful "I" statements. I find "I" statements particularly impactful when you have managed to control your emotions up to a certain point, and the other individual has said something inflammatory or attacking. At that moment, it can be powerful to make a statement such as, "What you just said makes me feel sad because it sounds like you think I don't care, but I do."

You can also add clarifying thoughts such as, "What I hear you saying is…." For example, "What I hear you saying is you are angry about your salary." Sometimes statements are made that are not accurate. They fall out of someone's mouth in the heat of the moment, and the person does not have time to retract the statement. Get clarity around a comment when necessary. Don't leave the conversation unsure about the point the other individual was trying to make.

Imagine if an employee said to you, "You don't even care about us as a team. All you're worried about is the payroll budget and ensuring we don't go into overtime." Most people's response would be, "That's ridiculous. Why would you say that?! Of course, I care, but you know I have to work within a payroll budget. That's my job, so we don't go bankrupt!" The response dismisses the other person's feelings. You might as well have said, "I don't believe anything you just said. Your accusation is false."

In this instance, communicate how you feel and clarify the meaning of what they just said. "What I hear you saying is that I don't care about anyone on the team. I feel sad when I hear you say that. I do care." Using "ridiculous" or "that's silly" in the statement devalues their opinion. While the individual did provide destructive criticism, it's important as a leader to coach that individual to successful communication, as it will benefit both of you. When you can word your response to convey your emotion professionally, you will continue to move the conversation forward in a productive manner.

Many leaders think that they are not permitted to cry during any conversation. Opening yourself up is not a weakness. It's a strength. If you feel tears welling up, acknowledge why it's happening by using an "I" statement. "I'm crying because I feel sad/angry/happy." Too often, people apologize for their emotions. Don't apologize for being human. Own your emotions but do your best to make them productive. If you are crying to a point where you can no longer communicate, you can use the exit strategy I listed previously. "I need to end the meeting here. I'm too upset and need time to process what occurred. I'd like to meet again tomorrow to pick up where we left off."

If you are in a leadership role and apologize for your emotions, you are telling others that they should not express their own emotions. Teach your team the difference between expressing emotions and being emotional. If you catch your team apologizing for their emotions, be sure to call it out. "Don't apologize because you are sad, frustrated, or angry." When we can embrace that we are human, it makes conversations easier. Use your emotions by utilizing "I" statements to make conversations more personal and impactful.

Create a Safe Space

When wanting to avoid conflict, you have to be cognizant of your body language and tone of voice. You may be saying you are okay, but your tone and body language are saying you are not.

Is there a desk between you and the other person? Are you crossing your arms in anger or anxiety? In order for someone to be calmer and feel like the other person is open to resolving the issue, they need to feel like they are in a safe space.

Two techniques that can be helpful when managing difficult conversations are mirroring and priming (Grenny, 2021). Mirroring is the art of describing what you're seeing. You can use this to describe what you are seeing. "You appear to be unhappy."

Priming is where you take your best guess at what someone might be thinking and say it in a way that conveys that it's okay to talk about it. I often use this technique when trying to get someone to open up to me. "Look, I get it; this situation sucks." By guessing what they may be experiencing, you are priming the conversation and giving permission for them to share. Create a safe space in which healthy conflict can occur.

Admit You are Wrong EVERY Time

We previously discussed the importance of accepting criticism. Unfortunately, many individuals cannot recognize they play a role in the communication issues. These individuals feel like they are always right and struggle with any ownership in a conversation gone bad. Often they can't grow in their leadership abilities because they fail to admit they need to grow. They are stifled because they believe they are always right and struggle with hearing criticism or feedback. With leaders, they see the team always being the problem. It's never them that is in the wrong. Leaders and those on the team need to admit when they are wrong, every single time. This is key to creating respectful relationships.

I once struggled with a manager. We simply didn't see eye to eye. She was exceptionally negative about everything and often presented a "doom-and-gloom" perception to every conversation. She also had a difficult time conveying her thoughts. It was hard for me to understand exactly what she wanted, and if I asked questions to clarify, she would act like I was the problem. Needless to say, communicating with her was hard. She was never at fault. She kept saying I was the problem.

Despite us both struggling to communicate with each other, she believed only I had communication issues. I did go and get help to improve my skills. It was early on in my career, so I went to a weekend workshop class and read some books. While my skills improved, hers remained stagnant. I often wish my manager had also worked to improve her skills. As an employee, I didn't understand why I was expected to improve mine while she never owned up to her failures in any of the communications. Because she felt she played no role in the communication issues, we continued to struggle. Even though I eventually left that hospital, I was grateful for learning how to communicate with someone I felt was difficult. Our communication did improve, but only because I improved my own skills.

Conversations involve more than one person. When there is a breakdown, it's never 100% one person's fault. It's often an issue with all persons involved. No matter how much you feel you are in the right, I assure you that you have some responsibility for the failure of a conversation gone bad. If you cannot see that you are wrong at times, then you are committing a tragic communication sin, the inability to improve your skills because you believe you are already perfect.

Unfortunately, most leaders do not like to apologize. They view it as a perceived weakness. When you are in a leadership role, apologies are more important than ever. Leaders are not only responsible for their behavior but also for the team. A leader's action has broad implications, and an apology does as well. When a leader apologizes to an individual, it will affect the personal relationship they have with that person and their relationship with the entire team. When a leader causes injustice to one member of the team and the entire team is aware, failing to apologize to one individual will cause distrust among the rest.

In a 2006 Harvard business review article, I read this great quote, "A leader's apology is a performance in which every expression matters and every word becomes part of the public record" (Kellerman, 2006). I like this quote because it reminds me of the importance of delivering an authentic and well-crafted apology. The entire team will know about the injustice or wrong that occurred to one of their own. Even if it was not that big of an issue, it's magnified because someone in a leadership role caused the mistake. When that team member announces that you apologized to them, the entire team will want to know exactly what was said. A leader's apology holds more weight than any other member on the team. The ability of a leader to apologize increases the trust the team has in its leader. That is why it is so important to offer an apology when it is due.

Why It's Hard to Apologize

The reason that any person has difficulty apologizing is that they believe they are right. The function of ego gets in the way of many people realizing that they played a role in or even caused the issue.

Intellectual humility is one's ability to acknowledge that one might be wrong. It does not mean you need to feel inferior. On the contrary, it's a strength to have intellectual humility. It means you have the intelligence not to fear being wrong at times.

A study by Dr. Tenelle Porter (2018) focused on high school students and their intellectual humility. She discovered that students with higher intellectual humility were more willing to learn and develop new strategies to enhance their understanding of their mistakes. These students also ended the school year with higher grades in math and were more engaged in their classes.

Benjamin Franklin has been quoted as saying, "Never ruin an apology with an excuse." I am guilty of sabotaging my attempts at apologizing by offering excuses. I sometimes even acknowledge that I am making an excuse when I say, "I'm not trying to make an excuse, but…". If you lead with that statement, you will certainly sabotage your apology.

6 Components of a Sincere Apology

1. Expression of regret
2. Acknowledgment of responsibility
3. Declaration of what you wish would have occurred
4. Declaration of what was learned
5. Offer of repair
6. Request for forgiveness

Expression of Regret

This is where you say the words, "I am sorry." Leave the "but" out of it. You can add in "very" or "really" or another adjective before the word sorry. "I am very sorry." That's where this expression of regret ends. Don't muddle it with anything extra.

Acknowledgment of Responsibility

Acknowledge two things here: what was the mistake and how it impacted others. "I am sorry that I changed your schedule without letting you know. I recognize that this has caused you a lot of stress." Use the words "I recognize" to acknowledge its impact on the team or an individual.

Declaration of What You Wish Would Have Occurred

"I wish I had told you about the schedule change over a month ago." Acknowledging what you wanted to happen or the message you were trying to send conveys that you were not purposely trying to be malicious. Very few individuals purposely try to harm others. The mistake was just that. It was a mistake. It was not purposeful. You show that you've consciously thought about the mistake and how it could have been avoided.

Declaration of What Was Learned

"I learned that next time, I need to communicate with everyone who is having their schedule changed way earlier." Make sure that you think about what you learned. The apology becomes more sincere when you can specifically illustrate how you are not only sorry but that you are taking something away from it.

Offer of Repair

Let's face it. Many mistakes we make cannot be repaired in a way that makes it better. If you are involved in a car accident that harms another individual, you cannot fix that. In most mistakes that occur, some level of damage happens. Much like a car accident, sometimes there are things that can be fixed, and other times there are things that cannot.

If there is an impact on a relationship, the relationship could heal back to normal, but it might take time. What about a medical mistake that resulted in the death of a patient? There is nothing that anyone can do to repair that. In those extreme situations, apologizing, recognizing what you wish would have happened, declaring what was learned, and requesting forgiveness are key. It is exceptionally important to acknowledge that no matter what is offered, nothing can fix it. Acknowledging that no repair is possible is an important step in healing and moving on.

Luckily, most mistakes in life are repairable. However, the repair may take time. In the example of changing the schedule where we did not give the employee much notice, we often cannot go back to the old schedule. There was a reason for the schedule change, but we failed to communicate it appropriately. The following month, we could offer an adjustment to the schedule temporarily for our error. Perhaps we allow one week to return to the old schedule or an extra weekend day off. We certainly can't give them back their old schedule permanently, but we can make amends by presenting a peace offering and asking for forgiveness with a genuine apology.

Request for Forgiveness

This is an often-forgotten part of the apology. How does the individual or team feel about your offer of an apology? If it's a group, some may be willing to accept it, others not. You cannot make someone accept your apology. They have to want to do so all on their own. If you have come from a place of kindness and sincerity and have included all the other five steps in a solid apology, you are at the mercy of the individual receiving it.

Asking if they accept your apology will get better acceptance. It says to the individual that you care what they think. Many individuals will lie when they answer. You may say, "Are we okay? I just want to make sure that you and I are okay to move past this." They may reply, "Sure, absolutely," when they clearly are not. Here's a key point. Don't argue with someone about them not wanting to accept your apology!

Too often, someone asks, "Do you accept my apology?" When the response is no, the individual attacks with, "What more do you want?! I said I was sorry. I told you what I should have done instead. I can't fix it, and you know that. So why aren't you accepting my apology?!" The other reply I hear is, "I don't believe you. You say we are fine, but I don't think you have accepted my apology."

If you start confronting them because they are not in a good place to accept your apology, there is no point in apologizing. In fact, you have caused the worst damage. You not only offended them and made a mistake, but you then started arguing with them about how they felt about your apology. The reality is that only the receiver can accept your apology. You cannot make them, so don't try ramming it down their throat.

Below are several appropriate responses if they do not accept your apology.

- "Thank you for being honest. I hope one day we can move past this, but I recognize it will take time."
- "Thank you for letting me know. I respect your thoughts and have learned from this mistake."
- "I'm disappointed, but I understand. I hope one day you will be able to forgive me."

All of these are centered around acknowledging how the individual does not forgive you and that you accept it but are hopeful that one day they will. If they do accept your apology, thank them. You should be grateful that they have the mindset to move past their anger, fear, sadness, or frustration and accept your apology.

Apologizing is never easy, but for a leader, it is imperative. For our team, it is equally important because it lays the foundation for other individuals to be honest. Honesty is one of the most important traits an individual needs to have to be trusted. If you are in a leadership role, apologizing will show your team that you are honest, leading to better trust and respect. Teach these skills to your team. It's important that everyone knows how to construct a proper apology.

Utilizing these tips will hopefully keep you out of conflict. But what about if a conflict does occur? In the next chapter, let's dive into how to manage and even embrace conflict.

Chapter Eleven

Embracing Conflict

The team is arguing or is not working well together. They may be loud and obnoxious or quietly stabbing each other in the back. Perhaps there are lines drawn on the floor and individual teams battling against each other. Regardless, some individuals or teams are in a conflict.

In the year 2020, we saw one of the most heated elections ever in the United States. While we all want to leave our non-work-related opinions and viewpoints at home, we must acknowledge that they do make up the core of who we are. The presidential election of 2020 destroyed entire families and relationships simply because of people's opinions of one particular candidate or the other. Many individuals could not resolve the conflict, so they elected never to talk to each other again. While it's sometimes okay that people never speak to each other again in their private lives, in a veterinary hospital, individuals must be able to move past their differences. They cannot simply choose never to speak to each other again. They must resolve the conflict.

All veterinary professionals want to work in a veterinary hospital that offers fantastic veterinary care with a healthy workplace environment. When teams realize that they all want a happy workplace environment, they can start to become aligned in their core values as a veterinary hospital team. Coaching teams through conflict, big and small, is one of the most important things effective leaders do almost daily.

As leaders, we have to recognize that conflicts will happen. We would be delusional to think everyone on the team would always get along. So instead of fighting against the conflicts, let's embrace them.

Recognize that not all conflict is bad. Conflict can be healthy and beneficial for the team. Conflict is good if it's done right. Good conflict can teach teams that they can still get along and provide excellent veterinary care to their patients even when they disagree. Good conflict can create new solutions and innovations. Good conflict creates change and can be a catalyst for motivating a group to work together better.

Healthy Conflict

Psychologist and author of *Conflict Without Casualties* Nate Regier (2017) wrote, "Conflict is simply the energy created by the gap between what we want and what we are experiencing." Too often, people negatively associate the exhausting emotional tug-of-war that can occur with unproductive conflict. However, in reality, when we figure out how to navigate the conflict, we often reap the rewards in return.

Unproductive negative conflict drains energy and costs companies significant money. A 2008 report from CCP Global Human Capital estimated the annual cost of workplace conflict in the United States to be roughly $350 billion in lost time and productivity (Meinert, 2017). That's some expensive anger. Even more concerning is that roughly 64% of individuals would rather compromise to avoid conflict (Meinert, 2017). Compromise to avoid conflict in veterinary medicine could cause a medical mistake, resulting in a loss of life. When a new doctor questions a senior doctor about a medication dose and the senior doctor becomes defensive, that may cause the newer doctor to compromise and agree even though they were correct, the dose was wrong.

When we are lucky enough to have productive, healthy conflict, we see our teams trusting and growing together. Productive conflict means the team can move forward with an issue and come to a resolution. In healthy conflict, people are attentive, open-minded, kind, and work towards a common goal of resolve.

Unfortunately, most individuals hate conflict. Some people have been taught that conflict of any kind should be avoided. Others lack courage and truly fear conflict. A good number of others try to avoid it altogether for self-preservation.

Our hospital grows stronger when we teach teams that conflict is necessary and even welcomed. No one wants a team of all like-minded individuals. When a problem arises, that team would all come to the same solution. We don't want people on opposite sides all the time, but we do want individuals who are different and who will buck the norm when needed. When hospitals and companies poo-poo those with differing opinions and label them as argumentative, they shut themselves down to great ideas and change.

As a leader, you must embrace conflict and talk to your team about how it can be beneficial. The concept of healthy conflict is the same as PKH conversations. Both come from a place of professionalism and politeness. Both help a difficult situation to be tackled with more grace. Both end with teams growing stronger together rather than apart. When teams recognize that it's okay to disagree so long as the disagreement is handled using a polite, kind, and honest approach, it permits them to be a more honest version of themselves. The flip side of this is that teams must be taught to accept that, at times, they will not be happy with the decision or outcome of a conflict. However, accepting to move forward rather than stay in a negative space of discontent is the key to successful conflict resolution.

Take this quick quiz on the next page to find out how comfortable you are with embracing productive, healthy conflict. The only rule to the quiz is that you want to try to check every box. For those you don't check, you should gain insight and work to improve those areas in the future.

	Responsibilities	Yes?
Conflict Mindset	I see conflict as an important part of a healthy team.	☐
	I confront difficult conversations directly.	☐
	I discuss several scenarios that could be true.	☐
	I remain open to different points of view.	☐
	I enjoy working with my teammates to come to a solution and compromise when there's a disagreement.	☐
Forum for Conflict	I encourage my team to bring up their concerns in public.	☐
	I ask my team for their opinions before making a decision.	☐
	I encourage my team to stay engaged in the conversation even when it's tough.	☐
	I don't allow my team to gossip to me, but I do embrace concerns and encourage them to resolve issues on their own.	☐
	I put issues on the agenda raised outside of the meeting for the whole team to discuss together.	☐
The Right Words	I have stopped saying "yes, but" when responding to something that I disagree with.	☐
	I use what-if questions to help my team think about other possibilities.	☐
	I help my team to understand the impact of the proposed actions.	☐
	I ask questions to understand the reasoning behind ideas I may disagree with.	☐
	I listen to my team's response after I have asked a question.	☐
Embracing Feedback	I know that giving feedback is part of my responsibility to my team.	☐
	I share observations to make feedback objective.	☐
	I am careful in how I provide feedback, so it feels kind and respectful.	☐
	I ask my team to provide me feedback to help me improve.	☐
	I enjoy listening to the feedback from my team.	☐

Adapted from *You First* (Davey, 2013)

How did you do? Are you comfortable with conflict? If not, never fear. Almost no one is. This checklist serves as a reminder of things you need to get more comfortable with. Just keep being mindful of areas you are uncomfortable in so that you can improve upon them.

Rules of Healthy Conflict

This is the cycle of how most conflict occurs in your hospital. Are you guilty of this cycle when you experience conflict? Let's talk about how to prevent and stop the cycle of gossip.

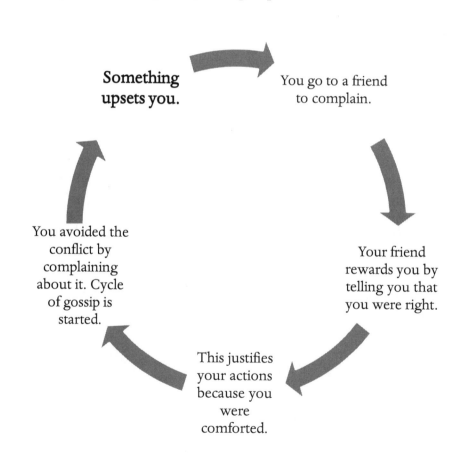

Something upsets you.

You go to a friend to complain.

Your friend rewards you by telling you that you were right.

This justifies your actions because you were comforted.

You avoided the conflict by complaining about it. Cycle of gossip is started.

There must be rules to conflict discussions. These rules are up to you and your team. People just can't go around screaming at each other and throwing things each time they get upset. I would suggest working on the rules of engagement during a meeting. This is important so that everyone respects and values the conflict rules of engagement. It is also a commitment to say that it's okay to disagree sometimes.

School of Babel (2020), an online website that provides resources to help leaders, suggests creating clubhouse rules. I love that saying. The team should create clubhouse rules so everyone has agreed on standards of behavior that will be utilized during a conflict. High levels of communication are a predictor of a high-performing team. Having an agreed set of rules that define the team's conduct helps to establish an understanding between members.

Clubhouse Rules for Conflict Conversations

- Be respectful and kind to all that are speaking.
- Listen and be attentive.
- Turn off all distracting tech (phones, smart watches).
- Rotate the conversation to allow all to speak.
- Do not interrupt others.
- Avoid accusations.
- Stay on topic.
- Remain calm and convey the feelings you are having by using healthy "I" statements.
- If needed, pause to take a five-minute break and collect thoughts.
- If you are silent during the conversation that means you agree.
- Think before you speak.

These are by no means the best or most perfect rules. In fact, they are generalized and not specific to any one hospital. Allowing the team to create their own clubhouse rules on how they want to communicate during conflict is important to creating healthy conversation. If individuals on the team struggle with voicing their opinion, you can always have them contribute by writing their ideas down. However, it is best done verbally with every single member of the team contributing. This is a powerful team builder and commitment to professional conversation.

We need to stop the vicious cycle of gossip that usually starts when someone has a conflict with another. When something upsets or bothers an individual, they turn to a trusted coworker and complain about the other individual. It seems innocent enough, and we all do it. We need to vent. The individual who listens to the complaint provides solace and a good ear, which rewards the person complaining. In the future, the complainer will continue to return to the person they received the favorable response from. At some point, the listener usually tells someone else. This causes the cycle of gossip to start, and it all started because an individual wanted to avoid conflict. Rarely does the team member who was upset confront the offender in an effort to resolve their concern.

It's easier to complain and gossip. Instead of having an honest and kind conversation about an issue they were concerned with, they talked about the issue to someone else who usually couldn't resolve it. That rewards them for their behavior by being a sympathetic ear.

John Maxwell is a best-selling author and speaker on the subject of leadership. I came across his "Ten Commandments of Confrontation" a few years ago and enjoyed every one of them. They are the commandments of how to keep conflict civil and productive. I think these could be added to the clubhouse rules or could sit alone on a wall to remind everybody of the importance of healthy conversation.

The Ten Commandments of Confrontation

- Thou shalt confront others in private.
- Thou shalt confront as soon as possible and not look for "a better time."
- Thou shalt stick to the issue at hand.
- Thou shalt make thy point and not repeat it.
- Thou shalt deal only with actions that can be changed.
- Thou shalt avoid sarcasm (especially in an email or text).
- Thou shalt avoid words like "always" and "never" because they are rarely accurate.
- Thou shalt ask questions and offer suggestions.
- Thou shalt not apologize for the confrontation.
- Thou shalt remember to highlight the person's positive contributions.

(Maxwell, 2016)

Promoting Productive Conflict

1) Have a conversation with your team about productive conflict. They should embrace having opposing viewpoints and opinions and understand it makes for a more creative and cohesive team. We certainly don't want everyone on the team to think the same thing all the time. Be sure to introduce healthy communication skills before introducing productive conflict conversations.

2) Create a set of clubhouse rules that all team members agree to. Working on this together as a team is pretty powerful because of the commitment of wanting to maintain a polite and respectful relationship with each other, even when disagreements arise.

3) During meetings, look for conflicts. Be sure to look for the eye rolls, the snarky facial expressions, or the whispering between team members. If you see something, say something! Don't call out the snarky face or eye roll. Instead, try saying, "You seem like you're not completely on board with this new policy," or, "I get a sense that you're feeling uneasy or unhappy about something."

Follow up with, "I know it's hard, but I would love to hear your thoughts because this is a safe space to communicate how you feel." If you are lucky enough to have an individual communicate what they think and feel, thank them immediately! This shows the rest of the group that you appreciate and value honesty. If you criticize or become defensive, you will shut the door to any future conversations.

4) When you see two individuals expressing differing opinions, praise them at an appropriate time. It decreases their guilt about having the conflict and increases their ability to have a healthy conflict because they were permitted to do so. So long as they are following the clubhouse rules of engagement, praise them for their professionalism and honesty.

5) Never pick sides! If two individuals or departments disagree, you should act as a mediator. The minute a leader picks a side is the minute when you influence the rest of the team's decision. Allow them to work through it together without your influence. Even if you think there's no way that you could influence a decision, you will. It is because you are in a leadership role. Act only as the mediator to help facilitate the discussion. Mediate that it's okay to disagree, but in the end, everyone needs to commit to the decision.

6) Talk to the team or individual about how they are feeling. It's uncomfortable to do so, but they will understand that you have their best interest in mind so long as you utilize a kind approach. You want to make sure their voices are heard so validate their emotions. "You are a valued member of the team, but you haven't spoken up during this conversation. I want to make sure that we hear from you. How do you feel about this?"

Moving Past the Loss

Guess what? You are not going to win every argument. As a leader, not only do you have to accept the losses graciously but so does your team. How do we coach someone to accept the decision that was made even though we disagree with it?

For example, a few veterinary receptionists argued that the veterinarians needed to take medical calls from clients instead of the receptionists fielding them. Despite countless conversations, the two teams were at a standstill. Finally, the practice manager decided it was in the client's best interest to have the veterinarians take all calls centered around medical questions. The veterinarians were not happy with the decision. In their opinion, they did not have the time to take more calls. How does a leader help a team or individual move past a loss?

Step One: Validate Emotions

Losses are tough. When a sports team loses, the coach usually starts by validating emotions. "It was a tough game today, and I know many of you are feeling down." For the previous example, talking to the veterinarians privately is important. "I know you are disappointed and likely even angry over my decision to have you handle all medical-related calls from clients." Acknowledging how one is personally feeling and allowing them to take time to sort through those feelings is important. That includes even your own feelings if you happened to be the one who felt like they lost during the conflict.

Step Two: Stop Pointing Fingers

Playing the role of the victim is easy, and many still want to keep arguing long after the conflict is over. The problem is, blaming others prevents teams or individuals from moving forward. Leaders must express to teams that moving forward is important and needs to be the main focus to move past a conflict.

Step Three: Focus on the Present

One of the most effective ways to let go of a conflict that did not go the way you wanted is to embrace the present. Instead of reliving the past and getting consumed with negativity, focus your energy on how you will embrace the new challenge or change. For the veterinarians of this story, we would want to move away from "this is going to be hard" to "let's talk about how we can streamline the medical calls and make it the best experience for you and the client."

When individuals put energy into helping with the change, they focus less on the past. While it's a difficult exercise asking the individual or team to list at least three positive things they could see with the decision that was made is important in reshaping their mindset. You should try this yourself when you struggle with the loss in a conflict. Unfortunately, if people are too bitter about the loss they may not be open to focusing on the positive. Only they can move past and accept the decision or outcome.

Step Four: Forgive Those Who Wronged You

Teams or individuals mustn't hold a grudge against those they lost an argument to. If you are in a leadership role, this sometimes includes forgiving yourself. Once teams no longer carry anger and resentment, they'll be able to move on. When you find yourself still angry over the outcome weeks or months later, you need to recognize you're likely missing this last step. Forgiveness is important to accepting and moving on.

The reality is that even some of the best coaches cannot help teams or individuals to move past losing a conflict. You cannot force anyone into acceptance. The individual is the only person who can move on and accept that the conflict did not go the way they hoped. Some choose to live with a grudge and be resentful and angry. As a leader, so long as we have coached to the best of our ability, we sometimes have to allow the individual to find which path they want to walk down all on their own.

Chapter Twelve

Just Stop Arguing!

How do you manage some of the more difficult conversations when they occur? What is our role when a team member struggles with something personally? How involved should we be? Why won't they just stop arguing?!

I struggled with presenting this information so that it provided useful tools applicable to most people. It's hard to teach individuals how to coach and communicate with others when using written word only. Workshops, webinars, and conferences are generally better tools for teaching conflict management and managing difficult communication.

Years ago, I created a lecture on understanding canine behavior so that individuals could better humanely and safely restrain dogs. I created the presentation because I saw that many in the veterinary industry struggled with picking up on the subtle signs dogs were trying to tell them. Unfortunately, the failure to recognize the clear warning signs dogs were displaying resulted in some individuals becoming injured or causing an escalation of the dog's behavior.

A veterinary technician attending my lecture came up to me at the end and said that it was a great lecture, but she really needed hands-on experience. She wanted to know if I was aware of any hands-on classes that allowed her to work with highly aggressive dogs. She said, and I quote, "It would be great if there were dogs lunging at me, and an instructor was there to help coach me. It would be even better if two dogs would get into a fight so I could see firsthand how to break it up."

For one of the rare times in my life, I was speechless. I had to muster all my strength to keep a poker face because my jaw wanted to hit the ground. I explained that I was not aware of any such classes, and they likely would not exist due to the high level of liability of hosting one. She seemed disappointed and mentioned she was going to keep looking because such a class would be invaluable. To this day, I have never heard of such a class existing where dogs lunge at people or get into fights for the purpose of training people on managing aggressive dogs.

I tell the story because I often imagine two veterinary team members screaming at each other. Like an aggressive dog class, I gather veterinary teams could benefit from an aggressive veterinary team members class. I picture two out-of-control veterinary team members flinging real insults and outsiders trying to coach them. Unfortunately, I don't know of any class that truly prepares leaders for the real thing, short of tabletop exercises at workshop events.

I decided to use scenario-based teaching to convey techniques that I have found effective for managing tough conflicts. The scenarios are real, and the outcomes listed used the techniques described for each scenario. My disclaimer is that not every technique will work for every person. You know your team best. These scenarios and how I managed them are merely one example of what may work. There are no guarantees in life except for death, taxes, the fact that chocolate is the best food, and unicorns are real. There are many different ways to mediate a conflict, so the solution presented is not the only answer, nor is it the right one. It's the one that worked for me.

No matter how many countless conflicts I've mediated and worked through with veterinary professionals, there are some where I fail. The teams or individuals remain conflicted. Remember that how they react is solely up to them. Sometimes despite our best efforts to coach them out of conflict, two team members remain conflicted without resolution.

Another key point to remember is that it may not be your conflict to resolve. If you are a veterinary receptionist manager and overhear two veterinarians having a dispute, your job would be to speak to their manager. That said, if two individuals are in a yelling match, it is likely everyone's responsibility to point out that they must stop such unprofessional behavior.

Leadership Must be Aligned

Conflict is hard enough to resolve, but it will be near impossible if the leaders aren't united. Whenever you are working to resolve a tough conflict in your team, talk to your manager and the leadership in the hospital. They may be able to collaborate with you on ideas of how to resolve the issue. Unfortunately, too many leaders think they are alone on an island. Collaboration with other leaders is often the key to success in managing some difficult issues. Find help in groups like the Veterinary Hospital Managers Association (membership fee applies) or social media groups dedicated to veterinary leaders.

Conversely, if the issue involves multiple areas of the hospital, the leaders responsible for those areas must first agree on the steps for resolution. For example, in many hospitals, the veterinary technician/nurse team might have a conflict with the veterinarian team. It could be the entire team or just an individual or two.

In this scenario, the medical director and veterinary technician manager must work together first. If the medical director only communicates to the doctor team and says, "You need to get along with the technicians," while the veterinary technician manager does nothing, no resolution will occur. The two managers must work together in these situations and agree on a solution. They then must present a unified front, which often comes as a joint meeting between the two groups. Failing to present a unified front will continue to result in negative discourse.

The worst offense is when one of the managers continues to agree with their team, "You are right. The doctors are difficult to work with. We are the better team. We all know we just have to manage their cranky doctor behavior." That type of communication will continue to divide the team.

The more leaders align together, the faster the conflict will be resolved. Unfortunately, too many times, other leaders don't support each other, resulting in the continuation of the dysfunction. If leaders could learn to communicate on the issues and find solutions together, teams would see a unified leadership front. Consistency in messaging is key to resolving any conflict. Let's run through some conflict scenarios and review one way you could work to resolve the issue.

But They Are the Doctor

A pet patient arrested, and the team was unsuccessful in their resuscitation efforts. During the CPR efforts, the doctor was barking out orders to the team. At one point they ordered 0.4 mls of epinephrine to be drawn up, but the technician drew up 4.0 mls and administered it. At the end of the code, the doctor angrily said to the technician, "We will never know if that patient would have lived or not since it may have been your mistake that killed them." They walked away leaving the technician stunned and crying. You are the practice manager and heard what happened and need to address the doctor.

Yikes! Did that make you cringe? The question is, what do you do next? The doctor is angry, and the veterinary technician is upset. To the doctor's point, they did make a mistake that did not serve the patient well. I can tell you more of the story: the veterinary technician excused themself to cry alone in a closed exam room.

While many managers feel that addressing this at a different time would be best, the best time is right after it happened. In an ideal setting, the hospital team has already learned how to utilize debriefing as a tool. I addressed this in my first book, but I want to present a high-level view of this exceptionally powerful tool again. In this situation, debriefing may be the ideal way to communicate with the veterinarian without causing more anger or frustration. It would also be a powerful tool to allow the veterinary technician to talk through how the mistake was made in a healthy setting. When you have two individuals with high emotions, utilizing a group tool can help ensure neither party feels attacked.

Debriefing enables a team to have a productive conversation and recognize the positive and negative aspects of that situation. In human medicine, debriefing almost always occurs after a CPR event. It allows the team to improve themselves by increasing their communication skills. It is a judgment-free zone where teams can learn about the good and bad that may have occurred during the code. It will increase the team's ability to work together during adverse times.

If the team was familiar with this important tool, you could request that they have a debrief. I will add that having a team that knows how to have polite, kind, and honest communication and one that also has a good level of trust between each other can help facilitate a constructive debriefing session. The first three steps require the facilitator to ask the following. The first two questions can usually be answered together.

1) What Happened?
2) How is Everyone Doing?
   -Point out a win that happened.
3) What Could Have Been Done Differently?

Team: "A dog arrested. We're not doing okay. It was pretty intense, and the dog didn't make it."

Facilitator Reply: "I'm so sorry. This must be hard for all of you, but I wanted to mention from an outsider's perspective, I was amazed at how quickly you started resuscitative efforts."

Now think about the third question. In this situation, we hope to talk about the medication error and that's exactly what happened. I asked the question and someone said, "There was a medication error during the code." The veterinary technician who made the mistake replied, "I really thought she said 4.0 milliliters. I feel like an idiot! I should have known better." A teammate of theirs replied back with, "It's hard to hear with everything going on. I wasn't even listening. Any one of us could have made that mistake!"

Another veterinary technician pointed out, "Since we don't have time to write things down, perhaps we need a double-check verbal system." The veterinarian who was involved in the CPR code, at this point, apologized and said, "I know I was just yelling out orders. I should have made a point to double-check that you heard me." Debriefing saved a conflict between two individuals, but my team also was familiar with the tool.

When your team is unaware of how to debrief, it becomes a more difficult conversation. The conversation will likely fall flat if the team has not built-up trust before this interaction. The veterinarian will not care as much about the veterinary technician with whom they hardly have a relationship. Instead, the focus will continue to be on the patient and how the veterinary technician may have contributed to the failed resuscitation effort.

The veterinary technician is unlikely to apologize if they do not have a good and trusting relationship with the veterinarian because the veterinarian said some harsh comments in front of everyone. Hopefully, the veterinary technician has a good support system to help support them through the trauma of making a mistake and being yelled at. If the team lacks a trusting relationship and a good rapport with each other, all a manager can do is try to coach the doctor on apologizing while attempting to console the veterinary technician.

If the veterinary technician and veterinarian have a trusting relationship, then communication can happen that day. Bringing them both into a room and acting as a mediator is most likely the best solution for both employees in this scenario. Allow the veterinarian to decompress for a bit and allow the technician to process their feelings before bringing them into a room together.

Once in a room, start from a place of kindness and compassion. "I caught the end of the CPR code on that dog. I am sorry. You both do amazing work every day and losing the patient is never easy." This immediately sets the tone for the interaction.

Turning to the veterinary technician and addressing them first will add to the tone you want for this meeting. "I know you feel terrible about the mistake. Can you tell me from your perspective what happened?" Allow the veterinary technician to process their emotions and recount the event. If you start with the angry individual, this adds anger to an already intense situation. Starting with the individual who feels sad or upset allows the anger to be diffused. The veterinary technician can apologize first instead of the veterinarian assuming the worst and continuing the insults. I learned this technique after countless failed mediation sessions. Start with the less hostile individual. It takes some of the anger out of the room by doing so.

Afterward, allow the veterinarian to share their side of the story. The goal is to figure out a way to decrease or remove the potential for this error to happen again. "Is there anything that could be done to prevent this mistake in the future?" This brings the two of them together to collaborate once again as a team. With any luck, the veterinarian will apologize for their verbal attack, and the technician will again apologize for the mistake. Hopefully, they will leave the room with no harm done to the relationship.

If the veterinarian struggles to apologize for their behavior, you must point out that the statement was inappropriate and could have been handled better. In the end, the veterinarian may remain angry and upset at the veterinary technician. It's up to them to accept the apology.

Why the Hell Did They Get Promoted?

XYZ has been working in the veterinary hospital for more than 10 years as a veterinary receptionist. They are a decent employee but tend to do exactly what is asked of them and not a thing more. XYZ sometimes likes to gossip and can be negative at times. While they are great with clients, they are not a great team member. They often make fun of others on the team or talk trash about the hospital. They tell the new employees that they are "essentially the manager" and that the "real" manager doesn't know what they are doing.

Most of XYZ's behavior has been manageable until recently. A coworker of theirs was promoted to a newly developed manager position. XYZ is irate because they feel they should have been promoted. The gossip has gotten out of control and the negativity is relentless.

The most recent concern was when a client asked XYZ how their day was going and they said, "Terrible. This hospital doesn't appreciate me so I'm likely leaving soon." They have been telling clients and teammates, "When I leave, this place is going to fall apart without me. I can't understand why they put them in a manager position. I do more than everyone on this team. This place sucks."

Everyone has had an employee like this in the hospital. It may be a jaded veterinarian that did not get promoted into the medical director role. It may be the veterinary technician/nurse who was passed up for the supervisor position. It could be the practice manager who did not get the opportunity to interview for the hospital administrator position because the owner hired someone from the outside. Regardless, when employees feel they are entitled to a leadership role and fail to get one, this often causes them to become angry and bitter.

How do we talk to an employee that has an attitude problem? How can we help them become more successful in areas where they struggle with their behavior? Many managers don't want to address behavior problems because they are in a gray area. How do you define too much gossip? How do you classify someone as having a negative attitude? These are tough conversations when it comes to talking to employees. While we don't want to insult their behavior, we do need to address it. Before addressing the veterinary receptionist's behavior issue, let's discuss behavior versus personality. It's important to understand the difference between behavior versus personality and what is and is not appropriate for leaders to focus on.

Behavior vs. Personality

Behavior and personality are two different things. It's important when you are having a conversation with an employee, you don't insult their personality. Too often, individuals don't understand the difference between behavior and personality. I encourage all managers to teach these differences to their employees. They then may be able to understand their personal role in owning each of these items.

Often, when leaders talk to a team member about their behavior, employees feel like it's an attack on their personality. Rarely is that the case. Instead, the manager has often sought to address a behavior issue that the team member must take responsibility for. Educating teams on the difference in each of these and their role is important in order to have productive conversations around behavior issues.

Personality

An individual's personality is stable and is what makes them unique and different from others. A personality helps to drive a person's behavior and is influenced by genetics and the environment in which they grew up. If you require your team to take a personality test, which I recommend that you do, you will learn there are a variety of characteristics that make up the individuals on your team. Some will be introverted, while others will be extroverted. Some will have a strong sense of urgency, while others will be more easygoing. All of these traits are the building blocks that make up any individual's personality.

As leaders, we cannot change the individual's personality in our hospital. We can coach them to break outside of their normal personality from time to time, but their true personality will always be there. For example, I have the ability to lecture on a stage in front of hundreds of people and be fairly comfortable doing so. However, my personality dictates that I am an introvert. At the end of a conference day, my favorite thing to do is grab some food and eat it alone by myself in my hotel room. Being alone recharges me. Many other speakers find joy in going out to dinner with their colleagues and attendees after they have a day of lecturing. Those are my extroverted colleagues.

If an employee has a personality trait that may cause them to struggle with change more than others, we can provide tools to help them accept change a little faster. However, they and we must recognize that it's still innately part of who they are. They will likely always struggle with change, and that's okay, but as a manager, we can help coach them with managing that change a little easier.

As leaders, sometimes you must have an honest conversation with two individuals about personality traits and how they are struggling to get along. I wrote about this in my first book and used an example of an extroverted individual clashing with an introverted team member. How I managed through that situation is the same as how one manages through many interpersonal conflicts. When managing personality conflicts, you cannot ask someone to change who they are because of another individual. Instead, you must help them see why they struggle with each other's personality traits. There are some individuals who will always be more empathetic than others. For those less so, we can coach them in opening up more and understanding what empathy is. Still, they are unlikely to be as emotionally connected as individuals whose core personality is empathetic.

Having the emotional intelligence to understand your traits is key to managing those traits. I am eternally grateful to my many friends who, with kindness and love, have coached me to recognize my high sense of urgency and how it can be both harmful and beneficial. If you want someone to score hard to get tickets to a concert, I'm that person. I will cyber-stalk all ticketing websites, have three computers and two phones ready to go, and get those tickets exactly when they go on sale. My high sense of urgency pushed me to write this book as soon as I finished the first. I recognize that writing one book for most people would be challenging enough. They would celebrate with a long break. Not me. No time to waste. My first book needed a sequel and getting this second book out as fast as possible was important. Getting up at 4:00 in the morning to write before my workday started was a must because a sense of urgency is part of my personality.

The downside to a high sense of urgency is that I get extremely upset if I'm late for something or if someone doesn't meet a deadline I have set. My anxiety builds, and I become difficult to deal with. My friends, have had to remind me that "it's not a big deal" and "not everyone moves at your pace." Learning to manage my high sense of urgency will always be something I need to be cognizant of because it is part of my personality.

Most times, an individual's personality does not disrupt the team. Most individuals can adapt to working with various personalities; some may even learn to embrace them. We can't expect everyone to act like us. We need to help our team get along with a variety of personalities in order to work effectively in a hospital team.

Behavior

Behavior defines a person's conduct and is learned and developed over the years. An individual's behavior may change throughout their lifetime, even drastically. For example, a teenager part of a gang and eventually incarcerated for theft may rejoin society and become a priest, lawyer, or mayor. Behavior can be temporary and can even adapt to the environment you are in.

I once listened to a friend talk to his boss on the phone. He sounded professional and knowledgeable, with a commanding confidence that I was jealous of. Then he hung up the phone and said a sentence that was barely English with a few slang words thrown in. He was a light switch in how he turned himself on and off. He morphed from one behavior to another with ease going from business professional to crass, funny friend. Innately he was still the funny kind person I knew him as in both scenarios, but his behavior was drastically different in the two scenarios.

How an individual presents themselves is the very definition of their behavior. This is often where many individuals get their personality confused with their behavior. They often blame their behavior on their personality, citing they cannot change it because "it is who they are." One's personality may drive their behavior, but the behavior itself is the person's responsibility at all times.

I spoke about my high sense of urgency. I have spent much time and effort learning to relax, moving slower, and recognizing when my "get it all done now" personality is driving those around me nuts. My personality does not permit me to yell at anyone because they are late by two minutes. How I react is solely up to me. That's my behavior. Yes, my behavior is in response to my personality's high sense of urgency, but I have control over that behavior. I don't get the right to berate someone for not meeting a deadline. Instead, I need to react appropriately and coach that individual. I need to have control of my behavior.

No personality trait gives someone permission to be rude, disrespectful, hateful, or angry to another individual. Those are all descriptive behavior traits. I had an employee tell me that she snapped at her coworkers because "it was just who she was." She was married and had two children. I asked if she snapped at them or her friends the same way she talked to the team at the hospital. The answer was no. Snapping at coworkers isn't a personality. It's behavior they elect to use in that one situation.

Leaders need to recognize and separate the two when we have larger conversations with employees. Leaders should never attempt to change someone's personality, but they can coach them. Bringing self-awareness to someone's personality traits can help them develop a skill set they would not have otherwise. Leaders need to break down that behavior—which, while dictated on some level by personality—can be controlled and managed at all times by the individual. Gossiping and negativity are not personality traits. They are toxic behaviors we need to address as leaders. Team members must have the emotional intelligence to recognize their responsibility in their behaviors in order for any change to occur. Unfortunately for some, they never accept that responsibility and instead blame everyone else for their behavior and actions.

Why You Did Not Get Promoted

Let's go back to the angry veterinary receptionist and address why they did not get promoted. You guessed it. This individual did not get promoted because of their behavior. They may be good with clients, but their behavior is unacceptable to the rest of the team. In past meetings, this individual explained that the reason for their gossip was that they were simply being honest and "weren't about to sugarcoat the inadequacies of the hospital." This, unfortunately, is someone who does not see they have any responsibility for their negative, toxic actions.

Honesty is one thing, but gossiping is another. Managing a conversation like this can be exceedingly difficult. Behavior conversations are never easy. Most people feel like their core personality is being ambushed. As leaders, it is up to us to explain that we are not insulting their personality. Instead, we need to coach them to understand that they can and need to control their behavior. Be sure to highlight what areas of their personality you value and appreciate.

We don't want this employee to stop being honest. Rather, we would likely want them to come to us directly. The employee isn't addressing their concerns to anyone who can impact change. Instead, they gossip to anyone who will listen and often to those who never asked for their thoughts. Using wording like the suggestion below will hopefully help drive the important points home.

"I have always appreciated your honesty and value your opinion. I'm not asking you to be less honest, but I am asking you to come to me since I am someone who can help make a change. Simply airing your grievances without speaking to anyone who can make a change is creating a negative environment. The team looks to you as a leader, but you are not exhibiting leadership behavior. I want to help you grow into a leadership role, but we need to work on the negativity. I want you to work with leadership in the hospital when you have concerns versus

complaining to the team. Let's create solutions for the concerns you have. Right now, I just keep hearing from others about the problems you are complaining about."

You have come from a place of politeness and kindness. You have provided this individual with a compliment and separated the behavior from the personality. Too often, in conversations like this, I see leaders confronting an employee's personality. For example, they may say, "The reason you were not promoted was because the other employee exhibits more leadership qualities and is more approachable." Statements such as this are obscure and can easily come off as a personality attack. What are these leadership qualities you mention? Instead, be specific as to why the individual did not get the promotion, what behavior they need to improve upon, and why.

If we, as leaders, can help employees gain self-reflection, we may have a chance at improving undesirable behavior. Unfortunately, often these employees are too jaded to see that leadership is coming from a place of kindness. They feel the hospital does not deserve nor appreciate them. Everyone else is at fault.

If we have tried several coaching sessions and have been unsuccessful, it is up to us to ask the difficult question to the employee. "If you feel so unappreciated, why do you stay?" For some, this question may be the ah-ha moment they need to recognize it is time for them to move on. Others may have the ah-ha moment of realizing they do like the hospital they work in and want to make improvements.

Unfortunately, others have no such moment and will stay at the hospital and be angry about it. They will continue to have thoughts that the hospital is out to get them. We must then decide if we need to say goodbye. I will address that tough decision in Chapter Sixteen.

Turf Wars

I arrived for an overnight shift some years ago. A few hours into the shift I spotted a dirty cage in the surgery ward. I asked the team who's cage it was. I was told, "No one is in that cage. The surgery department left it dirty." Another technician chimed in, "We're done cleaning up after them. If they forget to clean up their cages, we just leave them. It's not our job."

My response was swift. "Really guys?! It's in a dark corner of the room. I don't think they purposefully left it for you. They likely just forgot, but what you are doing is purposeful." I stormed off and cleaned the cage. When I returned a technician said, "You're probably right, but they are always forgetting." My reply was, "Does that give you the right to passively-aggressively leave a dirty cage in an effort to prove your point to them? All you are doing is creating a divide. Let's brainstorm on how to help them remember."

Many of you have experienced the "we're not cleaning that cage because someone else should" turf war. Unfortunately, without leadership intervention, these small micro wars can become full-out battles in the hospital.

Typically, when another employee asks about the dirty cage, they agree with the rationale of not cleaning it. "We will show them how they did us wrong by not cleaning the dirty cage! Then they will see the error of their ways and never forget again." Next thing you know, there's a hidden battle waging over dirty cages. When you say it out loud, it sounds insane and trivial because it is. One of the most common conflict issues I have addressed over my career is over turf wars.

The reality is there are a myriad of turfs in any one hospital. We see doctor turf, veterinary technician/assistant turf, leadership turf, and client service turf in most hospitals. Each turf is protected by at least one gang member on any given day. The gang member will protect their turf with words, body posture, manipulation, sabotage, and sometimes even verbal or physical threats. Invisible lines are drawn, and "our supplies" and "their supplies" are hoarded and hidden. Yet, they all work for the same hospital, driving towards the same goal. The issue of turf wars is not exclusive to veterinary medicine. It occurs in every business everywhere in the world. An article on Inc.com offered some sound advice on managing turf wars.

- Stop questioning the motives (aka assume good intention).
  - The surgery department did not purposefully leave the dirty cage. It's not like they walked out of the hospital laughing about how they "stuck it" to the emergency department. They just forgot.

- Agree there's an issue.
  - Turf wars are centered around real issues. Let's agree there's an issue so we can find a solution. The only issue is that surgery forgot to clean patient cages. They are not lazy. They are not a bad team. There's only one simple, non-complex issue. They forgot.

- Embrace productive conflict.
  - The team or individual must now discuss the issue using a kind communication style to find a resolution.
  (Vechey, 2012)

Forbes likes to call turf wars "silo mentality." I like that terminology because it hits home as to what the issue is. Turf wars occur because individuals are thinking too much about themselves or their own team, operating in a silo. "This type of mentality will reduce efficiency in the overall operation, reduce morale, and may contribute to the demise of a productive company culture," Brent Gleeson, a *Forbes* contributor, writes (2013).

Gleeson writes that almost all turf wars originate from the top-down, meaning that there is an obvious divide in leadership or a failure of one of the leaders to support the hospital as a whole. As tough as it is to realize, leaders need to accept that they may have played a role in creating the division between individuals or teams. Too often, leaders try to boost up their individual teams or even a particular employee by utilizing inflating ego tactics.

Silo Statements

- "We are the best team in the hospital."
- "We work harder than anyone else."
- "I know that other teams don't give you the respect you deserve, but you are the backbone of this hospital."
- "While no one understands what the overnight team does, I know they would fall apart without us."
- "I'm proud to be part of this team that runs smoothly and has the best medical care for their patients. The other department is so disorganized."

Do you see it now? Leaders use these inflammatory statements to boost their team up without realizing they are causing a divide. We need to change the language to ensure our team sees itself as part of the larger hospital team. Incorporate hospital team statements into your language that help to include rather than silo others.

Team Statements

- "We are part of the best hospital."
- "Everyone works hard, which makes us the best hospital."
- "I know it feels like the other teams don't give you the respect you deserve, and I can talk to them about that. Every team is needed to function."
- "While it appears no one understands what the overnight team does, I know they recognize our hard work. I know we miss many hospital celebrations because they occur during the daytime. I will talk with the practice manager about ways for our team to be included in the celebrations."
- "The XYZ department is struggling with organization, and I think our team can help them. Let's brainstorm on some ideas."

When leaders work to provide accolades centered around the entire hospital, it helps bring teams together rather than divide them. Even if you believe that no one understands how hard your overnight team works or that other teams are not giving your team the respect they deserve, you must keep those feelings to yourself. The reason why you or your team feel that way is because of turf wars or communication issues.

When there are issues between two departments, groups, or individuals, the best way to resolve it is for leadership to sit down together and have a conversation centered around polite, kind, and honest communication. As previously written, leadership must get on the same page first. When leaders of various teams get together, there will be disagreements, each defending their team. Leaders must work through the conflict towards the larger goal of stopping the conflict between their teams. Once they agree on a plan, leadership must present a unified front. From there, the leadership must provide a consistent "one hospital" message. Constant gentle reminders to teams will help to ensure the message is delivered daily. When teams go astray (we aren't cleaning that cage) a reminder of "we are one team" will bring them back aligned to the mission.

They Just Hate Each Other

Two veterinary technicians had been best friends for three years. They worked side-by-side together without any issues and enjoyed spending time together outside of the hospital. A position opened up in another department and employee A wanted the opportunity to try something different. After much discussion, it was decided that employee A would move to the new department and employee B would join her as soon as the second opening became available. This plan was discussed with the practice manager who agreed to move employee B over once a second position was available.

About a year later, a position opened up within the department and employee B moved over to work alongside her best friend employee A. Because employee A had a year of experience in the new department it was requested that she train employee B on the skills and knowledge that she needed to be successful in the new department.

Within four weeks employee A stormed into the practice manager's office and declared that she was no longer training employee B. Employee B stormed in shortly thereafter to announce that she no longer wanted to be in the department with employee A. They both stated that they hated each other and no longer wanted to work together. Employee B asked to be moved back to her old department.

While this is an interesting case because the two individuals were once best friends, the reality is this happens in every veterinary hospital. Some people flat-out don't like each other. It's hard to believe that two friends could so quickly decide they hated each other, but it does happen. However, it doesn't matter if they were friends before or not. When employees announce they no longer want to work with each other, it becomes a problem for them and the entire hospital team.

I am frequently asked, "How do you get two people to like each other?" If I had a foolproof method of how to get people to like each other, I would be a millionaire. Instead, what I can offer is some sound advice on dealing with a common problem in veterinary medicine.

As a leader, you don't care if they are best friends, but you do care that they have the ability to maintain a professional healthy working relationship with each other. There are three steps in helping individuals mend relationships:

- Ask why
- Agree on healing
- Coach them

Steps to Mediating a Conflict

Step One: ASK WHY?

Why do they not like each other? This is the most important step to finding a resolution. Employees are allowing their emotions to supersede their professionalism. Your job as a leader is to get them to understand that they don't necessarily need to be best friends but that they do need to be respectful and professional to each other. You must get to the core of why they are having an issue with the other person. Leaders often tell individuals, "I need you to work with each other so just be nice to one another." Until the employees get the opportunity to vent the issue and then work toward a resolution, they will continue to have issues working together. Meet with each employee separately and get to the root cause as to why they have issues with the other person.

There may be some valid reasons as to why the two are disgruntled. Maybe an employee made a racist joke causing another employee to feel uncomfortable. Maybe one employee bullied the other. Ensure that you always get both sides of the story by having separate meetings with each of them. In some instances, it may be clear that an employee was out of line, causing a break in the relationship. Bullying, yelling, cursing, racism, sexual harassment, and discrimination cannot be tolerated. If any of these are the cause of the relationship breakdown, the offender must be dealt with appropriately.

Luckily, it is not often one of those offenses that causes communication breakdown. Instead, it is a perceived injustice or slight against the other individual resulting in a disagreement. I would advise scheduling an hour for each person to meet with you. Avoid scheduling them back-to-back, as they will then run into each other, causing more discord. Here are some ground rules to ensure that the meetings are productive.

1) Keep your personal feelings out of it. It's about them, not you. You are welcome to express how their actions affect the hospital or the team. No offense, but they do not care that you are sad or disappointed that they are not getting along. Let the only emotions in the meeting be theirs and not yours. Remember, you should validate their feelings. "I am sorry you are feeling angry." However, expressing feelings and having a meeting centered on emotion are two different meetings.

2) Keep it professional. If the meeting becomes too emotional, offer to take a break. Allow them time to decompress and come back to the issue hours or even days later.

3) Keep it on topic. Too often, past histories get drudged up, or hearsay gets brought in. It's important to keep it on topic. If the employee starts talking about how they heard that the other employee yelled at a veterinary receptionist four years ago, politely stop them and have them focus on the current issues. "I am going to stop you there. I want to keep the conversation centered on the current issue, not what you heard may have occurred years ago."

4) Listen and keep your opinions to yourself. Nothing stops an employee from sharing more than a boss who keeps interjecting with their own opinions of what should or should not happen. While you may be offended by the individual, don't agree or disagree with that person. The minute a leader says, "You're right, she definitely should not have behaved that way," you are giving that employee the power to continue feeling jaded about the other individual. They will leave the meeting thinking, "My boss thinks she's a jerk too."

Step Two: AGREE ON HEALING

A leader can't simply tell employees to get along and assume they will. The only way that employees will heal their relationship is if they do it on their own. You can't force them or demand that they get along.

You may have an opinion on what you think needs to happen for the relationship to heal. Keep your opinion to yourself. They need to figure it out on their own. In their private meetings with you, they must agree that they want to improve the relationship.

Sometimes, an employee may refuse to communicate or maintain a respectful relationship with another employee. I have had an employee say they had no interest in working with that person ever again or even being nice to them.

If this happens, it is imperative that you, as a leader, draw a firm but clear line. While you appreciate their honesty that they have no interest in developing a respectful relationship with the other individual, that will not be tolerated. They need to work together, and they need to be respectful of each other. In the scenario above, this is what happened.

After individual meetings, employee A mentioned that she was willing to heal the relationship. Employee B said she was not interested in improving the relationship and wanted to return to her old department. The practice manager had to inform her that her old department had no opening available. She would have to work with employee A, or she needed to consider finding employment elsewhere.

It was a tough conversation with an employee who had been part of the hospital for more than five years. However, she had to realize that she would need to work towards a solution. As a leader, you must expect all employees to work together and act professionally towards each other. The minute you make exceptions to this rule is when your hospital team starts to break down. What's stopping two other employees from saying they don't want to work together? When employees get to work in a place where they no longer have to be respectful and kind to each other, it becomes an especially toxic workplace.

It's important that employees feel like it was partially their idea to want to heal the relationship. Here are some talking points to start broaching the conversation about how the communication breakdown will be repaired. The best way to get employees to agree on repairing a relationship is to ask questions where the answer will be yes every time.

- "It's been a struggle for the department to see you two so disconnected. Do you think it would be easier for you and the department if you both had a better relationship?"

- "It must be hard for you to work alongside someone you don't like. However, don't you think that if you had a better relationship with them, it would make your day easier?"

Once they have agreed that their poor relationship is difficult for them and the rest of the department, you now have some small hope of them wanting change. Ask them, "If we worked together, would you be open to mending this relationship with employee XYZ?" I want you to review this question again right before you have a conversation like this with an employee.

This question is important in the way that it is worded because it says to the employee, "I'm here for you, and we will work on this together." Just telling them to go and fix it themselves will never get results. Since you will have told both employees that you will be there for them, then going into the next meeting, they will each know you have both their best interests in mind.

Step Three: COACH THEM

Your job is not to play the game of telephone. Too often, leaders host a meeting and start by saying, "Latoya says you can come off as rude. She wants you to stop." That's how employees want their managers to handle the situation. However, unless the two individuals talk through their differences, they will never resolve the issue.

In the scenario above, the reason why the two employees disliked each other was over-training. Employee A was tasked with training her best friend, employee B. Employee B expressed to employee A that she was nervous and wanted to see how something was done a few times before doing it herself.

Employee A said, "I don't have all day to hold your hand. I had to learn all by myself. You'll be fine. Just do it."

Employee B felt like employee A's training style was abrasive and bullying. They told employee A, "I need you to train me, but you keep throwing me onto the floor. I don't know what I'm doing because you suck at training."

It all came to a head when employee A exclaimed, "You're impossible to train. I'm not dealing with you anymore." Fast forward to when they both stormed into the practice manager's office, and therein lies the story of why they were no longer friends.

Once you have gotten them to both agree that they need to improve their relationship, you will bring them into a room and act as a mediator. Set the stage with some ground rules. If you have created clubhouse communication rules, remind them that you've already committed to a healthy way of communication as a team. If you have not, remind them you expect them to act professionally, stay on topic, and not attack. After all, they have agreed to improve their relationship, which is a starting point.

"I thank you both for meeting with me privately before this meeting. I am happy you agreed to work on your communication and want to get past this disagreement." Statements like these set the tone. You have laid an equal foundation for both of them, and they both believe the other is committed to helping move past the disagreement.

Explain in your words what the differences are but leave the emotions out of it. This eliminates a heated exchange of them yelling at each other about why they feel the other had done them wrong.

You can continue with, "You both shared your grievances with me. It's my understanding that employee A, you feel like employee B is too difficult to train because she has requested extra time and wants to be shown how to do things more than once. Employee B, I understand that employee A is harsh in her training style and wants you to learn on your own. Is that the summary of the issue as you both see it from a high-level view?"

By summarizing the concerns and starting the meeting off professionally, you will have set the stage. Your job is now to get them to solve their problem. This is the hardest part. The best way to get them to resolve their problem is to ask specific open-ended questions. As much as we'd like to put them into a boxing arena to work it out, the reality is it will take time and perhaps several coaching sessions where you act as the mediator.

For example, to employee A you may ask, "Employee B has requested extra time to learn skills before she does them on her own. I know you say you don't have time to do this, but how can we make time, or can we better support you as a trainer?"

For employee B, you may ask, "I appreciate that you let us know you were nervous in the new department. Can you let us know what you need so you can effectively learn the new skills and knowledge?"

Humor goes a long way to breaking down barriers. If you know the two individuals well enough, you could joke, "Listen, I thought about just getting you both boxing gloves, renting a ring, and letting you two duke out your differences that way, but HR just wouldn't let me expense the ring. This leaves us having to talk it out. I get it; way less fun, but likely you'll both walk out with all your teeth." If you can manage to get them to laugh, it will improve the relationship.

Ensure they are both aware of each other's strengths and how they play an integral role in the team. Praise them for being kind to each other and wanting to work together. You can also try a quick team blast builder to get them to open up to each other. I described the concept of blast builders in my first book and listed quite a few for leaders to do during or after the meeting to build the team. In short, they are under five-minute team builders. These help to break the ice and hopefully get a laugh.

- "Tell me the naughtiest thing you did as a child that you may or may not have been caught for."
- "If you could live in any season of the year forever, what season would it be and why?"
- "What's your favorite and least favorite food and why?"

It seems out of character for a manager to ask team builder questions like these during a meeting centered around disagreement, but why not? It breaks up the tense emotion. When a leader is an effective moderator and brings two people together, they will create a stronger bond. Timing of the short team builder is key. You certainly don't want to do it in the middle of a conversation where one individual is crying or the other is angry. Therefore, I recommend it at the beginning or end of the meeting. "Before we start, I want to break the ice and learn about each other a little more."

Acting as a mediator and coaching difficult conversations was one of my main challenges as a manager. It was also one of the most important things I did. After years of practice and learning about communication, I pride myself on how much I've learned and improved. Getting two people to communicate better and even agree on something is very rewarding.

In the end, the only thing leaders can do is promote and teach our teams better communication skills and build trust and respect between members. Trust occurs from positive communication centered around knowing someone genuinely cares about the other person, hospital, patient, or client. Even if you have excellent communication skills, you will sometimes struggle to mediate a conflict between individuals. Take lessons from those times you struggle and continue to improve your mediation skills.

As leaders, we also must ensure we have the other tools in place for a healthy workplace environment. If we aren't promoting a healthy culture, individuals will likely struggle to get along. As much as we want to scream at team members who struggle to maintain a respectful workplace relationship by yelling at them, "Just F-ing get along because I don't have time to deal with your crap," that's not helpful nor practical. Everyone, including you and me, has struggled to get along with a coworker at some point. For some, we can navigate difficult communication and even grow our skills from the experience. For others, it takes a skilled leader to navigate the communication between two individuals.

Chapter Thirteen

Blame the Millennials

Lazy, no work ethic, and entitled. Is that your opinion of the generation known as millennials? It is certainly the opinion of many. I'm here to tell you that you are wrong. The mindset of blaming any younger generations for anything breeds toxicity in our workplaces. All generations offer something a little different that is beneficial to our workplaces.

I still hear a lot about millennials, but the reality is you probably aren't even blaming the right generation. When this book was published in 2022, the youngest millennials would have been 27 years old. In 2022, the oldest millennials would be 40 years old, with the mean age of that generation being 35 years old. Millennials have homes, children, and are contributing to society at this point. One of the lead scientists who helped create one of the COVID-19 vaccines, Dr. Kizzmekia Corbett, is in the millennial generation. They are environmentalists, scientists, engineers, and doctors. Lazy, no work ethic, and entitled hardly describes this or any generation. Millennials are saving the entire planet at this point and doing some pretty amazing things.

When I was in my 20s, I was told my generation (Generation X) wouldn't amount to anything. Older generations felt we were lazy, had no work ethic, and would be a drain on society. My generation was considered to be such slackers that would never accomplish anything that we were awarded the title of X, meaning "nothing," in the sense we were an X on society (Sanburn, 2015).

When an entire generation is told they will never amount to anything, what do you think that does for their view of older generations? It certainly doesn't have them skipping into workplace environments, ready to embrace them. On the contrary, it serves to create a further divide.

The myth that younger generations have less work ethic and productivity has been largely proven untrue. A study in 1992 showed younger workers had stronger work ethics than older workers (Tang & Tzeng, 1992). Similar studies since then have shown the same.

For your reference, here are how the generations are broken down. Depending on the reference, the years may be slightly different. For example, some references cite millennials starting in 1982 or 1983. In a study about the civic engagement of Gen X, the U.S. Census Bureau has defined this generation as individuals born between 1968 and 1979 (Tolbize, 2008). It seems there is still much debate between the exact years of Gen X, millennials, Gen Z and Gen Alpha. To create this chart, I utilized three to four references and took the most agreed-upon years between them. The reality is that a generation is not truly defined by its years until it is in its more senior years when the behavior of that generation has settled.

Generation Name	Years
Gen Alpha	2010? - TBD
Gen Z, iGen, or Centennials (Name not determined yet and the years may divide into multiple groups)	1996 – 2010? TBD
Millennials or Gen Y (Same Generation)	1982 – 1995
Generation X	1965 – 1981
Baby Boomers	1946 – 1964
Traditionalists or Silent Generation	1925 – 1945*
G.I. or Greatest Generation	1901 – 1924*

*Some references will group these two generations together, but more keep them separated.

Looking at the table, we can see four generations clashing at any given time in our workplace. While it would be nice to say that we should not have any bias or place judgment on anyone solely based on age, that is not possible. There are differences between generations. As a leader within a hospital, we must recognize the differences and work to create a cohesive culture within our veterinary teams by educating our team members on generational differences.

Multigenerational Differences

In the year 2022, we have four generations in our hospitals:

- Baby Boomers
- Gen X
- Millennials
- Gen Z, iGen, or Centennials

Each of these generations represents a different age group, set of values, and culture. It does not mean one is better than another. They are simply different, each with its pros and cons. When these employees come together as a veterinary hospital team, they come together each with different opinions, backgrounds, varied work styles, and dissimilar thought processes that potentially lead to workplace conflict. Recognizing how each generation is different may help leaders and teams create a more cohesive team while breaking down generational gaps.

Baby Boomers: 1946 – 1964

Baby boomers are now close to retirement. It is a generation shaped by the Vietnam War, the civil rights movement, the moon landing, television, and Watergate (Purdue Global University, 2020). They believe that work is expected and part of life. Overall, they are optimistic, competitive, goal-oriented, workaholics, and team-oriented (Purdue Global University, 2020).

They appreciate job security, particularly as they are getting older. Their focus is to gain manager and supervisor roles within their organization. Baby boomers often define their life by the job they hold. They find prestige and value in higher-ranking jobs because it means they have a successful life. They believe that you must sacrifice in order to be successful. Because they are used to the mindset that you are not successful unless you strive to be at the top, this generation may look down on younger generations who are not as motivated to take on leadership roles.

Baby boomers are best communicated to face-to-face or by phone calls. They may be more reserved in their communication because they value professionalism and respect in the workplace. Many are comfortable with emails at this point, though some may struggle with technology. They prefer traditional in-classroom, in-person learning.

Employers must provide them with specific goals and deadlines. Ensuring that hospital leaders have a clear schedule outlined for this generation helps them understand their daily goals and operation. Using creative approaches like allowing veterinarians to set their own schedules would cause this generation some frustration. They would be more comfortable with the hospital setting their schedule for them.

They also appreciate being in mentor and coaching roles for the younger generation. If they are not in a leadership role, they like to feel valued by their manager. Utilizing this generation to educate and guide younger generations of veterinary professionals is important. However, it can provide frustration because of the disconnect they feel with the younger generations. Hospital leaders need to educate those in the baby boomer generation about what to expect with learning styles and motivation for the younger generations.

Gen X: 1965 – 1981

I proudly fall into this category. My generation was shaped by the AIDS epidemic, the fall of the Berlin Wall, the dot-com boom, the early 1990s recession, and the latch-key movement (Purdue Global University, 2020). Many baby boomer mothers worked full-time, including my own. My generation was expected to let themselves into the house after school with the goal of not setting the house on fire until their parents came home. Both my sister and I managed to do that throughout our childhood. We proudly never set our house on fire.

Gen X tends to be flexible, informal, skeptical (particularly of a company or leader), and fiercely independent. We are willing to buck the system and try new things. We are relatively technologically savvy, though the younger generation is better at technology than us.

Many people are unaware that my generation started the work-life balance movement (Tolbize, 2008). Gen X watched their parents become overworked. My parents alone worked 50-60 hours each week. My generation made a commitment that we would never work that hard. We became committed to maintaining a healthy work-life balance. Gen X is driven to be in a workplace aligned with their personal views. As such, if hospital policies are implemented that go against our core values or greatly affect our personal life, we are quick to move on.

Gen X is driven by continuously improving our skills and knowledge (Tolbize, 2008). We are never satisfied with our current knowledge or skill. This likely explains why I felt the urge to go back to college as an adult and even challenge myself to write two books. My desire to keep learning and growing my skill is ever present in my life.

We can be communicated with by any means necessary, though we prefer emails to text. We may lose texts, so send them to our email box if you want something done. Gen Xs require immediate feedback. Hearing about something that could have been improved upon days or even weeks later tends to upset us.

Because we are an independent generation, we do not do well with micromanagers. We need autonomy to be able to perform our job to the best of our ability. We will challenge our leadership because we want our voices heard and expect our bosses to push our skills and knowledge to be the best they can be.

Millennials: 1982 – 1995

If you currently reside in this generation, my apologies. Admittedly, a vast majority of my generation has picked on the millennial generation. I often find it ironic since Gen Xs didn't appreciate being told they would amount to nothing. I can't imagine the millennial generation appreciates it either. Trust me when I say the millennial generation, like every generation, will turn out okay. Millennials are proving they are as productive and brilliant as all the generations before or after them. My ask is that we stop picking on this or any generation. I'm so sick and tired of the "kids these days don't know what work ethic is." By 2025, it is thought that millennials will make up 75% of the workforce, so we better embrace them (Forbes Workday, 2019).

Millennials were shaped by the Columbine high school shooting, 9/11, parental excesses, and the Internet (Purdue Global University, 2020). The irony of Gen Xs speaking negatively about millennials is that many millennials are the children of Gen Xs. The parental excesses handed to this generation can only be blamed on their parents. While these two generations seem light years apart, they are fairly similar. This is one reason why the years for these generations are not well defined and the years vary depending on the reference.

Watching so many horrors on television has helped shape this generation to be civic-minded and inclusive of everyone. Don't underestimate them, though. They are exceptionally competitive, and they are achievement-oriented. Millennials are exceptional multitaskers.

Similar to Gen Xs, millennials love independence and strive to have a great work-life balance. However, they struggle with their idealistic view versus the realistic view of what is presented to them. Letting go of their romantic views and being happy in reality can be an issue.

They also have a distrust for leadership, and as such, they place a lot of emphasis on trust and transparency. They appreciate when people take the time to get to know who they are and where they see their career path going. They are more confident than their Gen X predecessors and tend to work at a faster pace. At times, this trait may come off as demanding or even arrogant.

They love to feel valued and aim for their contributions to benefit society. While salary is important for them, they are motivated more by purpose and whether or not their job fits with their personal views. Providing them feedback and ensuring there is growth for them will likely retain them as hospital employees for longer. They also want to work in a happy workplace environment. They have a lower tolerance for negativity and toxicity than prior generations.

Millennials like fast ways of communication. Don't call a millennial on the phone. They are unlikely to answer. Instead, they prefer email, instant messages, and texts. Much like Gen Xs, they appreciate immediate feedback.

Gen Z, iGen, or Centennials: 1996 – 2010? TBD

This is the newest generation in our workforce, and as such less is known about them. There may even be two different generations within these years. At the time when this book was published (2022), the oldest Gen Zs were 26 years of age. This generation just entered the workforce, and we will have to wait until we can define the end year of this generation. Some references have already stopped this generation at 2005, some at 2010, and a few others have it being stopped at 2020. The reality is we don't know where the endpoint is and when the next one begins. Generations are truly defined once they are in their senior stage.

This generation has been shaped by all things technology, post-9/11 terrorism life, the 2008 recession (also known as the Great Recession), instant communication, and record-setting gun violence (Purdue Global University, 2020). Interestingly, this generation will likely not be shaped by social media. The influence of social media on an entire generation will likely be the one after Gen Z, which is currently termed Gen Alpha.

What we know is that they are the fastest multitaskers on the planet. They have the ability to rock technology in a way that no other generation can even come close to. That is, of course, until Gen Alpha gets a little older. I watch my nephews who are either in Gen Z or Alpha, and they know how to hack passwords, have mastered virtual reality, and navigate the internet with ease. I mastered riding a bike at their ages and pretended I was Luke Skywalker with a broomstick for a lightsaber.

Gen Zs are considered the first mobile generation. While they prefer instant messages and texts for short communication, it's interesting to note that they prefer face-to-face interactions for any deep conversations. If you are a manager of someone in this generation, refrain from sending them a text that says, "You need to stop coming in late." They find it rude and would rather be met with that information in person. Otherwise, they have embraced all things technology, and if there's an app that can make their job easier or more productive, they're willing to embrace it.

The difference between Millennials and Gen Zs is that while Gen Zs also want to feel like they have a purpose and contribution to society, they are more driven to take jobs that offer them a higher salary. Early studies show they are willing to sacrifice a little bit of their own personal views to make more money and have more stable benefits. This could be because they grew up during the 2008 Great Recession (BetterTeam, 2020).

Much like the two generations before them, Gen Z likes to work independently. They like to have freedom and be given the autonomy to do their work to the best of their ability. They also appear to be fairly competitive and require a healthy work-life balance like the two generations before them. When trying to improve a hospital process or implementing a new policy, if you have a lot of Gen Zs, you may be able to get good results with a little friendly competition.

One trend analysts see from Gen Z is that they like to be entrepreneurs. They want to work for themselves. They want to see if their new idea or business will be successful, and they don't mind the challenge of creating something new. For leaders in veterinary hospitals, we need to listen to this new generation, and if they have a new idea we think is of value, let them run with it. Like millennials, Gen Zs need to feel appreciated. They want to work in a healthy workplace environment and are willing to leave to find a happier workplace if necessary.

What about Gen Alpha? They are too young to enter the workforce. Only time will tell if that generation's name sticks and how they evolve. They are currently being called Alpha because they are the first generation born entirely in the 21st century. They are mostly the children of millennials. There's much speculation that the COVID-19 pandemic will be a significant event that will shape their generation.

Multigenerational Similarities

A study from 2017 polled Gen X, Millennials, and Gen Z. It was interesting to see a lot of commonalities amongst the generations. The survey asked:

- How important is it for you to be a leader in your company?
- Are you worried about whether your personality fits in at work?
- Do you worry about stress and work-life balance?

The answers to the three questions were largely similar between the three generations. Roughly 50% thought it important to be in a leadership role, about 50% said they worried about fitting in, and 50% worried about stress and work-life balance (Lighthouse, 2021). All three generations had the same views regarding the questions asked.

Since 1999, there has been a decrease in the view that work is necessary to feel satisfied (Smola & Sutton, 2002). There has also been a decline in all generations regarding the thought that working hard makes one a better person (Smola & Sutton, 2002). This includes the baby boomer generation, who grew up believing hard work made you a better person. As they are nearing retirement, many are changing their view that hard work is not necessary to prove their worth as a person in society.

Regarding how they like to learn, all generations prefer on-the-job or in-classroom learning (Tolbize, 2008). Gen X, millennials, and Gen Z all prefer immediate and frequent feedback (Tolbize, 2008). Baby boomers are comfortable with less feedback, even if it's only once a year. Other than the exception of baby boomers, all three other generations place more emphasis on work-life balance rather than working to take home a paycheck.

Baby boomers are happy with their leadership micromanaging them and, to some level, expect it. The leaders, of the Traditionalists or Greatest Generation, who oversaw the baby boomer generation often micromanaged their teams. If we find a baby boomer struggling, we may need to offer clear instructions with updates along the way.

The other generations want a strong, trustful leadership and the freedom to work independently. Micromanaging will deflate the younger generations. In fact, I once quit a job over a micromanager. If you're going to be a vulture-like leader to anyone in a Gen X or younger generation, you may lose some of them.

The issues that all generations are most closely aligned with are:

- They are all concerned when they hear change may happen. All generations share a similar trait: they can manage through some change fairly well so long as it's not too much change. They will be worried about it, but they will manage well enough. That said, all generations will struggle if significant change occurs in the workplace.
- All generations want to stay with a hospital because they believe in their work, feel like they are contributing, and are making a difference.
- All four generations embrace teamwork equally. No generation was better at teamwork than another.
- They all listed the same top three reasons they liked their work:
   o   They felt valued.
   o   Were provided recognition and appreciation.
   o   Worked in a supportive environment.
   (Tolbize, 2008)

The second one probably surprised many of you. Yes, even baby boomers want to be recognized and feel appreciated. Yet, I constantly hear boomers and Gen Xs saying that the younger generations need "an award for everything" and "praise all the time." It turns out we all need praise and recognition too! We all like to be told we are doing a good job.

When we look at the similarities between the generations in our workplace, they far outweigh the differences. That said, there are differences, with the largest being between the baby boomers and the other three generations currently working in our hospitals.

How to Bridge the Generational Gap

All leaders can do some key things to bridge the generational gaps in hospitals. The most important thing is that leaders need to be aware of generational differences and avoid generational bias. Generational bias means that an individual feels that a certain generation is either inferior to their own or displays a consistent negative behavior towards them.

As a leader, you must admit that you've probably done this in the past. The biggest issue comes when we act on that bias. When we hear other team members saying, "Generation ABC is so entitled and so lazy," we must stop that talk immediately. The minute we agree or remain silent, we are perpetuating what is a false bias.

I have a confession. When I decided to put this topic in the book, I thought I would find a ton of research showing work ethic has declined along with productivity in all industries. I thought I would find data that proved millennials and Gen Z were vastly different from my generation. I hoped to put in data concluding the younger generations were "slackers," but I found no such data. I was wrong in my beliefs. I'm embarrassed that before my countless hours of research, I believed most of the false information spewed about the differences between generations. I confess I was someone who used to say, "the younger generations have no work ethic." My apologies for being so wrong. I learned so much in writing this book. What I concluded is that we're not so different after all.

With age comes an increase in wisdom. Older individuals believe that they know more and have more life experience because that is largely true. Based on age alone, they have gained more knowledge and life experience than younger people. Therefore, an older individual automatically concludes that a younger person can't possibly know as much and therefore is inferior.

When someone new enters our veterinary hospitals, and we see them struggling to learn skills, we may blame it on their generational traits. The reality is it's just someone trying to learn new knowledge and skills. It has nothing to do with work ethic. Generational bias needs to stop with leadership. Until leaders can call themselves out and stop their own bias, the rest of the team will continue to perpetuate the lies.

As leaders, one of the best ways to stop any bias is to get to know each one of your employees. Really get to know who they are. We, as individuals, say that we never want someone to have a bias against us, yet it's hard for us not to have biases against others. You may have a baby boomer veterinarian who is exceptionally tech-savvy. You may have a Gen Z who struggles unless they are micromanaged, and they welcome the constant attention from their boss. Simply getting to know each individual and how they want to be coached and managed will help eliminate the bias and make you a more effective leader.

If possible, consider cross-generational mentoring. Consider a mentor program where an older veterinarian is the mentor to a younger veterinarian new to the hospital. The same holds true for veterinary technicians/nurses or veterinary receptionists. Pairing them up with someone with more experience and knowledge who can help guide them will help decrease the generational gaps.

Lastly, educate your team. Hold a meeting and discuss the differences between generations as well as the similarities. Also, allow the generations to have a voice in that meeting. Discuss key issues they may be struggling with between each other.

Allow each generation to talk about how they like to be communicated to. Do they like their feedback to be immediate or delayed? Do they want to be talked to in person or over email? When learning a new skill or knowledge, how do they like to learn?

Let's use the example of introducing a new app into the hospital. A Gen Z employee learned about a brand-new veterinary app and wants to introduce it to the hospital. The leadership agrees and allows the employee to introduce it at the meeting. The Gen Z employee would likely explain what the app could do and then would say, "Download it and figure it out. It's pretty easy."

Meanwhile, your baby boomer employees are freaking out inside their heads. "Just download it with no instruction? "Madness!," they think. For a baby boomer, hands-on training and showing them the new app would be the best method for them to learn about it.

Another generational difference is that those in the baby boomer generation must understand that the other three generations need to take a break, eat food, and decompress from time to time. Baby boomers often feel that working straight through breaks is "normal." It doesn't mean that the other three generations have a poor work ethic. In fact, they have a healthier work ethic. Taking care of oneself doesn't mean a bad work ethic, but it's a hard concept for a baby boomer to understand when their previous Traditionalist bosses told them to "keep working all day, every day."

I would like to apologize to Gen Alpha and even those whom we have not met yet. You will be made fun of and told that you will never amount to anything. I gather since social media will play a large part in your life and shape who you are as an individual, there will be plenty of wisecrack jokes about how all you do is live on computers.

No matter what is said about Gen Alpha or future generations coming into our hospitals, we should all be aware of one undeniable fact. They will turn out fine. They will be amazing employees and reshape our work environments, likely for the better. So, stop talking trash about younger generations. Instead, bridge the gap and work to create understanding.

Chapter Fourteen

Performance Reviews Are the Devil

Few employees love filling out performance reviews. Most employees dread them. Once a year, employees are expected to rate their performance and receive feedback from their manager. A raise may or may not accompany the performance review. I have only met a handful of employees that truly welcome the experience.

One of the main points of doing performance reviews is to improve performance, correct? Another reason may be to gain insight into the employee's career goals. Once a year, leadership sits down with an employee one-on-one uninterrupted and dives into how to improve the employee's performance. Ultimately, these reviews are a way to justify salary changes along with motivating employees to higher performance. This sounds pretty important, right? Unfortunately, the way that most performance reviews are rolled out causes little to no improvement in the employee's performance.

It may surprise you that performance reviews don't have much data or science supporting that employees improve their performance based on the review. So why are we doing them? After all, most leaders have to invest countless hours and energy into compiling the reviews, developing a strategy, and meeting with the employee. It's exhausting for everyone involved.

Jack Zenger, a contributing editor of Forbes, wrote an article about the validity of performance reviews in 2017. Zenger cited a 1965 article in the *Harvard Business Review* titled "Split Roles in Performance

Appraisal." In this article, three highly respected psychologists analyzed the performance reviews of General Electric. They concluded that reviews that included criticism by a manager negatively affected the employee, and praise did little to change or alter the employee's performance. While praise doesn't appear to alter performance, it does improve the manager and employee relationship.

Future studies showed the same. In addition, Zenger found that when employees were actively involved in setting their own goals, their performance increased substantially (2017).

Since then, numerous studies have been conducted looking at the success of performance reviews. In the last few years, several surveys have concluded that neither employees nor their managers like the process of performance reviews (Zenger, 2017). According to a Gallup survey, only 14% of employees strongly agree that performance reviews led to them improving, while 33% of employees had a decrease in their performance following their review (Sutton & Wright, 2019). Yikes! It seems we are demotivating our teams by standard performance review processes. If employees aren't motivated to improve their performance after an annual review, then what's the point of having the review? Even worse, that same Gallup survey found:

- Only 29% of employees strongly agreed that their performance reviews were fair.
- Only 26% strongly agreed they were accurate.
  (Wigert & Harter, 2017)

This means the vast majority of employees leave the review meeting thinking the review was unfair and didn't represent them at all. Employees cited five main reasons for their distrust and dislike of the annual performance review:

- Infrequent feedback
- Lack of clarity
- Manager bias
- Adverse reactions to evaluation and feedback
- Too much focus on pay incentives

(Wigert & Harter, 2017)

To add insult to injury, most managers are never trained on how to put together, let alone deliver a performance review. This leaves the entire process disorganized and, frankly, just made up.

Is there a way to make performance reviews effective for the employee? There has been a trend in progressive organizations to abandon traditional performance reviews and replace them with discussions about career growth and the future (Zenger, 2017). The focus has shifted to career development plans rather than center reviews on the manager's view of the employee's performance. Together, the manager and employee work to set goals for the future.

Gallup studies have shown that when performance feedback is only applied a few times a year, it becomes insignificant to the employee (Sutton & Wright, 2019). However, when the formal performance review occurs after a year of motivation, constructive feedback, and other meetings, it clearly communicates to the employee what they need to improve upon. In my first book, I spoke about the importance of providing constant feedback and having multiple career conversations throughout the year. Gallup found that when managers provided weekly feedback instead of just one annual review, employees were:

- 3.2x more likely to be motivated to do outstanding work.
- 2.7x more likely to be engaged at work.

(Sutton & Wright, 2019)

There needs to be a shift from performance management to performance development. Leaders struggle to manage undesirable behaviors during a singular performance management meeting. In performance development, leaders work to develop and coach an employee's performance throughout the year. We should be focusing on developing our teams, not managing them.

It's exciting that so many companies are attempting to repair the damaged annual performance review system. However, some of these newer methods are worse than the older annual performance review processes. I recently talked to an employee of a major international technology firm. He spoke about how his company recently announced it would no longer do any performance reviews. He, a Gen X who needs feedback, said, "They didn't put any framework around how employees would receive feedback. I'm concerned that I'll have no idea how I'm performing. Getting to sit down once a year and have an in-depth conversation with my manager was something that I looked forward to. At least I knew how I was doing." I agree. When employees are not provided any information on how they will learn and develop their performance with their manager, it leaves them feeling unsettled.

The key is we need to learn how to optimize employee performance within our individual hospitals. I don't think completely throwing away performance reviews is the way to go, but I also don't think once a year is the right way either. I also strongly disagree that the review should be focused on coaching unwanted behaviors. Instead, I think there is a balance, which I will discuss in more depth in this chapter and the next.

I want to challenge you that likely the current system you have is broken. Your team doesn't like it, and I gather you struggle with it as well. While I don't have the exact best way to repair it, I know that the best performance management systems involve frequent, meaningful manager-employee conversations.

Creating a Better Performance Development Plan

When completing this chapter, I thought about my work in various leadership roles and how it felt to be an employee completing a performance review. Over the years, I have personally filled out many performance reviews for myself. My employers have required me to complete 360-reviews, standard performance reviews, and Behaviorally Anchored Rating Scale (BARS) assessments.

One of the more recent performance reviews I filled out only had two questions, "Rate your performance as you see it throughout the year," and "Why did you rate yourself this way?" It then offered a scale from one to five, with five being outstanding. The performance review offered "suggestions" on how to approach answering the second question, leaving it veiled in mystery as to what the individual could or should write.

This review was nearly impossible for me to fill out. I was asked to assign myself only one grade for my entire role that year. What happened if I felt I had great technician skills but was not necessarily the shining pillar of success when it came to being part of a team? Was being part of a team even included in this rating? What about my skill as a leader? This review was so obscure it left me frustrated and angry. As such, I did what peeved employees would do. I circled the number three and left the other question blank.

My manager was angry with me and said, "why did you write nothing," and "why did you score yourself a three?" I said I knew I was at least a slightly-above average employee. If the scale were up to five, that would mean I was above average at a three. I felt okay leaving the other section blank since it did not say it was a requirement to complete it. She didn't appreciate my passive but aggressive take on the review. As such, she rated me as a three and left her written portion blank to show me a lesson. You know what happened with my review? Nothing. To this day, it likely lives somewhere in a cyber-cloud where no one cares that Amy rated herself a three. No one followed up with me. The review meant nothing.

While I wish I could say this was the worst review process I have ever had to partake in, I cannot. I once went 10 years without a single review despite asking for feedback. Talk about a drought! I'm a border collie, and by nature of being a Gen X, I need feedback and want some guidance as I'm always seeking to improve myself.

As previously stated, this chapter will not provide the exact way to develop a perfect performance development plan. There is no such thing. Currently, both large and small businesses alike are trying to figure out what better looks like. What research has shown us is that the once-a-year performance review is broken. I will share with you some thoughts of things that should be included in what I consider a good solid performance development system and what some companies are experimenting with, but in no way are these suggestions the bible. Take this information, look at your system, and make the changes you think will work best for your hospital.

To dive into this chapter, I looked towards leaders with far more knowledge than I in human resources science. This chapter is based on hours of research, my education taught in my master's degree in management and leadership, and my own personal experience. That said, if the suggestions here don't work for you, that is okay. The discussion of changing the archaic process of performance reviews has just started in the past decade. We're all trying to figure out what to do.

Let's dive into some key aspects of creating a good performance development plan. The exact system you use is less important than ensuring leaders hold regular constructive conversations with employees about improving performance. Equally important is that leaders work towards coaching team members throughout the year.

KEY ASPECTS FOR GOOD DEVELOPMENT PLANS

Focus on Positivity

Stop centering your conversations around the past or negativity. Neither the employee nor you can change the past. Reconsider what you are calling this annual get-together. Do you really want to call it an "annual review?" Are you truly reviewing the entire year? Wow, that's a lot.

The infamous PIP (Performance Improvement Plan) acronym clearly states to any employee that you have some improvement to do, and we are about to tell you about it. While some hospitals use PIPs exclusively for employees who need to improve in some way, many use this term to describe their annual review process. Why can't it be called a career growth plan, personal development plan, or career development plan? Are we not looking to develop them or their career?

Why not get creative with the title? I've always liked Awesome Conversation Time (ACT). We are ACTing together, the employee and us, to determine what we as employers could do better and what the employee may need help with improving. Imagine an employee saying to their teammate, "I'm off to have my awesome conversation time." Sounds more fun than an "annual performance review." The meeting should focus on future career growth and developing the individual's talents. But wait, when do we get to tell them everything they have done wrong throughout the year!? You don't.

No Surprises

Annual performance reviews should offer no surprises. The reason why so many employees dread the annual performance review is that it is full of surprises. The employee opens the door to the office. They enter with fear and trepidation. They see a person sitting behind a desk in front of their computer. "Sit down," the person says. Insert scary horror music here.

The reality is there shouldn't be anything new to discuss in the way of improvement. Yes, there can be some focus on what needs improvement, but those items have already been discussed when they happened, right? (Hint, hint, wink, wink.)

The reality is most managers keep all feedback locked down tight and save it up to verbally vomit on their employees once a year. There should be no surprises when you have an annual performance review. If there are, you have failed as a manager. You should be continuously providing feedback throughout the year. During this meeting, you can continue to coach through an issue you previously addressed, but let's not make it an office of horrors and negativity.

It's a Year-Round Plan

Throughout the year, we need to offer feedback and check in with every one of our employees. Part of our performance development plan needs to include that we continually coach our employees. A once-a-year coaching session isn't going to cut it. We should establish expectations from day one when they are hired and work to create accountability in every team member. That doesn't occur with one meeting a year.

Don't Focus on Money

Your compensation will always be tied to your performance. That is a fact. Unfortunately, too often, the annual review is tied to money. Why are salaries only adjusted only once a year? Why can they not be adjusted based on performance throughout the year? Why do they have to occur at a specific time each year? I challenge all of you to consider compensation and the best way to support it.

Let's dive into two key definitions: raise and adjustment. A raise is when an employee gets an increase because of something they did that warranted them getting paid more than their current salary. They could have picked up more responsibility, improved their skill, or gone above and beyond.

An adjustment accounts for inflation or because the employee was not previously compensated correctly (was being paid too much or too little).

Employees should expect that their salary increases yearly at least to keep up with the inflation rate. Failure to account for inflation means they are making less each year. This is the most common salary adjustment. Unfortunately, I find that most veterinary hospitals tell employees they are receiving a raise when in fact, they are being paid the exact same or even less.

In 2022 the rate of inflation was about 8%. If a veterinary technician was earning $20.00/hr this means that their salary would need to increase to $21.60 (a difference of $1.60) to be compensated the same. Most employers increase salaries by $0.50 to $1.00. This means that the $20/hr employee is doing the same work for less money. Sadly, I find very few employees ever receive true raises. More commonly, they receive salary adjustments.

The other reason I dislike tying the annual review to a salary change is because in most veterinary hospitals, the manager has decided on the change before the meeting. What's the point of the meeting then? In essence, the manager has already reviewed the employee's performance and assigned a valuation on their work before even speaking to them.

There's no point in having the employee discuss how they think their performance ranked over the year. The manager has already made up their mind as to what the performance is worth. In most hospitals, the manager requires the employee to defend their performance, share what they feel they excelled in, and what they need help with. None of which will change the salary as the manager is sitting there with a sheet of paper with the decided salary information on it. This is just another reason employees dislike once-a-year reviews.

Incorporate the 3Cs & the 3Fs

3Cs	3Fs
Clear Collaborative Coordinated	Frequent Focused Future-Oriented

The 3Cs

I wrote in my first book about the importance of ensuring every employee has an accurate and thorough job description that is **clear** in outlining what is expected at work. When we are developing plans for our employees, they must clearly understand the expectations of the role and any plans. Studies have shown that the best managers **collaborate** with the employee on the plan. However, when a manager comes to the meeting with a plan already in place (just like the salary already set), there is no buy-in from the employee.

Ask open-ended questions so that you can help them to develop goals that will be best for the hospital and themselves. It's imperative that before the conclusion of any performance-based conversation, you and the employee are aligned and **coordinated** on the next steps. Too often, managers have the "annual review," verbally vomit all the concerns of the past year to the employee, ask "how they feel," throw a salary at them, and then say, "See you next year." Instead, be sure you are collaborative, clear, and coordinate with them in the plan.

The 3Fs

Suppose leaders incorporate the 3Cs (clear, collaborative, coordinated) into a **frequently** evaluated plan **focused** and structured around goals. Then imagine if it looked to the **future**. That type of development plan would likely create a team of unicorns.

Stop thinking of a performance development plan as a once-a-year occurrence. Having a meeting once a year to do a deep dive into career paths and goals can be rewarding, but it can't just be once a year. Instead, your development plan should include meeting with each team member several times a year. If you say you don't have time, you either have too many team members that are your direct reports, or you are not being provided the time to manage your team.

The best managers engage frequently with their employees, ideally every day. I recognize this is not always possible in veterinary medicine because you may be working different shifts. In my first book, I wrote about how the best managers check in with their employees at least 15 minutes every week. I know it can be hard. You have a lot on your plate. However, a Gallup study found that employees who received daily feedback from their managers were three times more likely to be engaged than those who received feedback once a year or less (Wigert & Harter, 2017). Frequent feedback also increases trust between the employee and their manager.

Natural opportunities are the best for increasing employee engagement and performance. When I say frequent feedback, that does not mean micromanaging or constant critiquing. Your praise should far outweigh the critiques. Negative feedback does not motivate employees, but positive feedback does.

Some of my employees preferred meeting privately. It made them feel valued and cared about. For others, I would simply check in with them on the clinic floor. Ask each team member how they would like to be communicated with. Praise them, offer feedback, and show them that you care deeply.

To make your plan focused, ensure your plan isn't too complicated. You can't coach everything all at once. For example, in one annual review meeting that someone shared with me, a veterinary technician was provided the following areas of improvement:

- Less gossiping
- Improve client communication skills
- Work on improving math skills, particularly CRI skills
- Be more positive and less negative
- Learn advanced skills like central and arterial lines
- Work with current technician manager on creating SOPs

After I saw this list, I addressed the manager who wrote it and asked, "How do you expect the employee to fix each of these concerns? Do you have simultaneous plans going at the same time to improve every single one of these items?"

The answer was no. She had simply provided the employee a list of items she wanted to be improved upon and assumed it would get done. There was also no mention of anything the employee did well or resources to work on the items listed. This could be why the veterinary technician left the meeting crying. More frequent meetings will result in less bombarding of items that may need to be coached.

A comprehensive study looking at performance reviews concluded that when feedback focused too narrowly on past mistakes, employees tended to feel demotivated and often performed worse in the future (Sutton & Wright, 2019). As a manager, you should be excited about their future. Your enthusiasm should spill over in the conversation, so they also get excited. The best development plan conversations are those that are positive, encouraging, and focused on the future.

Communicating to the employee about how they will achieve their goals by focusing their expectations on a specific goal will motivate them to embrace their improvement process. When employees understand you want them to reduce their negativity because it's a trait unbecoming of a leader, and you are hoping to transition them to a supervisor role in the future, they become more motivated about the goal. They can see their future supervisor self and recognize you are helping them achieve that goal. Simply telling a negative employee to please be more positive will hardly improve the behavior.

As a manager, you can express your vision to them once they have shared their vision. Many times, employees don't see their potential. During my annual meetings with my employees, I always wanted to hear from them first about where they saw themselves in five years or how they wanted their careers to develop. After listening to them, I often would say the following, "Here's where I see you in five years." Then I would share my vision. I always thought big for each one of them. Many would say they couldn't become a manager, obtain their veterinary technician specialty, or lecture at a large national conference. They didn't see that future or any for that matter. Collaborate with your employee and determine what is the best future for them.

Taking Care of Yourself

Remember that development conversations can be exhausting. Be sure to put safeguards in place to help protect you from emotional chaos. Employees may still be nervous about the meeting, even if the conversation is overwhelmingly positive. I had an employee who cried every year even though she was amazing. I never had a negative thing to say, but her nerves would cause her to cry every year. I would advise against back-to-back meetings if you can avoid doing so. You want to allow extra time in case a meeting goes over and time for you to decompress. Finally, be sure you take care of yourself as you navigate the meeting you just had.

The Making of a Unicorn

Making a unicorn team member doesn't occur overnight. It requires time and dedication. That is the very problem with only having one performance review a year. A leader cannot cultivate a team of unicorns if they only meet with them once a year. It's not possible.

In a few of my leadership roles, I tragically only held a performance conversation once a year. I called them annual reviews, and they had all the toxic parts I just described that are damaging to our teams. I focused on the past and thought only about what needed to be improved upon. I had a salary ready to give them even before meeting with them. I verbally vomited my review, asked them their thoughts, and told them to "fix" everything I just cited as concerns. I was wrong. I look back at how I used to develop my team members, and I regret the method I used. I did everything I wrote not to do.

Unicorns only appear if they can trust the people and environment. Unfortunately, too many leaders send their potential unicorns scurrying away because they focus on a few things that need improvement rather than the fact they make rainbows.

I know I have repeated this a few times in this chapter, but I will repeat it once again. My recommended performance development plan is not perfect. It may not even work for your hospital. What I know is it worked well for my team for many years.

Those I met with throughout the year said that they felt like I cared about them as a person and their career paths and that I focused more on the future than the past. One former employee told me she felt I was a goal-oriented manager instead of a mistake-oriented one.

With the lack of information on what works best for reviewing veterinary employees, I felt strongly that a plan should be included in this book to serve as a template for other leaders to start developing their own. If your current plan is working well, wonderful. There is no need to change it. If you have a plan and it is failing, then take the parts you think would work well for you and your team and utilize them.

I love this quote by author Peter Lerangis (2015). "Trust is a fragile thing—difficult to build, easy to break. It cannot be bargained for. Only if it is freely given, it can be expected in return." How can you expect your employees to trust you if you never meet with them? They won't. Building up the relationship between you and every one of your employees is more critical than performing an annual review. Ensure that you are truly developing each individual relationship and that you care deeply about each member of your team first. If you can't get that part right, then there's no point in a performance development plan. Meeting frequently is the foundation for developing your trust and relationship with the team so that a development plan can be effective. There is also a high correlation between building trust and having high emotional intelligence. Emotional intelligence is often the foundation for building trusting relationships.

Most importantly, have a way to actively make unicorns. Winging it or meeting once a year won't change anyone's behavior. Once you are done reading the next chapter, you can refer to Appendix Two, where I have created a quick step-by-step guide for a full-year development plan.

Chapter Fifteen

The 3-1 Development Plan

After years of trial and error, the 3-1 is the method I developed and settled on as an effective way to help grow employees. I did not develop this plan overnight. It took many leadership roles, research on my part, reaching out to colleagues in similar positions, and countless tries with other failed performance-based systems to land on the 360-feedback method incorporated into what I refer to as the 3-1.

Again, don't try to fix something that isn't broken if you and the team are happy with your current process. Also, don't feel obligated to use every detail in the 3-1 plan. Instead, pick out the parts you think may work for your hospital. Lastly, this plan only works if you have a team that understands polite, kind, and honest communication. If your team is a cesspool of negativity, then the 360-feedback gathered from the team will be centered around anger, negativity, hatred, and bias.

THREE

The three in the 3-1 requires you, as a manager, to meet three times a year for 30 to 60 minutes to focus on the employee's goals and performance. This means if you had 15 direct reports, you would need to carve out 23 to 45 total hours in the entire year to develop your team. Looking at it that way, it's not so daunting of a task. What I have learned is the more 1:1 sessions you have with your individual team members, the less time you spend putting out fires.

Ideally, each of the three meetings would be once a quarter and focus on career development and coaching their performance to get the desired result. This means you need to set aside eight to fifteen hours for conversations each quarter. That's it. To put this in perspective, you will work a minimum of 480 hours a quarter. Setting aside 15 hours for development conversations is nothing.

These short meetings should be largely positive. After all, any performance-based issues would be addressed at the time of the incident. Don't pile up all the performance-based issues and dump them on the employee once a quarter. Instead, coach those separately, but use these meetings to revisit and check in. Ideally, don't use the whole session to focus on something that needs improvement. Those need separate meetings and coaching together.

A Gallup study found that meetings centered around negativity resulted in demotivated employees. In turn, this lowered their self-esteem, lowered receptiveness to feedback, and lowered performance (Wigert & Harter, 2017). On the flip side, studies have found that when employees leave a meeting feeling positive because the meeting was achievement-oriented, they perform better in the future (Wigert & Harter, 2017). Could it be that a largely negative meeting demotivates an employee while a largely positive meeting increases their motivation? Yes, it's that simple.

This is an area in my plan that I have had time to reflect on. Towards the end of one of my management positions, I started only meeting with a few employees twice a year. I knew these employees well and was comfortable that they would come to me if there were issues outside of our meetings. We developed such a wonderful working environment that I felt I could decrease the number of meetings per year and still feel like the performance plan was ideal. This is something to consider if you integrate more frequent development meetings throughout the year. To me, these three meetings spread throughout the year were hugely impactful and really improved my trust and relationship with the team.

ONE

Once a year, you should put together a more formal performance meeting. I've tried several performance-based systems over the years, and the one that provided me with the most information as a manager was the 360-feedback process. In both *Radical Candor* and *What Got You Here Won't Get You There*, the authors describe their fondness for the 360-review process (Scott, 2019, Goldsmith, 2007.) The 360-feedback process can be quite intense, but for a good reason. It is meant to give the employee and manager an in-depth look into their strengths and weaknesses so that a development plan can be created.

While I do like the 360-feedback process as a way to evaluate employees, this is where I insert a big word of caution. If your team is not getting along well and gossips often, the 360 process may backfire. You must have a team dedicated to helping each other by offering kind feedback, not cruel feedback. If you do not, then fix the communication of the team first. In order to be successful, the entire 360-feedback process is based on PKH feedback. If teams do not welcome honest feedback, this review process could be a nightmare in your hospital. While I think this is one of the best ways to review employees, I only feel that way if your culture is healthy first.

Besides the team's culture being in a good place, the employees must be prepared to let go of the past, tell the truth, pick something to improve, and be supportive and helpful for it to be effective (Goldsmith, 2007). If the employee is not in a good place to receive information, this system can backfire in a big way. If people are unable to let go of the past, they should not be able to participate in the 360 review. The process is about developing for the future.

For me, I started integrating the 360-feedback process after a year of working to repair a very broken team. They were still very broken but at least open to change and had committed to being kind to each other. I like this review style because the manager's review of the employee is only one small factor in the overall process. The largest amount of feedback comes from the employee's peers and themselves.

360-feedback

What Is It?

It is an intense review process in which the employee will be reviewed by:

- Themselves
- Their coworkers
- Their direct manager

Do we expect employees to review each other fairly? Can that really happen? The answer is yes, but only if the team is open to PKH feedback. I know of veterinary hospitals that have tried implementing 360-feedback only to have the comments received be malicious, rude, and bullying. That defeats the purpose. There is also a right way to implement it and a dozen more wrong ways.

The Benefits Of 360-feedback

It Increases Emotional Intelligence

There is no doubt that the 360-feedback method helps people become more self-aware. Individuals will have to look internally at themselves. It evaluates their thoughts against what their coworkers' and manager's thoughts are. Thus, the individual gets a full view of themselves rather than a one-sided view from their manager. I have certainly had employees not gain any emotional intelligence from this process, but the majority who are open to receiving feedback will gain insight.

It Lists Both Strengths and Weaknesses

Too often, performance plans are focused on what needs to be improved upon. This one-dimensional perspective of who the employee is appears to demotivate employees. By including strengths, managers can identify individuals who may excel in certain areas and elevate them even further. Especially in veterinary medicine, where you may not always work with every employee, having the employee's coworkers participate in the feedback process will provide tremendous insights for the manager. Having employees realize that their coworkers said kind things about them helps to grow the team.

It Boosts Morale

I will say that if this process is not done correctly, it could have the opposite effect. However, if done correctly, I have found that this almost always boosts an employee's morale. Coworkers are required to list the strengths of their fellow team members. Therefore, every employee will get to hear positive accolades directly from their coworkers during the meeting. The only time this backfires is when the manager doesn't construct the feedback correctly and/or focuses only on the negative. We want employees to understand that some areas do need to be improved upon but that they are also great at a large number of things.

It Adds to PKH Culture

If we have already started talking to our teams about polite, kind, and honest communication, this will add to the culture we strive for. In addition, the 360-feedback helps to boost transparency and openness within the team, creating a more cohesive environment. The nice thing about this feedback system is that it is delivered in a safe environment between the manager and the employee. This results in controlled transparency, which builds trust.

It Gives Employees a Voice

If a review of an employee only has the viewpoint of a single manager, it fails to give the employee a voice. The 360-feedback method allows employees to voice what they view as their strengths, what they would like to improve upon, and what they would like to see in the future. Too often, the big one-time annual meeting is focused only on what the manager wants because they think it's what is best for the hospital. The 360-feedback system allows employees to have a voice.

It's Future Focused

Past performance is not the center of the conversation and is seldom discussed. Instead, this method seeks to do a deep dive into the employee as a person. No leader has a perfect method that helps to coach every single employee to succeed. Each person is unique, so no one method will work for everyone. However, a manager's feedback from a 360 can help shape conversations around how to hone the strengths, bridge the gap in some areas that need improvement, and focus on the employee's future in the company. Looking toward the future is more important than dwelling on the past.

It is a Launching Point for the Rest of the Year

The 360-feedback becomes a launching point for the rest of the meetings throughout the year. You are promoting continuous growth and improvement by offering meetings throughout the year. The employee knows it's not just a one-and-done. They are more motivated to work on areas of concern because they know you will be checking back in with them and cheering them on.

It's a Way to Change Your Company's Culture

For many, this feedback system is completely different from the archaic painful performance reviews they are more familiar with. This review centers around how an individual works within a team rather than by themselves. They will hear their coworkers' feedback on how their performance affects the team. They must also look at themselves internally and hear their manager's thoughts. While that is a lot to digest, the whole goal is to ensure that you are encouraging the employee to be the best version of themselves. The desire to be the best team member for the hospital can change the company's culture.

The Cons of 360-feedback

It can Deflate and Demotivate the Employee

One of the biggest disadvantages of 360-feedback is that if it fails, it fails in a big way. In almost every other review method, the manager takes the lead in reviewing the employee. Sometimes the employee reviews themselves, but the discussion is centered more around the manager's views. When the review is bad, the employee can justify it by saying that the manager doesn't like them, it's biased, it's only one person's opinion, etc. When the 360-feedback is bad, it's hard for the employee to deny the negative feedback. Multiple coworkers provided feedback along with the manager. If the manager fails to provide feedback in a constructive way, it can destroy the employee's morale and trust. Therefore, how you deliver the 360-feedback is important. Filtering the feedback, so it's productive and healthy, is imperative to the plan's success.

It Can Create a Negative Culture

When the feedback is centered around negativity, it can divide an entire team and destroy an entire hospital's culture. Remember that this feedback needs to be centered around PKH communication. If it's cruel honesty, it will ruin your hospital. As a leader, you must filter the feedback. It's not lying; it's ensuring success. While we want transparency, we also need positivity.

It's Not 100% Accurate

When you seek the opinions of coworkers, each one will hold their own bias against the employee being reviewed. There may be internal politics that you are unaware of, so step gently onto the ice when you start reading negative comments about a particular employee. Be aware that they may have been manipulated on purpose to diminish the employee being reviewed. Be careful with the data you are collecting.

It's Time Consuming

Compiling the feedback into a version the manager and employee can easily digest takes time. That said, many business companies are now offering online 360-performance systems. These companies handle the work for you, but at a price to the hospital. The hospital has to do some legwork to prepare the feedback form. Employees log in, complete their portion of the review, and the software program compiles all the data and presents it in a neat and tidy package to the leadership.

How to Perform 360-feedback

All three components of the 360-feedback process need to hold equal weight. If the manager's feedback supersedes the coworker's feedback, then it diminishes the point of the 360-feedback system. I believe that every veterinary hospital member should be held to the same feedback system. By this, I mean that the hospital should utilize 360-feedback for veterinarians, client service representatives, practice managers, owners, and veterinary technicians/nurses/assistants. No one should be exempt.

Everyone should want to gain insight from their colleagues to help improve themselves and the team. As managers and leaders, we cannot expect our employees to embrace receiving 360-feedback if we skirt away from it.

The nice thing about the 360-feedback method is that it allows you to modify and improve the process each year. Talk to your team and collaboratively approach this new process. Explain your goals and be honest that some aspects may miss the mark. We want them to be comfortable and even embrace developing their performance plan. Most of my employees were nervous at first but also eager to hear what the team had to say compared to just my opinion. It's exciting and scary all at the same time, but many aspects of the plan can be altered to make it more successful.

The other thing of note is that employees and even managers complete performance reviews based only on the past few weeks' interactions. While we hope our employees look at the entire past year's picture of the employee, that's not realistic. Most everyone who is asked to review themselves or another individual provides feedback based on current events. Few managers can look at the entire year of an employee's performance objectively. Instead, there is a bias from the manager regarding how they are doing during that particular month. No one can be expected to remember how an employee performed over the entire year. Keep that in mind when you sort through the feedback. The feedback is based on the last month's performance and may not truly represent the entire employee's body of work over the year.

For example, if an employee has been experiencing burnout for the past month, has been negative, and coming in late, this will reflect in the review. As a manager, take all comments and thoughts, including your own, and do your best to reflect on whether "do these comments define the person's true performance, or was this a blip on the radar?" It is certainly worth addressing any small blips now but hardly defines the individual's career at the hospital.

One way to decrease the moment-in-time reviews is to…wait for it…have more frequent meetings! Yes, by holding more meetings throughout the year, you can look for consistency, or a lack thereof, in behavior and performance.

Employee Reviews Themselves

This was one area that I radically changed over the years. Many call this the employee self-assessment. This is where the employee looks internally at their performance over the past year and reviews it. Here is the twist that I added as the years went on. I also had the employee review the hospital. This part of the review would be separate and compiled into one big review of how the employees viewed the hospital and what they thought could be improved. As the years continued, I was able to map out trends utilizing this data on how the employees viewed the hospital by assessing such areas as their stress level, morale, the pros and cons, and their viewpoint on leadership.

Adding in this part of the review for the employee was a game-changer because it asked the employee their opinion of the hospital. It took away the focus being solely on the employee assessing themselves and brought it back to how they felt being an employee in the hospital. For many employees, reviewing oneself can be difficult. It's hard to look internally and then express it on paper to someone else. Having them review the hospital in addition to themselves took away some of the stress that they experienced when reviewing themselves.

For an employee self-assessment, I want you to think about questions that would work best for your hospital. I would suggest asking them no more than 10 questions. Utilizing an online form for employees can make it easier for managers to compile the final data. In most of my leadership roles, I failed to embrace technology. When you have 15 employees all submitting hand-written paper reviews, typing them up into one feedback form is exceptionally time-consuming. In my defense, I started veterinary medicine when dot matrix printers were the only type of printer, landlines still existed, and computers had a green font against black screens. Some of you know what I'm writing about. That said, I wish I had utilized easy-to-use survey forms like Google forms or Survey Monkey. Please review the sample 360-feedback review example in Appendix Two for examples of some questions to ask. Most are centered around what the employee views as their strengths and areas of improvement.

If an employee decided to omit a particular question, I never chastised them for it. It meant that they were uncomfortable sharing that information. As a manager, I needed to help them become more comfortable.

As far as filling out the review of the hospital, I found that my employees never had a problem providing their thoughts. I gather if an employee is hesitant about filling out a review of the hospital, it would be because of a lack of trust and worrying about retaliation from leadership. At no point should we place harsh judgment on an employee for not completing a self-evaluation or not evaluating the hospital. Instead, recognize the reason they failed to complete a section is that they are afraid or uncomfortable.

The best part about having employees review the hospital was that I could compile data over time and make the following statements and conclusions. For example, in 2018, the data I pulled together allowed me to discover the following:

Largest Areas of Concern
Lack of communication (b/t departments or b/t staff & management)
Lack of doctors
Conflicts between departments
Personal schedule concerns

After I compiled the data, I would present it to them for transparency. With transparency, the employees got to see how they ranked the hospital, their perceived work-stress level, and what they enjoyed the most about the hospital.

Why would I not want to deliver this information to my employees? Hiding this information will cause almost every employee to believe that filling out the hospital review is pointless. Not being transparent about the hospital's issues causes teams to distrust management. The point of hosting an employee engagement survey was so that I could tackle some of the big items with my team's help. I needed their help to decrease the communication issues in the hospital. I did not hide behind an office door pretending as if everything was okay. I took full ownership in trying to rectify every issue employees cited as a concern. That's how you build trust.

Manager Reviews Employee

This was also an area that I changed over the years. As a manager, I used to fill out a different evaluation form than the one the employees completed. When I look back, I remember having an epiphany one year, thinking about how pretentious it was to review them on different criteria compared to that of their coworkers. At that moment, I decided to use the same evaluation form that their coworkers used to evaluate a particular employee. Why should a manager be any different? Does my opinion as a manager mean more than that of the coworkers who work side-by-side with that individual daily? It likely should not.

A manager may have different insights, but the criteria that is being reviewed should likely remain the same. The review will be different solely because the leader will review the employee through the leader's eyes instead of the coworker's. Therefore, there are no sample questions for this part of the review. Just use the same questions that the coworkers use.

Coworkers Review Employee

As you develop this part of the review, I recommend that you change it no more than 10% from year to year as you modify your feedback forms. Maintaining a similar question set year-to-year allows you to track yearly employee performance easier. If you overhaul the questions each year, you will have difficulty tracking consistency.

For years, my manager and coworker feedback form consisted of a total of six different sections. In total, there were close to 45 questions and comments sections that I expected employees to fill out for each other. Yikes! I look back and now recommend only having 25 questions tops.

All sections used a point scale system, one to five. This allowed me to assign an actual value. Without technology and online forms, I had to calculate every value by hand. Time-consuming is an understatement. Again, you need to embrace modern technology so the 360-feedback form does not suck countless hours out of your life. Consider an online company that offers 360 feedback reviews or create an online form to compile the data.

Review Appendix Two for sample questions and examples of questions. The goal was for you, the manager, to have the employees evaluate the employee in such a way you had a comprehensive picture of the performance of that particular individual.

Who Completes the Evaluation?

I am often asked how many coworkers per employee should complete the feedback form. Part of that answer lies in how big the team is. If there are only five employees, having every team member fill out an evaluation for every one of their coworkers is feasible. My rule of thumb was that any particular employee should not have to complete more than three evaluations. In a team of 30 individuals, this may seem like a small percentage, but anything more than that I felt, took away from the experience. It takes time for employees to fill out evaluations. You want them to think about each one rather than be rushed or annoyed they have to fill out 25 reviews. To keep track of who I assigned to review each employee, I kept a spreadsheet that looked like this, which used the initials of the reviewers:

Name Being Reviewed	Reviewers
Joan Newson	AK, CV, BF, JL
Jason Steick	JL, KA, AK, BF
Bridget Stagon	AN, AK, DJ, MS
Jaquinda Jones	DJ, CS, BF, KA

As you can see, BF has reviewed three of the coworkers, so I would likely not assign BF to anyone else. I also liked ensuring each employee had the same number of people reviewing them, so it was fair.

Remember that this feedback form was for the entire hospital. Pulling the entire hospital in to evaluate a single employee helped decrease the overall workload. For example, the front office, veterinarians, and their peers also reviewed the veterinary technicians. In the case listed above, I would ensure that 75% of the reviews came from their direct peers and 25% from other departments. Once you receive the employee, manager, and coworkers' reviews, the next step is to compile the data.

Compiling the Data

It is up to you how you want to put together the data for the individual employee. However, I would strongly advise against providing all the feedback provided by the reviewers. In my opinion, the review must be filtered. Providing unfiltered reviews will likely result in employees feeling dejected or overwhelmed. Be sure to filter out each review the same way for each employee.

When I spoke about how 360-feedback could go awry, one big reason is that the manager fails to filter the data appropriately. I've had managers provide every comment to the employee. For example, if Erin wrote on Jeremy's review, "He is lazy, and I don't know why he's not been fired yet," the manager would provide that comment to the employee. You can see how quickly 360-feedback could ruin an entire hospital. You must filter the comments from coworkers, or you will ruin your hospital.

Providing too much honesty can be damaging. We don't want Jeremy to know that Erin thinks he should be fired. How would that benefit him or the team? As a leader, it is your job to look for trends in the reviews. If several employees reported the same concern they had about another employee, it is worth noting during the review or, at the very least, investigating further. If only Erin feels Jeremy is lazy, then it likely isn't worth a mention, but keeping an eye on Jeremy's work ethic is likely warranted.

I always left out comments that were one-offs. For example, if only one employee cited a particular concern, I would not include it in the final report until I could investigate it further. It's not to say I dismissed it. Instead, I noted it and kept watch of that particular concern. If there were a valid negative comment, I would tailor it to ensure it landed well. Telling employees that they may lack motivation at times and asking what is going on is far different than saying, "you are lazy."

I once broke my cardinal rule of not including any one-offs. I had an excellent employee who was a leader on the floor. The team loved her, and she rarely received any negative comments from her coworkers. As I was perusing the coworker's feedback, I laughed out loud as one of her coworkers wrote, "Her shoes keep squeaking on the clinic floor, and they are driving me nuts. Can she please get shoes that don't squeak on our floors?" It's not like her shoes purposely had a squeaking sound in them. It's that the shoe material happened to hit the laminated floors in such a way it made a subtle squeak when she walked. I had a good laugh and thought she would as well. I included it in her final feedback and handed it to her during our meeting.

When I got to the part about the squeaky shoes, I laughed and said something to the effect of, "You're a rockstar. The only critique that you got was about your squeaky shoes. If that's all you need to improve upon, you're doing great! This is the least negative comment ever!"

As a leader, remember that what you find funny is not what your employee may find funny. Criticism is criticism, and employees will always see it as such. I had failed. She didn't find it funny. One of her coworkers was annoyed. This upset her. It didn't matter that the rest of the review was glowing.

In her mind, someone disliked her because of her squeaky shoes. It didn't matter how many times I reworded it or tried to minimize the criticism. In the end, it was criticism. She left the meeting, trying to figure out who she had offended. When I look back, it was stupid to include it. I didn't follow my rule of "look for the trends in comments and ignore the one-offs." Did I, as a manager, really expect her to get new shoes because of one squeaky shoe comment? No, but in the end, that's what she did. She bought new shoes. I felt terrible.

This is why it is imperative that reviews are filtered. Leaders must look for trends in the critiques. You can provide all the positive accolades you want, but when it comes to critiques, they must always be filtered. It certainly does matter that an individual was annoyed by the squeaky shoes, but it's up to that individual to speak directly to that employee. I learned that criticism lands hard no matter how small we think they are. That employee brought up the squeaky shoe comment to me the following year as one of the first talking points. "Did anyone mention my shoes this year?" she asked. "No, apparently, your shoes are doing okay this year," I laughed. She again did not laugh.

If there were alleged harassment, abuse of any kind, or discriminatory concern over racism or bias, I would always discuss it with the individual before the feedback meeting after investigating the matter. If there were a formal HR department, I would always put these types of comments on their radar. Leaders mustn't let even one comment suggesting that an individual acted in a way centered around discrimination or abuse slip by you.

Employees sometimes use the 360-feedback system to air all grievances. Unfortunately, some individuals may lie to get someone fired or demoted because they do not get along with them. Always investigate both sides of any accusation.

So how should you compile the feedback and deliver it to an employee? I have included an example below, but first, let's talk about how to deliver the comments and accumulate the points.

The verbatim comments that offered areas to be improved upon were only included if they were polite, kind, and honest. I never included anything blunt, angry, or rude. That said, I did try to include as many verbatim comments as possible for transparency so they wouldn't leave wondering "what was really said."

While my point scale system worked for my teams, there is no data suggesting that you must use this same point system. To come up with the average score in a certain area, I added up all the points awarded and divided them by the number of those who had provided a rating to come up with the average. For example, let's say the section rating dependability had three questions, and five people filled out a survey.

Reviewer	Question 1	Question 2	Question 3
1	4.0	3.0	3.5
2	4.5	2.5	2.5
3	4.5	4.5	4.0
4	5.0	4.0	3.0
5	4.5	5.0	4.5
Total pts	22.5	19.0	17.5
Average section pts	4.5	3.8	3.5

It's pretty easy to create an excel spreadsheet in which the data populates and comes up with this total for you. Since there were a total of five reviewers, you would divide the total of all the averages by five to get the average for that section: Looking at question one: $22.5 \div 5 = 4.5$. The employee would meet job requirements because the scale "meets job requirements" was between 4.0-4.5 points.

The Meeting

Of course, we as leaders, always hope that every performance meeting we have is an easy one. When they are not, it can be exceptionally emotional and difficult for both the manager and the employee. Regardless of whether it was great or there were areas for improvement, my talking points with any employee included:

- Talk through the feedback form line by line and pause for feedback.
- Hear their feedback on any criticism that was received.
  - Ask, "Do you feel this is a fair statement? How can I help you improve in this area?"
  - Develop a plan if time allows or set a separate meeting to discuss options and plans.
- End with future goals. What are the employee's goals they want to set for themselves for the next six months to a year?

Example of a Finished Review

Performance Review Scale

   1.0 - 2.4: Probation Period Needed

   2.5 - 3.2: Poor Performance

   3.3 - 3.9: Needs Improvement

   4.0 - 4.5: Meets Job Requirements

   4.6 - 5.0: Exceeds Job Requirements

Part One: Coworkers Review Employee

Dependability   *4.4*   *Meets job requirements*

You conduct yourself in a professional manner and are someone that can be depended on.

Initiative   *4.0*   *Meets job requirements*

You can complete tasks without any supervision. Your lowest-rated area was cleaning.

Job Knowledge   *4.7   Exceeds job requirements*

Your knowledge base is excellent, and your technical skills are wonderful. You continue to improve your knowledge.

Planning, Organization, & Problem Solving *3.5 Needs Improvement*

When it is busy, you remain organized and focused. If a client is stressed, you may come off as short-tempered or appear stressed yourself at times.

Teamwork   *4.2*   *Meets job requirements*

Everyone stated you have a positive attitude and are a wonderful team player. You are polite and compassionate to your pet patients. You are open to hearing other people's opinions and ideas and always educate others.

Comments

"Can become stressed if there is a demanding client."

"Very personable."

"I love learning from her. She's so smart!"

"Very motivated except for cleaning, constantly learning and trying to improve her knowledge."

"Willing to do anything that is asked of her."

"Is a wonderful team member who is always teaching others."

Part Two: Employee Review of Self

Self-Review

You have a great understanding of your strengths and weaknesses. While you listed one of your weaknesses as "difficulty in teaching others," I disagree. You are a fantastic teacher and have a great way of explaining things to others on the team. Just make sure you have more confidence in your knowledge.

Part Three: Manager Summary

Manager Summary

You have a strong knowledge base and good technical skills. You are motivated and a hard worker. You maintain a positive attitude and offer excellent care to the hospital's clients and pets.

Part Four: Future Goals

You have an innate ability to educate the team. Let's talk about how to strengthen your teaching abilities throughout the year.

After reviewing this feedback, you can likely see why this employee walked away feeling especially valued as a team member. She knew her team cared about her. I wanted to challenge her by growing her skills as a teacher, so I made a note at the end to talk to her about how to tap into her gift even more.

She expressed that she was interested in doing a continuing education class for the team on interpreting bloodwork. However, as you saw, she cited that she didn't feel like she was a good teacher, so we talked about imposter syndrome and how to get her more confident in her teaching abilities.

She was not a credentialed veterinary technician, so at every meeting, I would ask her if she had any interest in going back to school. For financial and personal reasons, it was not something she was interested in pursuing, and I respected that. I never made her feel like she was less than, but she knew that she would receive an increase in salary if she became credentialed. Regardless, I treated her like the leader she was rather than a failure for never becoming credentialed. I wish the hospital had offered to help pay for her education, but unfortunately, it was not a benefit they were willing to pick up.

Remember that your goals for an employee may not align with theirs. There has to be a collaboration between employees and managers for them to be successful. As much as I wanted her to go to college, I respected her for the hard worker she was and elevated the skills she had. Here are some pointers to ensure the meeting is successful:

- The positives ideally should outweigh the negatives.
- Negative comments are filtered to ensure they are delivered in a PKH way, and only trends are included.
- Only one to two and no more than three areas of improvement should be included. Anything more, and you've lost the employee.
- The end of the meeting needs to be centered around the future. Get them excited and challenge them. They should feel like you care about developing them.
- The discussion goes two ways. Ask their thoughts on areas of improvement and get them to express their feelings about both the positives and negatives. Show you care deeply that you are proud and there to coach them.

You will use the larger meeting to help create coaching and guidance throughout the other three meetings. Essentially every quarter, you will set aside time to speak to each team member. One of those quarters will be a deep-dive into a development plan that encompasses the 360-

feedback. That's how you keep in touch with your team, address issues early, and constantly invest in developing them.

For some employees, you may need to schedule a follow-up meeting before waiting until the next quarter. This may be an employee who is struggling with something where you need to coach them more frequently rather than three months later. It never hurts to have more meetings. It only hurts to have less.

When Do They Get More Money?

As I mentioned a few times, one of the big turn-offs for me in the old-school annual review method was that the employer (without speaking to the employee) decided the fate of the employee's salary for a whole year.

I also recognize that many of you may not have any influence on an individual's salary even though you are responsible for providing their performance review. To this, I say, "Hogwash." If someone else is deciding the fate of your employee's salary while you are the one presenting the feedback, then what's the point of the annual review at all?

Any manager responsible for an employee's performance must be directly involved in that employee's salary changes. Having a manager who only coaches but has no say in compensation doesn't make sense.

When you are looking at salary adjustments, ask yourself:

- What criteria are you using to change the salary?
- Are you increasing everyone's salary by a certain percentage across the board?
- Is there a way to ensure raises (real raises, not the cost of inflation) are fair?
- How about randomly picking names out of a hat as to who gets more money?

<u>The last question was sarcastic.</u> Please don't pick names out of a hat, though I feel that's what many managers do because they cannot verbalize why some individuals received changes in their pay and others did not.

Most of the time, department managers collaborate with the practice manager or owner on raises. If only the owner or practice manager makes the decision without the input of those coaching the teams, then they hardly consider the individual and their contribution to the hospital. Therefore, it becomes a very biased, one-sided view of the employee.

I want to challenge you with some thoughts regarding changes in pay. Ideally, start thinking outside the box with how you deliver salary increases.

- All salaries should be minimally increased yearly with the rate of inflation. Otherwise, you are paying your employees less each year.
- A true raise is above the rate of inflation.
- Salary can be adjusted more than once a year.
- Salary raises should be awarded when change happens. This may include when:
  o An employee takes on more responsibility.
  o The hospital experiences great financial success.
  o An employee moves into a new role.
  o An employee improves their performance through knowledge, skill or goes above and beyond.
- The employee should understand why the salary was adjusted rather than not having any understanding of what they did to receive the change in pay.

Do I think everyone deserves a raise every year?

No. However, at the very least I do expect salaries to increase to compensate for inflation.

Do I think that changes in salary should be tied to the 360-feedback?

No. I think any salary change would be better received after both the manager and employee have had time to digest the thoughts of the 360-feedback meeting. The manager should consider how the employee received the feedback and obtain their insight. For example, a manager may walk into a meeting thinking, "this employee doesn't deserve any pay increase." After speaking to them about how a particular employee has bullied them, they may realize that the reviews were largely biased. Conversations with employees matter and should play a role in salary changes.

To me, salary adjustments can be given out at the next meeting, or a quick follow-up meeting can be scheduled to present the new salary. Salary adjustments become more impactful if they aren't already decided on before the meeting because it means the manager considered all factors. It means the employee got to have a say in the 360-feedback, and from there, we decided how to adjust their salary.

Final Thoughts

Remember that your performance development plan should be a year-round one, not just a one-and-done one. The 360-feedback system helps to drive performance and goals throughout the year, but it's not the start or end of the development plan.

There also does need to be some kind of development plan. Too often, employers get busy, and the employees are left not receiving any feedback, for years and years. This leaves the employee guessing about their performance.

When issues arise (which they will with almost every employee at some point), the feedback surprises them. The employee was on cruise control, and their manager is verbally vomiting a list of failures. All employees would rather have frequent check-ins than be caught off guard.

Any good performance development plan seeks to challenge individuals by growing their skills and knowledge to their fullest potential. Development plans should be embraced by employees, not feared. They should get excited because they know that their manager will see something of great value in them. My recommendation is the following:

- Two or three 30-minute meetings spaced three to four months apart, checking in with the employee about career goals and areas of improvement.
- One 360 feedback meeting as a big check-in.
- Consider one follow-up meeting focused on the 360-feedback.
- Repeat.

Remember, there are plenty of other ways to create a well-designed development plan for your team. The key is to have a plan. Make it consistent and fair. Ensure it's universal for all employees so that some employees aren't being reviewed with a completely different system than others.

No matter the system you decide to implement, ensure it has all the important components of a healthy performance development plan. If you have a system that works well, don't change it. The 3-1 performance development plan took me years to create, and it worked well for my hospitals and teams, but it doesn't mean it'll work well for every hospital and every team. Look at your system and seek to improve it so that it will work even better for you and your team.

Chapter Sixteen

Saying Goodbye

Saying goodbye to an employee is the worst part of any leadership role. If it is part of your responsibility to terminate employees, I am sorry. I have deep empathy for you because it was the worst part of any leadership role I ever held. We must remember that no matter how hard we try as leaders, being part of our team is not a journey everyone wants to take.

How you decide to fire someone will define you as a leader. You are about to inflict suffering on someone that was part of your team. They will lose their insurance, their paycheck, and part of their ego. They need to communicate their termination with their friends and family. Your team will learn about how you fired this individual. If you fail to show your team that the termination of an employee is a difficult decision, they will lose respect. When you fire someone, you must show that you care about the individual and the termination process.

Unfortunately, I have known managers who have terminated someone, walked out onto the clinic floor, and announced, "John is finally gone, everyone. Thank goodness! We can finally move on from that saga." Don't be that manager unless you want to lose the respect and trust of your team. Even if the team likely agrees with you that letting that particular employee go was what was best for the hospital, never verbalize it. Instead, reflect on how best to support the team and control the narrative, which we will discuss in more detail in this chapter.

It Should Not be a Surprise

Unless it's an egregious and intentional error, termination should never be a surprise. In my first book, I talked about some of the major offenses that should result in immediate termination. Here they are for your review:

- Physical assault on anyone (clients, staff, pets). This includes if a staff member throws something across the treatment room floor.
- Theft of any kind. This includes hospital documentation (pay ranges, pricing structure, etc.), money from a colleague's locker, pharmaceuticals, etc.
- Working under the influence.
- Vandalism (buildings, cars, etc.).
- Severe verbal threats.
- Harassment: racist, religious, sexist, or other discriminatory language or behavior.
- Falsification of company records or medical charts.

To me, these are offenses that should result in immediate termination. I always hope these employees are fully aware of why they are being terminated on the spot but sadly, sometimes they are not. All of the listed offenses pose a threat to the hospital, people, or animals. When I lead a team, I do not take lightly any direct threat to those I manage. Thankfully, we are often not terminating for any of the above reasons.

Most of the times we have to make a decision to terminate it is based on poor performance that has occurred over a long period of time. How do you know it's the right time to terminate an employee? You should review these 10 pre-termination questions to help guide you.

10 Pre-Termination Questions

1) Have we given the individual polite, kind, and honest feedback on their performance in the past?
2) Have we demonstrated to this individual that we care about them and their work?
3) Can we be certain that we have been crystal clear in our communication so that they understand what the issue is?
4) Do they understand the severity of their actions and that termination is a possibility?
5) Do they understand how their performance impacts their team and may be hindering their growth?
6) Have we as a leader sought advice from others if it was a situation we were not familiar with?
7) Have we truly tried to coach them to our best ability to be more successful and included tools, training, and resources for them?
8) Have we provided reasonable and obtainable goals as part of our coaching efforts?
9) Have we asked them for input on how to rectify the issue?
10) Have we exhausted all options?

If the answer is no to any of those questions, I suggest not terminating and ensuring that we've done our due diligence to coach this individual to better performance. Trust me when I say that every single question needs to be evaluated before terminating someone. By doing due diligence we should not have any regrets about terminating someone. We may still feel badly and have empathy for the individual, but we did all the work needed to not regret the decision.

I would also say these questions should be answered before considering demotion of an individual to a lesser position. Did you, as a leader, do everything to help that employee be the best they could be?

People often wonder why the second question is included. "Have we demonstrated to this individual that we care about them and their work?" This is important because if employees do not feel like their manager cares about them, what's the point of improving? If employees feel their manager doesn't care, they are unlikely to improve their performance. All employees need their leader to care about them as a human being, not just their performance.

The third, fourth, and fifth questions are centered on communication. Too often, when we provide feedback, we dance around the actual issue at hand because we don't want to offend an individual. However, if we offer an apology first when we are trying to correct a performance issue, we diminish the impact of our communication.

"I'm sorry that I have to talk to you about an interaction you had with our new client service representative. You get along with everyone else, but I heard you snapped at Cassandra. What happened? I'm sorry I even have to bring it up. You understand why I have to, right?"

The above paragraph is a common example of the type of communication that occurs all the time from hospital leaders to their employees. Unfortunately, this leaves the employee believing that it wasn't a big deal. You apologized several times for having to talk to them about it. Does this employee understand that if it continues, further action will need to be taken? Do they understand what they need to do in the future?

Question six challenges leaders to ensure they seek resources for themselves when dealing with a challenging situation. For example, coaching someone through a communication concern is vastly different than coaching someone who's made a medical mistake. As a leader, if you're not familiar with how to solve the problem, get help. Reach out to fellow hospital leaders and ask about what has worked for employees with a similar issue.

Questions seven through nine ensure that we, as leaders provide tools and resources to help improve performance. We always need to ask the individual for suggestions on how to improve in the area they are struggling. For example, I once had a veterinary technician who was struggling with client communication. Clients complained that she sounded derogatory and even demeaning in her communication. I worked to get to the bottom of why her behavior had changed. She hadn't received any criticism from clients in the past. However, over the prior two months, we were getting a good number of complaints. Finally, she confided in me she was burned-out.

I coached her through her burnout and found in-person seminars where she could develop her communication skills. She worked to improve her behavior and reduce her stress level. Together we were able to provide tangible solutions rather than me saying to her, "I need you to stop doing what you're doing and just be nicer to clients."

The last and final question serves as a reminder to ask ourselves: did we really do everything? Have we, as the manager or supervisor, done all that we can to help this individual? If we have answered yes to all ten questions now, we can consider termination.

Demotion Instead of Termination

Very few individuals require a demotion, but sometimes they do. Demoting an employee occurs because of poor work performance that has occurred over a substantial length of time, hospital restructuring, or financial reasons for the hospital. Regardless, the demotion will result in a change of title and role that is likely to be extreme for the employee.

Unlike a termination, the employee brings a large value to the team, and leadership wants to retain the employee.

Refer to the 10 questions before considering a demotion. If you have struggled with an employee's performance for only three months, you have hardly put in the time or effort to help coach and develop that individual.

Like termination, I believe demotion should be a last resort. It's a unique situation in that you have tried everything to help coach an individual, and you value them enough to want them to stay on board, but not in that role. If they aren't a great employee, it's better to terminate. You should only consider demotion when they are a good or great employee, and you truly don't want to lose them. You also have an idea of how to utilize their talents better. If you don't know what those talents are or how to utilize them, why are you trying to hold onto the employee?

Here are some key steps you must take to ensure the demotion is successful.

- They need to know you care and appreciate them. Any demotion will hurt. However, an employee who knows they are valued is more open to hearing about why the demotion is occurring.

- You must have a plan developed for the employee's next role. Leaving it up to the employee to pitch ideas is confusing and leaves the employee feeling like there are plenty of other options when there may be only one or none.

- Be sure you have a transition plan for the employee's role. Under no circumstances should you ask your employee to meet with their peers for them to delegate their responsibilities to them. It's painful to the employee who

was just demoted and humiliating for them to be subjected
to watching their coworkers pick up pieces of their job.

- Lastly, document everything. If not done properly and fairly, demoting an employee could find you in hot-water legal soup. It's best to contact an employment lawyer to make sure you do it right.

Demoting someone could go one of two ways. You may find them a role they are better suited for in which they shine. I have seen this occur successfully with someone in a veterinary technician manager role who was not thriving. After more than nine months of coaching, she and her manager discussed whether she was the right fit for leadership. The employee felt cared for and had been coached for months. She knew she was struggling and continuing to be a manager was too much of a headache for her. She welcomed the conversation when her manager asked her if she wanted to step down. "Yes, please," she exclaimed. "Being a manager isn't what I thought it would be."

The second way it could go is you could end up with an employee in a role they are unhappy in. They may sabotage themselves or the hospital. They may end up quitting. In order for them to even have a chance of being successful in the new role, they have to believe you value them. Otherwise, they are more likely to end up in a role where they feel like they don't belong and become angry and bitter about it.

When employers have taken the time to coach and talk to employees, the demotion conversation is better received because the employee clearly understands the issues. They often know they aren't the right fit. When an employee is blindsided and not provided much feedback, it leaves them uneasy and full of questions resulting in a range of emotions from sadness to anger. Ensure you do right by your employees rather than making poor leadership decisions that impact not only the employee, but the entire team.

I'm Too Short Staffed to Fire

Listen, I get it. Since the dawn of time, all veterinary hospitals have been short-staffed. There are periods of being just a little short-staffed and periods of crisis short-staffed. And, if it's the hospital's highest-grossing veterinarian, it becomes an even harder decision to terminate. Think of all the revenue and business the hospital will lose by terminating a seemingly popular doctor with clients. The four common reasons why veterinary leaders are afraid to terminate are:

- Eventually, the employee will get better.
- I'm short-staffed, so any warm body will do.
- I care deeply about their personal lives and don't want to ruin it.
- They make the hospital a lot of money.

I'm here to tell you that none of those reasons are acceptable for keeping an employee that is no longer performing well. If you truly have done your due diligence and can answer yes to the ten questions previously listed, termination is likely best for both the individual and the hospital. The 10 questions should take months to years to ensure every criteria is met. In the end, sometimes people don't work out, or it's best for them to move on.

I know many of you are faced with that high-performing veterinary receptionist, doctor, or veterinary technician/nurse. They are brilliant, and their skills cannot be matched. There's only one issue. They are one of your most toxic, negative, poisonous employees. Unfortunately, once a team member becomes a hazard to the company's culture, it is likely time to say goodbye. I understand that losing revenue or causing someone financial hardship by terminating them is difficult for any leader to manage through. However, we as leaders have set expectations for the team, which must be continuously set and reinforced. When we allow a team member an exception because we lower the bar for their behavior or performance, we have done a disservice to everyone else. If you have gone through the list of 10 questions and are sure you've done everything you can to help this individual, then it's best to part ways. Their toxicity is ruining your hospital.

I have witnessed and delivered many terminations in my career. While they are difficult to manage through, I have never seen a hospital go under because of one termination. If it is a high-performing doctor, the hospital should certainly expect to financially struggle to some degree. I have watched some of the highest-grossing boarded surgeons, cardiologists, internists, and other specialists get terminated and have concluded that one person does not drive the entire business. Could one termination result in a hospital closing its doors financially due to lesser income? Maybe, but I have not witnessed it. I have witnessed the complete opposite happening.

More often, the hospital thrives better than it ever has before. Yes, sometimes it may take a year or more for a hospital to bounce back after losing a key player to its team. I once witnessed a $250,000-a-month grossing surgeon be terminated, and, to add to the insult, it was the hospital's only surgeon. Three months later, they were better than ever and looked back with no regrets. Granted, the surgeon was throwing things at the team and cursing every day, so getting rid of this individual was necessary.

How does the team react to one of the most talented team members being let go? The most common reaction is that the team is shocked for about a week or two. After that there is a return to normalcy and even improved performance by the remaining team only a few short weeks later. Most teams describe a feeling of being happier, carefree, and lighter without the negativity looming over them.

While it can feel better for the team to let someone go, if you are looking forward to the termination or have no trepidation, I am concerned about your moral compass as a leader. Terminating someone should make you sad, anxious, or worried. Leading up to any termination, I often spent countless sleepless nights running through everything in my head to ensure it was the only option. I didn't want to regret terminating someone because I felt like I didn't try to help them to the best of my ability. Every time I fired an individual, I worried about my team and how they would handle it. I worried about how they would view me as a leader. Thankfully most of the time, they were not surprised and respected my decision.

It's hard to put personal feelings aside when you know someone is a single mother, the breadwinner of their family, or the caretaker for their dying parent. How do you terminate someone like that and still manage to sleep at night? The answer lies in the fact that you care deeply and empathetically for the individual you are terminating. You have tried, and maybe even they have tried, but the performance is not improving. They cannot be successful at the hospital and keeping them there hinders them from succeeding in their career. They are also hindering the team from being as successful as they could be. At that moment, it's hard to recognize that you are helping them, but you are. You want them to be successful and find a hospital or even a career that they thrive in. As hard as it will be on them, you, and the remaining team, everyone will be better for it. It may not seem like it at first, but it will be.

The Goodbye Conversation

I'm not going to get into all of the legal issues that result from terminating someone without a justifiable reason or in an inappropriate way. There are plenty of human resource (HR) books out there that will educate you on how to terminate someone to prevent legal action. The Veterinary Hospital Manager Association (www.vhma.org) offers a lot of advice in this area. My focus is not on the HR aspect of termination. Instead, my focus is on the human aspect of termination.

With that said, I want to ensure that you research your company's guidelines on the appropriate steps to terminate someone. More importantly, ensure that you adhere to the state and federal termination laws. For example, firing someone over 50 because they need to sit down more may cause your hospital to have a lawsuit. Terminating someone who wears a hijab when there is no written dress code policy could land you in court. Ensure any termination falls under state and federal guidelines and adhere to your company's policies. Be sure you are well versed in your state and federal employment laws, which can change. Make sure you do not end up with a wrongful termination lawsuit on your hands. You can avoid these by ensuring you have fair and equal policies for everyone on your team, and everyone works under the same rules and regulations that meet the state laws. You have documented your interactions, attempts, and coaching of performance issues. When in doubt, reach out to a professional who can help guide you if termination is legal and the right decision.

Letting someone go is the hardest task any manager must do. If you have done your due diligence, it will not be a surprise to the individual. The termination needs to be planned for and thought out to ensure that it is done in the best way possible. If you are met with a scenario where termination on the spot is necessary, do your best to follow the guidelines below.

Inform your HR Team / Practice Manager

You have decided to terminate. If your hospital has a human resource team, you must adhere to the policies in place for appropriate termination. Make sure your grounds for termination are in line with company policy. If you do not have a human resource (HR) department, be sure to write a hospital policy. By having written policies and a "how to handle" guide on terminations, you can be assured that everyone will be treated the same.

All senior leaders should be notified that an employee is about to be terminated so that everyone is on the same page. Too often, I see a veterinary technician/nurse being terminated, and the medical director was never notified. I often hear from veterinary technician/nurse managers about how they were not notified that a doctor was terminated. If we truly have cohesive leadership, these decisions would be discussed with everyone on the leadership team. The leadership team should be trusted to keep the confidentiality of this information until the termination is complete.

The employee's final pay must be calculated. Next, collect all documentation and paperwork you'll need for the employee's departure. Once everyone has been notified that a termination is going to take place and all paperwork is in order, then the meeting can be set up.

Set Up the Meeting

Ideally, the sooner you do the termination, the better. I know all too often of hospitals that have wanted to terminate someone but try to schedule it at a convenient time. I once heard from a veterinary receptionist about how she learned that she worked a full month after the decision had been made to terminate her. The hospital's rationale was that any warm body would do, and they had hoped to find a replacement in that month. They failed to find a replacement and finally decided they needed to let her go. When she was let go, her manager said, "We wanted to let you go sooner, but we couldn't find a replacement for you."

Throughout that entire month that leadership kept her employed, she created more issues. She said to me, "I wish they had just terminated me. The only reason I was there was to take home a paycheck. It would've been better if they had just fired me so that I could move on, and so could they." I agreed with her. Unfortunately, many leaders wait on terminations for what they think is the best time, resulting in the unhappy or toxic employee causing more damage to the team.

When you set up a meeting, the employee will want to know what the meeting is about. They probably have their suspicions. Keep the answer vague. When an employee asked me what the meeting was about, I would say, "I need to talk to you in person about a concern." This sets the tone for the meeting.

Do you always need to set up a meeting ahead of time? No. There were more times that I never set a meeting. Instead, I would terminate an employee right before the start of their shift. The advantage of terminating right before a shift is that the employee does not have to worry about the meeting. Too often, when we tell our employees we need to meet with them for something serious, they fret and call other people on the team to see if they know anything. It can sometimes get awkward. As someone who knows what anxiety is like, I would rather my employer pull me aside without advance notice. I know if they set up a meeting about a concern, I'd not sleep and be anxious until the meeting happened. So how do you know when to set up a meeting versus right before a shift?

I always tried to look at it from the employee's perspective. If the employee were someone who worried a lot and was anxious, I would more likely terminate them right before their shift. Having them worry for even a day was not something I wanted to do to them. Being terminated is a miserable experience enough, let alone spending a day or more worrying about it. I explained to the employee why I terminated them right before they started their shift, and they usually thanked me for being so considerate. I knew them well enough that they would have had a panic attack or worried about my request to meet for countless hours. While they were not happy to be terminated, they appreciated my not causing excessive worrying.

I also never terminated after a shift. Making an employee work an entire shift just to save the hospital is selfish. They end their shift tired, often cranky, and now they find out it didn't matter whether they worked. They were just terminated. The last shift they worked was just because their employer needed a warm body.

Terminating right before a shift can backfire. Employees start to get wise to you, and if you show up on a day or time you don't normally work, they start to figure out that you are about to terminate someone. I always ensured that my shift varied widely so that the team thought it normal when I would come in on a day off or a time I didn't normally work. When employees asked what I was doing there, I always replied with the generic, "Catching up on a few things." Then when the employee that I was terminating arrived, I would quickly grab them before they could even put their things away and say, "Before you head out on the floor can I speak with you?" Whether you decide to schedule a meeting in advance or terminate by surprise right before a shift is completely up to you. I also think it depends on what is best for that individual.

There may be times when you will need to terminate over a phone call. This is not ideal, and if it's necessary to terminate over a phone call, ensure the employee knows they should be in a private area to talk to you. They should be aware that this is a serious meeting for which they need to allocate time. Cold calling them when they are at their kid's birthday party is unethical. Please don't ever text or instant message a termination to an employee. It should go without saying but some managers find these methods acceptable.

Most references will tell you that it's important to have a second person present for the termination. This ensures that everything was done legally and fairly. Particularly in the United States, lawsuits are numerous because terminated employees often feel it was unjust and unfair. I never had a second witness in the room with me for any of my terminations, but only because all my employees were not surprised by the termination, and none were expected to be volatile. If you feel that the situation may spiral out of control or the employee may seek recourse, I strongly suggest a second person witness the termination.

Ensure that the environment in which you are firing is private and is free of distractions. Silence your cell phone. Turn off your computer screen. Ensure that no one can barge into the room or disrupt the meeting. Don't keep a desk between you and the employee. Sit near them. Again, they should know you care about them as a person. Too often, terminations feel like a money transaction to employees.

One hospital I worked in believed in open-door policies for their managers' offices. As such, they either removed the physical doors or had all the office doors constructed as glass doors. The hospital thought they would be modern and encourage transparency by having glass offices and no doors. Unfortunately, this made it exceptionally awkward when an employee needed to be terminated or a serious conversation needed to happen. There was no way to have any privacy. While I agree with open-door policies most of the time, there needs to be a door in place, and hospitals need to have private offices. Walking by a glassed office with no door and seeing your coworker crying is hardly the modern-day experience anyone wants.

The Actual Meeting

This is where utilizing PKH communication skills is so important. You must start off being polite and kind before you dive into the honest part as to why you called the meeting. The first thing in any termination meeting should be to let the person know they are being terminated. Do not apologize. I know you will feel genuinely bad, but you need to leave the emotion out. This is not about you. It is all about them.

Offering too much context might seem like the right thing to do, but it can ultimately cause the employee to become angry and defensive. You had already informed them countless times before this meeting about the issues. There is no need to review the issues again.

Start With the Bad News

"As you know, we have met several times about your poor performance. I know you have tried, but your performance has continued to be unsatisfactory. Unfortunately, we have come to the decision that we need to terminate your employment." In this example, you were polite. There was no name-calling or mudslinging. You acknowledged their efforts which was kind. You were honest and brief to keep it factual. Stay away from ambiguous wording such as "things aren't working out" or "it may be better if you work someplace else."

I always use the word "terminate." I know that it's a harsh word, but there is no confusion when you say it. In some of my early terminations, I would use the words "let go." "Unfortunately, we have decided to let you go." I found that some employees would reply, "You mean I'm being fired?!" Saying the words "let go" doesn't soften the blow. The result is the employee is still fired. It's up to you what words you decide to use, as these are merely my thoughts and experiences. There are plenty of people who would advocate not using the word "terminate" and instead "fired" or even "let go." Regardless, be clear in your communication.

Allow Them to Share Their Feelings or Thoughts

You just told them they are being terminated. It's important they are allowed to share their thoughts. Not allowing them to say anything is unkind and will leave them fuming. I have known many managers who told employees they were terminated and concluded with, "I need you to get your belongings right now, and I'll escort you out."

While I believe in allowing them to share their feelings or thoughts, I strongly suggest that you do not change your mind about the termination. It may be difficult not to want to change your mind, especially if they discuss hardships and how the termination will cause even more. It may be quite emotional. Be sure that you don't continue to justify over and over why they are being terminated. They already feel bad enough, and you've already explained it to them in prior meetings. You don't need to defend your decision. You also do not need to have them accept the decision. In fact, many employees do not. Despite your many hours of coaching, many employees will feel the termination was unjust.

Stick to only discussing the recent performance-based issues. Do not add anything new, as that is unfair. If you bring up something new, the employee will think, "This is the first I'm hearing of it. If I had known, I could have fixed it and not been fired." Too many times, I see employers adding in issues such as, "You also gossiped a lot." It's unnecessary to bring it up, so don't. Stick to the performance issues you have been working on and why a termination is warranted now.

When talking, keep your explanation short but specific. There's a fine line between explaining why they've been terminated and simply making them feel worse. You want to avoid getting into an argument or a long discussion. The decision has been made, and it is non-negotiable. While clear feedback is important for them to improve, it should have already been given at this point. The employee may vent and ask questions. Listen and repeat the same message.

For the employees I had to fire, I often found they apologized for not improving their performance and easily accepted the termination. I had countless employees say, "I understand. It's my fault." I even had a few that wanted to tell me on their way out what a fantastic manager I was because they knew I truly cared about them. The only reason I had many terminations go well, and dare I say even easy, was because I cared about every one of my employees, and they knew it. They knew that I didn't take the decision to terminate them lightly. They knew I wanted them to excel. They also saw my dedication in trying to improve their performance over months, if not years. They understood I had their best interest in mind and had tried my best to coach them.

Terminating a Good Employee

It is rare, but sometimes, a veterinary hospital may need to terminate an employee because they could not afford to keep the employee or service. I once knew of a veterinary hospital that lost its only oncologist, and despite months of trying to hire a new one, they were unsuccessful. They started to let their veterinary technician oncology team go, which was exceptionally difficult for them. The oncology team didn't want to work in other departments, and without any work for six months, there wasn't much more the hospital could do.

Another reason could be the hospital was purchased by a company. Through the sale of the hospital, terminations may occur because the new company may bring in its own leadership or personnel. Usually, I find this is not the case, but it certainly could happen. In most acquisitions, the new owner retains the original staff because it is much easier to do so.

In these cases, termination is not occurring because of a performance-based issue. These truly are miserable terminations for everyone involved. The employee being fired is often unaware and taken by surprise because their performance was adequate. If an employee is to be terminated over non-performance-based issues, we must try to set this employee up for success as a future hire in another hospital.

If you have the time, research jobs for them before the meeting. Present them a list of jobs that they qualify for and that you think would be a good fit. This seems excessive, but this is a termination that you don't want to have to make. If you can give them a head start on the job search, they are more likely to come back to you when or if you can rehire them. It's also just a nice thing to do. It shows that you genuinely care. This will be the message that they leave the practice with and likely tell other veterinary professionals. You can also consider having a reference letter ready to go for them. They need to feel cared about because this was not a decision you wanted to make.

The After-Action Items

Once the termination has occurred, you need to clearly define the next steps the terminated employee needs to take. When is the effective date of termination? Unless it's an employee that you are terminating because of reorganization, budgets, or the sale of the hospital, termination should almost always be immediate. In the case where the oncology technicians were terminated because there was no oncologist, they were given two weeks' notice to prepare for their last day. I would recommend all performance-based terminations be effective immediately.

The Consolidated Omnibus Budget Reconciliation Act of 1986 (COBRA) allows terminated employees to extend their health insurance coverage after they depart. It is important that you have the COBRA paperwork ready to go. Too often, I see veterinary hospitals skipping this step and sending their employees packing without knowing how to extend their health insurance. Awkwardly, the employee then has to come back to receive the information or request that it be sent to them. Again, I cannot express enough that you must comply with state and federal laws during this process.

Be sure to explain to them when they will receive their last paycheck and when all their benefits will terminate. The next part is the hardest. If it is a performance-based issue, you need to escort this individual to get their belongings and then out of the hospital.

For safety reasons and to minimize issues, every workplace is advised to escort the individual out of the building immediately following termination. Allowing an individual to linger, share the story with coworkers, or think about what just happened will only result in anger, confusion, frustration, and even retaliation.

A colleague once told me a story about how she terminated an employee but failed to escort them out of the hospital. After saying goodbye, she shut her office door and started to process her own emotions around the termination. About one hour later, a doctor knocked on her door to inform her that her surgical team refused to work. It seemed that the terminated employee talked to a large number of the team and caused them to believe that the termination was unjustified. In one hour, the terminated employee convinced the team that she needed to be rehired. The team felt so connected to this individual and wanted to show their support that they decided to stage a sit-in. They stated they were not going to work until the employee was rehired. What a nightmare.

What happens if an employee snaps? I know of a veterinarian who was terminating a doctor who, upon hearing about his termination, jumped up from his seat, threw the chair, and started screaming obscenities. "I'm going to make sure this f-ing hospital burns to the ground. You'll all be ruined. This is a f-ing joke, and so is everyone in here. I am the only thing keeping it afloat."

Volatile situations like this can be scary and pose a real risk. Try to remain as calm as you can. In that moment, the only thing you should do is to get this individual to leave the building immediately, even if you have not fully wrapped up the conversation. "I understand you are upset, but I'm going to ask you to leave at this point. I will send the information to you about your final paycheck and any benefits information." If they refuse to leave, you should contact the police. Let them know that you will be contacting the police due to their refusal to leave.

When an individual is screaming, threatening, and throwing items, it is safest to get them out of the building immediately. Once gone, lock the doors to ensure they do not reenter, and you are sure they are gone. Be sure to address the concern with the team immediately and inform them under no circumstances is the terminated employee allowed back in the building.

While you cannot stop the former employee from reaching out and connecting to the team after they have left the hospital, you can control the narrative in the moment by escorting them out of the building. As they go to leave the building, they may speak their opinion or even scream about it. It will be limited compared to allowing them free reign to stay in the hospital for an unknown amount of time. The good news is most employees are reasonable regarding termination, especially if we've had numerous prior conversations around their performance.

To escort them out, I would say, "I'm going to walk with you to get your things. If you want to say a quick goodbye to everyone, you are welcome to, but I need to escort you out of the building once you have finished getting your belongings." I always worked in a hospital with a back entrance and would give that as an option to the employee should they not want to walk through the main treatment area. Before you terminate an employee, figure out how you would like the exit to occur.

Thank Them & Wish Them Luck

This should be genuine because it is. I never thanked an employee if they did one of the cardinal sins I previously talked about, resulting in immediate termination. Otherwise, I truly did have gratitude for them being part of my team, even if, in the end, they drove me completely bonkers and made me want to rip my hair out. Most employees contribute to the hospital's success at some point in their career. It's important to acknowledge that.

I always wanted every one of my terminated employees to be successful in another hospital or wherever life took them. In my career, I have rehired two terminated employees back as part-time staff. You may think me crazy, but the reason for firing them was that they were burned-out and angry. Despite all the coaching sessions, I could not make any headway. They were both excellent employees. That was the frustrating part. They both had stopped being excellent at some point, and neither they nor I could get them back on track.

After they joined other hospitals, time and perspective helped to heal their burn-out. Years later, they contacted me and asked if they could work part-time. After talking it through with them, they informed me about how they were in a better place and missed the hospital. So why not rehire that individual for a part-time role?

People grow and change throughout their life. Most likely, the person you are terminating doesn't enjoy their job, or at the very least, they are frustrated. Sometimes we need to let employees go so that they can grow. The employee may hold a grudge and never talk to you again. However, if we do our due diligence, care deeply about an employee, and the termination is accepted, then it is often something that they can grow from after some time has passed. Once they have had time to process their feelings and thoughts, they may even come back to your hospital as a much better employee.

Coping With Your Feelings

As I have mentioned countless times, it is terrible having to terminate an employee. As a leader in any position, this is hands down one of the most difficult and emotionally challenging tasks that one must do. It can feel exceptionally lonely being a leader at any time, but I found I felt the loneliest after I had to terminate someone.

Hopefully, you have a solid leadership support system in your hospital. After you terminate an employee, you certainly can't go out to the clinic floor and vent your feelings to the staff. Instead, you need to find ways of digesting and processing your emotions. Having a leadership support system within your hospital will help you do that. As a veterinary technician manager, I was lucky to have great support from my practice manager. While she was not present for the termination of my employee, I knew I could rely on her afterward to discuss how it went and share my feelings if necessary. I also knew that she always supported my decision and was a great listening ear for me.

There are plenty of online social media leadership groups and even leadership organizations to gain support from if you struggle with a difficult termination. In addition, many of my friends have mentors in similar leadership roles in different hospitals that they go to for support and guidance when it gets tough.

Be sure you shoulder only your burdens. The termination probably had many emotions. The employee probably shared hardship, feelings, or even stories about how the termination would affect them and potentially ruin their life. As an empathetic individual, it's easy for you to let your mind ponder how they feel and how the decision will affect them. It's easier to say that you must focus on your burdens, not theirs. However, recognize you do have your burdens to shoulder. Terminating an employee will impact you. Be sure you prepare yourself with how to manage that stress afterward.

Take Care of Yourself

It's okay to take a break and take care of yourself. You are not letting your team down. They need you at your best, so you can help lead them through the change that just occurred.

Everybody has different ways of managing stress, and it is important that you figure out what works best for you. Be sure it's a healthy way of handling stress. Too often, we drown our sorrows in drugs, alcohol, or overeating. All of these self-coping mechanisms add more stress and problems to our bodies. I find solace in the outdoors. In the darkest moments in my life, I always gravitate to running trails or scuba diving in the ocean. I stay busy to avoid thinking too much in the silence. I encourage you to find what works for you.

If possible, go home after the termination and take care of yourself. You have been through something emotional and energy-draining. Working at your best potential in the hospital afterward is probably not realistic. If that's not possible, give yourself a break in the evening. Have your spouse or family take care of the kids and let them know that it's all about relaxing and taking care of yourself for this one night. Do your best to keep your mind off your troubles. Recognize that the sick stomach and heartache are natural, but do not let it pull you to a dark place. Find a way to relax and devote your energy to yourself and the team. It's okay to focus on you for a bit.

Managing the Change

How your hospital recovers from the termination will be largely based on how you personally recover. When you have less stress and are organized with a plan, your team will see that and reciprocate with less stress themselves.

Change is always scary. Even if it were a poor performer that most of the team struggled with, it would be difficult for them to move forward because there is some level of change. When an employee is terminated, other employees recognize it could happen to them. For those that may be on the edge of not performing well, it might be a wake-up call that shows them that termination is possible.

The thing that combats the fear of change is control. Once we get things back in control, we feel better about the change. Being able to control the narrative post-termination is important because it allows the hospital to move forward productively and healthily as opposed to chaos and disruption.

Remember that it was for the best. It sounds like it's a way to justify a difficult decision to make yourself feel better, but it is true if you were able to answer yes to the 10 questions posed at the beginning of the chapter. You put in countless hours and effort trying to coach this individual, and they were not improving. Sometimes an individual is not right for the job or hospital. It may be that it's not the right time in their life for that particular job in that hospital. Regardless, it is for the best because now they can find something that they excel in, and your hospital can find someone better suited for that position. Be sure to convey to your employees that the decision was difficult and that you wish the terminated employee nothing but the best.

Filling the Hole

You just terminated an employee. Likely there is a hole that needs to be filled. This can be scary because veterinary professionals are in short supply. Make sure you come up with a plan before you terminate the employee. In those rare cases, it may not be possible to because of such a horrific performance issue, resulting in termination on the spot. However, most of the time, we have been planning months, if not years, for this termination.

If possible, develop a plan before the termination but be careful not to set it in action until afterward. I know too many managers who were burned because they reached out to a colleague, hired a new employee, or connected with a co-worker and gave them a "heads up" that they would need them on the schedule because there would "be some changes." Of course, the terminated employee figured it out before the manager could notify them. That said, you do need to figure out how to manage the shift and upcoming schedule without the employee that has just been fired.

Having a plan in place will help the current employees adjust better to the change. The unknown is scary for them. Doctors who lose a veterinary technician/nurse will want to know who's seeing appointments with them. When a client service representative is fired, the others want to know who's picking up the extra shifts. Make sure you have thought out some ideas to mitigate the response immediately following the termination.

- What roles and responsibilities did this individual have, and who will now fill them?
- Where will you be advertising for the open position?
  - Ask your team for ideas of places to advertise or if they may know an individual who may be a good fit. Consider incentivizing them with a bonus if they find someone.
- Get them excited about a new team member joining the hospital.
- If the termination will result in schedule or hour changes, notify the team of the new change.

Managing the Post-Termination Gossip

What do you say to the team after you just terminated one of their coworkers? This can be just as hard as the actual termination. Often, the team is aware of the issues that a particular employee is experiencing. Let's face it. There's a lot of gossiping that happens within the walls of a veterinary hospital. If someone is not performing well, everyone knows it. Often the individual struggling complains to their team members about the injustice happening to them. Regardless of whether they agree with the decision, there will be gossip and worry. The more plans you can communicate to your team, the less fear and rumors they will have about the unknown.

Being Honest, but Not Unprofessional

Too many leaders simply say, "Amy was fired today," and that's it. You cannot afford to be silent, but you also cannot afford to gossip and break confidentiality either. If you remain too silent, this opens the door to gossiping. While employees know they don't have the right to learn why the other employee was terminated, they still want to know. Here are a few tips on how to talk to your team.

- Be careful with your words. Be deliberate in your word choice. Remember, you can always say you cannot tell them all the details due to legal reasons. "They were not a good match" is usually all the explanation the team needs. The team worked alongside the individual. They are aware of the issues.

- Leadership needs to be unified. The team that is most directly impacted by the termination should be communicated to first. However, the rest of the hospital needs to be notified shortly thereafter. Since the leadership was unified in the decision prior to the termination, a communication plan should have been created so that it can be implemented immediately following. For example, if a veterinarian is terminated, the veterinarian team should be notified first. The medical director will then inform the technician / nurse manager and client service manager that all veterinarians have been notified so they can proceed to inform their teams. Ideally, this is done on the same day. All leaders must communicate the same message and be supportive of each other. Failure to do so creates a divide in the hospital, confusion, and chaos.

- Prevent the hospital-wide freak-out. If the person was terminated for financial, restructuring, or acquisition reasons, people will freak out and for good reason. They will no longer feel their job is secure. Convincing them will take a lot of time and building up of the trust. If the termination was because of a performance-based issue, then be vocal to your team that their positions are secure. Assure them that you tried your best to coach the individual but that you had to let them go. Reiterate it was a difficult decision and one that you did not take lightly.

• Stop the gossiping. It's going to happen, so you must allow for some to occur, but anything highly toxic or damaging should be addressed. Employees should know that the reason the individual was terminated was valid. If the employee was terminated immediately, inform the team that "the termination needed to be immediate because the offense was so egregious that it went against the moral code of the hospital." While the team will gossip, they will also understand that the immediate termination was warranted, and that leadership stands by its values.

• Let them know you care and that you tried to work with the individual to coach them. Employees should know that leadership did their best to try to help someone improve. Often teams are unaware of all the efforts that go into helping an individual improve a performance-based issue. Don't go into details but certainly, let them know that you and your fellow leaders tried your best.

• Keep an open door. Ensure your team members know they can come to you with any questions or concerns. You may get a few that come to you wanting to know more details but explain to them that their job is secure and that your focus will be moving forward in a positive way as a team. Letting your team know that you are available to them for any questions regarding the termination will show you care about how they are doing.

• Be aware of your mood because it will impact the team. Be sensitive that some individuals may be best friends with the terminated employee. Consider how the firing affects morale and team environment. Remember that you are a coach. Your job is to build up your team when the score is low. They will undoubtedly worry about who's going to fill the shift. Your job is to assure them that there is a plan in place. Be somber but not sad. Walking around as if someone died will have the opposite effect. On the flip, don't be joyful or celebratory. Acknowledge that the termination was a big deal, but don't dramatize it. Also, minimizing the termination by not allowing conversation around it will show employees that you simply don't care about them once they leave.

- Reassure, reassure, reassure. It's going to be okay. Hospitals manage through terminations all the time. It may seem impossible to manage at the time, and the hospital will fail. When I was younger, I was working when a senior veterinary technician was fired. I remember thinking that there was no way the hospital team would heal. Fast forward more than two decades later, and I've now lost count of how many people I have seen terminated. The hospital always heals. It may not be easy or quick but healing always occurs.

Chapter Seventeen

Keeping It All Going

You just spent a year or more working through tough conversations with those exhibiting toxic traits and worked to coach them. You've mediated conversations between individuals who despised each other. You are a master at resolving conflict and utilizing PKH in everyday conversations. Once we have created an amazing culture, how do we keep it going? How do we prevent a backslide?

Part of creating and keeping a cohesive team is recognizing and rewarding our superstars. We need to reward them with more than just promotions or money by challenging them and elevating them to being the unicorns that they are. How do we keep a team at the top once we get it there? What do we do with our superstars once they have reached their potential?

How to Keep Unicorns Happy

Now that we know what a unicorn is, we must ensure we never lose one. Too often, leaders start making some headway with a toxic team and sit back to relax. While you may be able to breathe a little easier, maintaining a happy team still requires work. Leaders must elevate their unicorns and be on the lookout for any Red Bulls lurking around the corner (a 1982 movie reference from the cult classic *The Last Unicorn*). In all seriousness, how do we keep our team happy once it is??

Treat them As Equals

This is a good rule for everybody on your team. I never had to pull out the "I'm a manager card." In fact, through the countless leadership roles I have held, I have never once had to remind a single employee that I was the boss, and they were not. I peruse veterinary leadership social online groups from time to time. On more than one occasion, I have seen a veterinary manager write they had to remind their staff that they were the boss, and that's why XYZ was happening. The minute you say, "I'm the boss, and that's why," is the very minute that your unicorns disappear.

Let's realize the real issue. You are reminding them that you are the boss because they are underperforming in some way. You've asked them to do XYZ, and they have said, "no." Stop and ask yourself, "Why did they say no?" Is it because they feel it's not part of their job, they don't have the time, or are they feeling undervalued?

The best leaders lead by example. We treat our team members as equals by listening to your employees' opinions, seeking them out, and treating them with the trust and respect you want.

No one person, including the manager, is more important than another on the team. If you lose even one member of the team, then the hospital struggles in some way. This is true of the owner, veterinarians, client service representatives, technicians, and other team members. Every single person is equal to each other on a team. We maintain our happy team culture because every member of the team believes they are an equal part of the hospital's success.

We keep our superstar unicorns at their peak performance only when they realize this. If they feel like they are less than or not as valued as someone else, we lose them. If they don't feel equal to us as leaders, they will not be as motivated to lead.

Provide Consistent Feedback

Unicorns know they are awesome. I mean, it's a freaking unicorn. They have a horn, magic powers, and rainbows that may or may not come out of their backside. Most unicorns are not egotistical. They are quite humble. They know they are awesome because the team relies on them, and they get joy from the team asking for their opinions and help. A unicorn has earned the respect of others through its hard work and dedication.

While a unicorn knows it is a superstar on the team, it still requires constant feedback, like any other employee. They want to know how they can improve and what they excel at. Too often, managers sit down with their unicorns only once a year during an annual review and tell them how awesome they are and then send them back out into the pasture. That's not good enough. Hopefully, this book has driven home the point that good solid performance development plans happen year-round.

Unicorns want to constantly improve themselves. Therefore, it's imperative that managers not forget about them. Provide constant feedback to them as they do to other employees. Otherwise, most unicorns will leave and find someone else who appreciates their awesomeness.

Ask for Their Opinion

They didn't become a unicorn by not knowing anything. They worked hard to become the superstar that you see now. Leaders must remember that sometimes the best solutions don't come from other managers or supervisors. Often, the best solution and ideas come from the employees working in the trenches.

When you are stumped with an issue or there is a problem within the team, a unicorn should be brought into your inner circle of trust so that you can seek out their opinion. Your unicorns are those on your team who hold the hospital's value high. They often avoid negativity and gossip, so you should trust your unicorns. Superstars need to feel valued by leadership. One of the best ways to do that is to ask for their help when the team or hospital struggles.

Why can't you pull a few of your superstars aside and ask, "We need to add in a shift during the weekday, but I'm struggling with when the best time would be. What do you think?" Think about how impactful it would be if you reached out to one of your best employees and asked, "The team seems negative lately. What are your thoughts as to why?" In these moments, you treat them as equals and value them because they have proven to be an amazing team member. Their trust in you will only grow. Let employees offer ideas for fixing systems that may not be working. They probably have some great ideas.

Whenever Possible, Let Them Define Their Duties

What?! Why would we ever let them define their job? Don't we just lock all employees in a cage and ensure they work within the confines of the job we have provided them with no freedom to leave its walls?

In veterinary medicine, there's only so much wiggle room with what can be defined. A surgeon must always perform surgery. A client service representative will have to manage all aspects of the front office area. A veterinary technician/nurse has to be a veterinary technician/nurse. All employees understand that they must do certain essential tasks to remain employed.

But what about those special tasks that pop up? We all have them in our hospital. The refrigerator needs to be cleaned out. We have to perform yearly inventory counts. Perhaps a new standard operating procedure needs to be developed around how patients are handled who potentially have leptospirosis (a zoonotic disease). A new piece of equipment just showed up, and no one knows how to use it.

The best suited individual for the task is not always you. If you are struggling with delegating, please read my first book, where I address how to delegate. As a leader, finding the best suited individual is your job. The best-suited individual is someone who wants to do it and has the skills and knowledge to do so.

If you do have someone in mind to take over a special task that you need help with, ask them what their opinion is and whether or not they would find any value or interest in taking on the task. If the answer is no, that's okay. You will find someone who is ready to take it on rather than forcing it upon someone.

Many of the unicorns in our hospital define their duties all the time. They frequently will approach their manager and suggest they have an idea about a better way to do something. Hear them out rather than saying, "That's not really your job." If you think it's something that may help benefit the hospital, your next response should be, "Do you have any interest in taking this on?" They probably do because they were passionate enough to bring it up to you in the first place.

Unicorns are problem solvers. They are not the employee who just complains negatively about things and walks around saying they wish this or that. Instead, a superstar usually has superstar ideas of how to fix it. Of course, they may not share or even have thought of ideas when they come to you with a concern, but you should challenge them. I bet somewhere in their magical brain are some great magical solutions.

Most recently, an individual approached me and asked how they could get their hospital ready in case a disaster struck. They wanted to create a mini-disaster team within their hospital and didn't know how to start. I provided some resources to her, but then I encouraged her to bring her idea to her practice manager and regional manager. She did just that and got full support. She went on to develop a standard operating procedure for the entire company that focused on how to respond to a disaster. Without realizing it, she defined her duties because of her passion.

The best way to demotivate a unicorn is to force them to do something they have no interest in doing. Just because they've been there for ten years and are a senior client service representative supervisor doesn't mean they wanted to take on the responsibility of training new hires.

They may feel stressed or don't enjoy training at all. When we force a superstar into doing something because they are considered a senior employee in the hospital, we demotivate them. They wonder what they've done wrong to be forced to do something they don't want to do. Our superstars are just that because they often don't say no, but if we keep forcing things on them, they will start feeling undervalued and unappreciated. That's when our unicorns start looking elsewhere. If you add more to their plate, make sure it's something they want to do. If they are unsure or you sense any hesitation, let them know they can give it a try. If it's not something they end up wanting to do, they can always take it off their plate.

Appreciate Your Unicorns

If you decide to take your unicorns for granted, they are going to go elsewhere. They know they are unicorns, and they know they can get a job anywhere. Too often, our unicorns work the hardest of anyone in the hospital. Unfortunately, managers become complacent with their excellent work ethic and fail to pay them any attention.

As a manager, while we cannot destress their external lives outside of the hospital, we must create an environment that encourages and rewards the hard work of the people who are functioning at their best every day. Your unicorns are helping your hospital be the best it can be, so show them some love.

They want to know that you know they are superstars. They want to feel like you can't function as well without them. The reality is you cannot. Like any healthy relationship, they want to feel needed. Be sure you frequently tell your unicorns exactly how much you value them. Praise them, give them a bonus, buy them their favorite coffee, and make sure they know you value them. You do not want to lose your best hitter on your baseball team because you'll struggle to win games. Think outside the box and reward your superstars.

Challenge the Unicorns

I describe myself as a border collie. If the sheep don't move after a while, I will find another game to play. Border collies like to be challenged. They love to think. They enjoy problem-solving and being part of a solution. In fact, I once left a job simply because I was bored in my current role. The team was amazing, there was no drama, the salary and benefits were good, but I was bored. No one and nothing was challenging me. Unicorns and border collies are virtually the same. Trust me on this.

All good leaders know how to challenge their superstars. The problem is that many leaders have forgotten to ask their unicorns whether or not they felt challenged in their skills and knowledge. As a manager, ask your superstars, "Do you feel like you are growing here, or are you bored?" If the answer is that they are bored, then dive into the reason immediately before they decide to leave.

To challenge your unicorns, ask them where they see their career going. Next, develop a career path for them to grow and help them get there. They may not know how to challenge themselves; this is where you come into play.

Many hospitals challenge veterinary technicians / nurses to learn new skills. One hospital I consulted with challenged one of its superstar veterinary technicians to go back to school to become certified in performing echocardiograms. She became certified and now performs echocardiograms for the client. That's right, a veterinary technician performing ultrasounds of the heart. After scanning the heart, she submits the images to a board-certified cardiologist for review. The world of telehealth is so cool! All this superstar veterinary technician did was express her love of cardiac medicine and how she loved the hospital but wished she could do more with cardiology. Talk about a great challenge for both her and the hospital; the tremendous value in return is equal for both. As an aside, the doctors of this clinic are paid a base salary plus a percent of the revenue they bring in. This veterinary technician is now compensated with a base plus percent of revenue because she's making a lot of money for the hospital. It is things like this that change the culture of the hospital and industry for the better.

As leaders, we need to think outside the box to avoid losing our unicorns to boredom. Have conversations and figure out how to make their passions work inside your hospital. Challenge them to be the best possible.

Developing a Team of Leaders

I have written a few times about the importance of focusing your energy on developing a team of leaders. When we have a team of superstar unicorns, the hospital is amazing. But how does one go about doing just that? How can you develop people so they feel like a leader, like a superstar?

You Must Value People Above All Else

This one is hard for many of us. After all, we went into veterinary medicine, where our focus was on veterinary patients. But, as a leader, we now have to put people first.

You will never successfully create a team of leaders if you don't put people first. If your primary focus remains centered around veterinary patients, you will have struggles managing a team of people. People first, and you will create a much better team all around.

Commit Resources to Develop People

I have seldom had a veterinary hospital do this. At least not at first. When I make this suggestion to a hospital, the immediate question I'm asked is, "What is it going to cost?" The answer always is, "Not as much as the return you will get in developing your team."

Have you ever considered having your entire team learn about a profit and loss statement, so they understand how it's impacted? Developing a person is an overlooked area that could truly improve the team dynamics for the remaining members of the team. It costs money to have a great team. Your team isn't going to understand communication unless you invest money and time in the people who are in your hospital.

The hospital needs to commit to developing the different teams within the hospital. How many hospitals pay for a pet first aid course for their veterinary receptionists? What about educating them on basic anatomy and physiology? If you are a veterinary receptionist reading this, I know you just screamed, "yes!"

Paying for continuing education is one thing, but how else can we commit to developing people who will support them and the hospital? By committing resources to our team, we can then start to develop leaders. Have conversations about developing the whole person. We will discuss well-being in the next chapter.

Provide Leadership Opportunities to Your Team

We can't develop a team of leaders if we provide them with no leadership roles. I want to challenge every hospital to redefine what a leadership role is. Some of them are obvious. They come with the title of supervisor, shift lead, medical director, and manager. But what about a leader who is responsible for educating new hires? How about a leader of a medical error reporting committee? Any thought of a leader for the cheer committee? Why shouldn't everyone receive some type of leadership training?

In my first book, I listed several free resources available for those interested in leadership roles. Click on this QR code more to pull up a list of resources on my website. Scroll down on the page and look for "Leadership Resources."

There are countless ways to develop leaders within your hospitals and provide them opportunities to use their leadership skills. You should always be on the lookout for potential leaders and ensure we have opportunities for them.

Place a Value on Leadership

At meetings, we should praise those who go above and beyond. Reward those that may be heads of committees or responsible for certain areas of the hospital for their extra efforts so that the whole team sees the value of leadership. Too often, employees are assigned more responsibility that comes with no extra value. At first, they will feel good contributing more to the hospital, but after time they will wonder why they have received no praise and nothing in return. Elevate those that are leaders in any capacity.

Respect the No

Everyone has boundaries. Leaders and employees are often at odds about trying to protect their boundaries. Too often, veterinary hospitals fail because they assign more tasks to senior veterinary team members even though they were told no. Those tasks often feel like a burden and a punishment. I had a veterinary receptionist call me because her manager asked her to come in on her day off. She said, "no." The manager replied, "I know you don't want to come in on your day off, but you're the best person. Who else is going to do it?" The answer is no. Respect the no.

When you disrespect an individual's boundaries, they will feel unappreciated. Thoughts of "I'm the only one who does everything here" will race through their head. They will become disengaged and burned-out. For many, boundaries are the very thing that keeps them from burning out. Respect the no. If you have someone who always says no, then dive into why. Figure out what they are willing to say yes to. You can't develop leaders in your hospital if you burn them to ruin.

Provide a Safe Environment

Team members should be comfortable taking risks, asking questions, and sharing ideas. This is the importance of teaching teams how to communicate effectively. Veterinary hospitals should encourage open dialogue, and team members should not be made fun of but rather praised for speaking up. Leaders are created because they feel safe sharing their thoughts. No leader was ever effective in remaining quiet. To develop our leaders, we must ensure we have a psychologically safe environment.

Every day, leaders must work towards creating a safe environment for all employees where they can be themselves, voice their thoughts, and be appreciated by their team. They can do this by ensuring they have a healthy work environment that promotes PKH communication and that bigotry, racism, and hatred do not exist.

Actively Commit to Developing Leaders on Your Team

If that is not your focus, it will never happen. Look at every person on your team and figure out where they would be best suited to be a leader in the hospital. Find their superpower, harness it, and utilize it, so it helps both them and the hospital. Everyone has a strength. The minute you elevate their strength is the minute you start creating leaders.

Unleash Your Leaders

You must allow the leaders on your team the autonomy to perform at their best. You must trust them. You will need to check in with them from time to time but stay away from micromanaging them. Don't suffocate your leaders. Instead, set them free with the tools and resources you've provided for them to develop even further.

Care Deeply, but Don't Cross the Line

Even the best employees, at times, are going to struggle. That includes managers. Life is complex, and that also includes home life. Leaders often ask their employees to "leave life at home," which is an impossible ask. Homelife affects work, and work affects the home. The minute leaders recognize the two are intertwined, they can better coach their team. Leaders need to care deeply about each person's success on their team. With that said, it is possible to care too much and even easier to cross an invisible but inappropriate line. How do you know if you care too much or have crossed a line?

I have seen countless leaders turn into psychologists and social workers in an effort to help guide and coach their teams. Unfortunately, while many see it as trying to be helpful, they don't realize that they are prohibiting the person from getting the appropriate help they need while exhausting themselves in the process.

During the global pandemic, stress and anxiety were at an all-time high. Veterinary leaders were challenged daily with teams that were, and continue to be, burned-out and exhausted from work and the stress the pandemic played on every aspect of human life.

It is imperative that hospital leaders break down the stigma around mental health. Mental health refers to one's health and wellness centered around their mental state. It is not mental illness. Mental illness is a diagnosable disorder that can cause psychological and behavioral issues. Mental health is how you are currently doing. It could be good, or it could be bad.

Unfortunately, when a team member approaches a manager about their mental health, too often, leaders think they may be suffering from mental illness. That's rarely the case. Leaders or any employee within a veterinary hospital are ill-equipped to manage mental illness, and very few even have the resources to help mental health when it's struggling.

True mental illness needs to be handled by a professional who is skilled in doing so. Counselors, social workers, and psychologists help those with mental illness with their toolbox of resources. I once spoke to an employee who informed me that their practice manager was exceptional because he was on the same antidepressant drug as her. He understood what she was going through. She then said her practice manager helped her adjust her medication dose. Yes, this is what crossing the line looks like. Your job as a leader is not to manage mental illness. That's a trained professional's job.

As a veterinary leader, your job is to refer individuals on your team with mental health and illness issues to professionals. Be kind and offer compassion to those suffering from mental health concerns. They should know that you support them but that you will never offer suggestions to them on how they should manage their mental health. Keep that line very well-defined at all times. Crossing it could put you in some hot legal water. So how can we support those suffering from mental health and illness?

At some point in everyone's life, their mental health fails. Leaders at all levels need to talk about the importance of mental health at meetings, invite others to talk about it, and actively work to gather resources for their teams. When leaders talk about the importance of mental health throughout the year, they remove the stigma and instead develop a hospital culture focused on the team taking care of themselves. It's okay for team members to be sad, depressed, or angry. All of these feelings are part of mental health. Instead of you being the only resource, your job should be to provide appropriate resources.

When you notice a team member struggling, ask them how they would like to be helped.

- "What would be most helpful to you right now?"
- "How can I support you through this?"
- "Let's discuss our resources and what else might benefit you."

Unfortunately, the last part rarely happens. The leader feels that they can solve the issue. Hours later, tears have occurred, emotions are all over the place, and the leader is just as exhausted as their team member. The main role of any leader dealing with an employee struggling with mental health is to provide the resources that will best help them. None of those resources are you, the leader.

I have found that, particularly during the height of the pandemic, veterinary leaders spent countless hours in what they described as "counseling sessions" for their team members. I once had a practice manager tell me she had just finished a four-hour meeting with a doctor where she coached her through some issues in her personal life. The practice manager was not skilled nor trained in how to be a life coach, counselor, or therapist. Yet, for four hours, she acted as such.

Leaders often fail to draw the line. I certainly don't want you to be callous or uncaring. Instead, I want you to recognize that your primary job is only to listen and provide appropriate resources. You are their manager, not their counselor. If you find yourself providing counseling sessions, the fault lies with you when you are two hours into a meeting with an overly emotional employee who is sharing their deepest home-life secrets.

Over my career, I've had meetings where employees cried or screamed about their problems at home, with family or friends. I could feel their anxiety and stress. I've had a few employees that have struggled with grief when they have lost a parent. My heart was broken alongside theirs. As a leader, you will absorb some of their pain and suffering simply because you care deeply. Getting yourself too involved by trying to fix their problem will do both them and you a disservice. Listen to them but keep your opinions out of it. Get resources that will help them. Let them know you are there to listen and care about them. That's it.

Deborah Riegel, a contributor for the *Harvard Business Review*, writes about creating an environment in which employees feel cared for without managers crossing the line.

Be clear to your employee that you are there to listen to them and offer support. Remind yourself not to cross the line.

Do not judge them. The minute you place judgment on the situation, or their feelings is the minute they will lose trust and respect for you. For example, I once had a veterinary manager friend tell me that when her employee shared with her that her home life was falling apart because she had cheated on her husband, she blurted out, "Why the hell would you do that?!" Suffice it to say, the employee quit shortly after that. The only judging you should do is judging their performance at work.

It's not about you, so don't try to relate to them. If you can relate, ask permission before "stealing the show." Ask, "I had a similar situation once. Do you mind if I share?" Never try to one-up them. What you experienced may be similar, but it's not the same.

Don't ask for too many specifics. You are there to support them and listen. While you may want to know who's getting the house in the divorce settlement, it's not your business to know, nor does it pertain to their job at the hospital.

Be present when they are talking. Cell phones should be silent, and the screen should be face down. Pull yourself away from behind a desk. Sit in front of them and pay attention to what they are saying.

When they ask for advice, you may offer generalizations or broad ideas but avoid formulating a plan. Let them know you are not comfortable offering advice. I once had a medical director confide in me that she spent two hours in a meeting formulating a plan with her employee about how she could best leave her husband and get the most out of the divorce. That's a firm no. Don't give that level of advice.

Instead, say, "It sounds like you are going through a lot. I'm here to listen, but I don't have any advice to offer other than I want you to take care of yourself. Do you have a support system outside of this hospital? If not, I can provide you with some resources." Your advice should be broad and not specific to the situation. Above all, always offer the advice that they need to take care of themselves and provide resources on how to do that.

(Riegel, 2020)

Chapter Eighteen

Cultivating a Healthy Workplace

Work will always be stressful. Every day veterinary medicine deals with life and death situations. Great leaders ensure that they have a healthy workplace environment that centers itself around keeping mental health in top-notch shape.

Protecting mental health in veterinary medicine starts with the individual. If you are in a leadership role, you must take care of yourself first. Veterinary leaders, no matter what tier they are on, not only have to deal with the day-to-day stress of the hospital, but they also have to deal with the stresses of managing a team. Many times, our medical directors still perform surgery and see cases in our hospitals. They are also expected to manage a team of veterinarians. In one day, they will manage a complex surgery while being short-staffed and trying to resolve their team's concerns.

Leaders need to treat themselves with kindness and make efforts to protect their mental health. I see too many leaders who preach to their teams about health and well-being while failing to take care of themselves. Make a date with yourself and be sure not to break it. Spoil yourself just a little bit. Tell your team that you are unavailable because you are taking care of yourself. They will understand. Find healthy ways to reduce your anxiety by grounding yourself in the moments happening right in front of you.

The reality is too many leaders burn out, become bitter shrews, and are unbearable to work with and for because they fail to manage their own well-being. You can't help your team if you are an angry mole. Be your best self so you can then focus your efforts on your team's well-being.

We are fortunate to be working during a time in which health and well-being has been pushed rapidly to the forefront of the industry. The industry is finally talking about the high suicide rates, burnout, and compassion fatigue that plagues veterinary medicine. It's long overdue, but better late than never. In addition, the pandemic has caused an even louder discussion on the importance of mental health. There are countless online support groups and continuing education offerings centered around mental health. In addition, you can find blogs and podcasts to help you navigate your way to improved mental health.

Toxic Positivity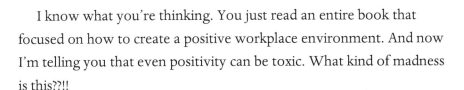

I know what you're thinking. You just read an entire book that focused on how to create a positive workplace environment. And now I'm telling you that even positivity can be toxic. What kind of madness is this??!!

Toxic positivity is a relatively new term that takes positivity and pushes it to an unhealthy level. Unfortunately, many industries, including veterinary medicine, have seen an increase in negative workplace environments. In an effort to combat the negativity, employers have started to focus on positive workplace environments. This sounds like a good thing, but how positivity is introduced into some environments can be harmful and damaging.

Employees are told to "be positive" and "get on board with the amazing change." Culture champions are introduced, and programs are implemented. Catchy phrases, slogans, and even paraphernalia start trickling into and onto break rooms, walls, clothing, and water bottles. Most of the time, the team is excited about the new wave of positivity.

Leaders are smiling, patting people on the back, and exaggerated statements of admiration fill the hallways.

The hospital has done it! Positivity has filled every nook and cranny. The team is happier. There is little to no gossip. People are smiling once again. Yahoo!! The hard work has paid off.

But then Tom walks into his manager's office. He has a concern. He feels that the new veterinary assistant isn't performing well and may not be the right fit for the hospital. What he is saying is not positive.

His manager replies, "You need to be patient and kind. She's new. Have you made sure you helped her? Are you doing the best you can with training her?" Tom says he really has tried, but he's still struggling with the new employee.

His manager concludes the meeting with, "She's part of our family, and we don't give up on family. How about you find a better way to welcome her in?" Tom leaves the meeting discouraged. Two weeks later, the new employee made a serious medical mistake. Tom returns to his manager's office with an increased level of concern.

The manager replies, "Remember, she's still fairly new. The rest of the team loves her, and she's so positive. Let's find a way to help her. After all, she has a seat on our happy bus!"

At this point, Tom leaves and vents to a few of his coworkers. He's concerned this new employee may kill a patient. He's frustrated and doesn't know what to do. A few days later, Tom is called into the office.

"Tom, I have some concerns. A few employees have told me you are being negative about our new hire. This isn't the culture we have here. I think you're bringing in some of your past baggage from your other toxic hospitals. Our culture is supportive, positive, and welcoming to new hires. I was looking at our culture scale rating system, and you are about a seven to eight instead of an amazing nine to ten. We need our employees to be a nine to ten on our positive culture scale. I'd love for you to read our happiness handbook again and consider if you are the right fit for our culture."

Toxic positivity is positivity taken to an extreme. It is an unhealthy obsession with positivity where an individual cannot tolerate anything negative or uncomfortable. When it happens in our workplace environment, it deprives us of the ability to look at negative, uncomfortable things. Leaders decide to eliminate all the bad and negative things by closing the door to healthy debate, criticism, and conflict. Managers are disillusioned that "nothing is wrong," and should anyone have a concern, they must be the problem. After all, the hospital is perfect, and everyone is happy. They minimize the issues, dismiss concerns and discipline anyone who dare utters a negative word. Management only sees unicorns and rainbows, but the reality is the unicorns are vomiting and shitting all over the hospital, and it turns out that's not a great thing after all.

Unfortunately, veterinary hospitals are not immune to this extreme form of positivity turn toxic. Toxic positivity is becoming so mainstream that psychologists are studying it, and business websites like Harvard Business Review and Forbes are writing about it.

A Forbes contributor wrote, "Toxic positivity is in effect putting on blinders, and it serves to increase negative emotions and isolate those around you. While we all recognize the peppy cheerleader in the group, and sometimes cheerleading does help you get through the day, it's important to set safe boundaries for yourself and those you work with to enable transparency and collaboration. Let's embrace authentic communication and work together to create healthy cultures of dissenting and diverse opinions (Colella-Graham, 2022)."

Ramming positivity down the team's throat will only cause it to backfire. It needs to be introduced genuinely. If it feels like employees must agree 100% with everything in order to feel like they belong, it's likely toxic. If individuals are not comfortable voicing concerns, because they fear going against the beliefs of the group, then the positivity is not real.

Toxic positivity shuts down change and quiets those with concerns. The team is left walking around agreeing with bad policies and harmful procedures because if they try to voice concerns they are told they are the problem, not the bad or harmful policy. They say too much of anything can be a bad thing, and in this case, it's positivity. We want our team on board with the positive changes we are doing, but we cannot dismiss concerns and criticism.

Psychological Safety

Leaders should not only want but recognize they need a psychologically safe workplace environment. Countless studies have found that more creative solutions will occur when there is more diversity of thought, and individuals feel comfortable sharing ideas. Psychological safety occurs when members of a team do not embarrass, reject, or punish others for speaking up. It is imperative that every veterinary hospital is a psychologically safe workplace.

According to a Gallup poll in 2017, three out of 10 employees strongly agreed that their opinions don't count at work (Dvorak, Pendell, 2019). And remote work settings (which are much more common now, given the global COVID pandemic) have worsened the problem, particularly for women.

During the pandemic, many workers found themselves on virtual calls. Even within a digital space, psychological safety can struggle. Catalyst conducted a survey in 2020, which found one in five women reported feeling overlooked or ignored during video meetings (Connley, 2020).

There are four stages a person must go through to achieve Psychological Safety (Clark, 2020).

Four Stages of Psychological Safety

Stage 1: Inclusion Safety:

In this stage the person feels included. They can be who they are and feel accepted by others.

Stage 2: Learner Safety:

The individual feels safe asking questions and receiving feedback. They learn they can make mistakes and it's okay.

Stage 3: Contributor Safety:

The individual feels safe using their skills and knowledge to make a meaningful contribution. They are giving back in this stage.

Stage 4: Challenger Safety:

In this stage the individual feels safe to speak up and challenge the status quo when they think there is an opportunity to change or improve.

Much of what we have discussed so far in this book helps to promote psychological safety. It's important leaders make psychological safety a priority. Talk to your teams about it, and be sure you model the behaviors you want to see for your team.

Teaching PKH communication will grow psychological safety within your team. It's centered on kindness, politeness, and honesty. Hospitals that educate their teams on healthy communication styles will more likely have team members with the courage to speak the truth.

Praise individuals who challenge the norms. Provide a creative space for when challenge occurs. Leaders who stifle conversations because "it's how it's done" reduce psychological safety in the workplace.

Ensure teams are educated on DEI. Embrace productive conflict. Encourage dialogue and healthy debate. Work to resolve conflicts productively. When people feel safe to speak up and challenge, they will be more likely to contribute more. It's equally important that these individuals respect when a decision is made and agree to disagree.

Veterinary Social Workers

Veterinary medicine has started to embrace the field of social work. Licensed social workers are trained to handle and respond to mental health crises, navigate the many layers of conflict resolution, and increase communication skills in teams. More and more veterinary hospitals are employing licensed social workers as a member of their team. There's no downside to doing so. Human medicine professionals started working alongside and utilizing social workers themselves decades ago. It's about time veterinary medicine catches up.

Having had the amazing opportunity and experience of working alongside veterinary licensed social workers, I can confidently say that hiring a licensed social worker on your team will help decrease the daily mental stress and anxiety individuals feel. They are trained in conflict management and communication skills and can help coach and guide your team to improve those competencies.

Unfortunately, I have found that many employees who have available veterinary social workers are often hesitant to utilize them. This is because of the stigma about mental health and a lack of understanding of what a social worker can do.

When you suggest to an individual that they talk to someone about their mental health, many assume you think they have a mental illness. Again, these two terms are separate. I will admit that, at times, I have struggled with my own mental health. At times I've been depressed, and I've struggled with managing anxiety. I've been sad and angry for periods of time in my life. Most everyone has.

I gather you have struggled with yours. We likely both have experienced times where we had weeks of grief, anger, bouts of depression, lack of motivation, and/or overindulgence. It's safe to say that I may have gone through all these mental health struggles on more than one occasion. None of these things meant I was mentally ill, but just that I struggled with my mental health like most others. Talking to someone trained and with a license to improve your mental health is always beneficial, yet there is still a stigma in doing so.

In human medicine, doctors and nurses work alongside social workers every day. I gather one day, it will eventually become the norm in veterinary medicine. Still, it will take time for the stigma to decrease and for more hospitals to embrace social workers to help round out their teams.

It's interesting because we have no problem asking someone how they broke their leg and how long the recovery will be. We often readily offer help to individuals with a medical illness or injury. However, when it comes to mental health issues and the struggles that we all have gone through, we do our best to change the subject, ignore them or run away from them.

As a leader, I was not always the best in having a hospital environment where mental health was freely discussed. As my leadership skills grew, I worked to help create a safe environment for my team. As an instructor for Mental Health First Aid (MentalHealthFirstAid.org), an international program focused on decreasing the stigma and opening up conversations, I can see the importance and value in conversations within the hospital.

As a leader, it is your job to create a culture where team members are comfortable asking each other, "You don't seem like yourself. Is everything okay?" From there, we need to teach ourselves and our teams that each of us can be an ear and a shoulder to lean on. Everyone can be a support system for those who need it, but no one is the solution to the issue. Everyone has the ability to provide resources and point individuals to the care and help they need. Together we can support and lift each other up and let those trained in mental health do the rest.

Steps to Creating a Healthy Culture

It starts when leaders commit to creating a healthy workplace environment. The Center for Disease Control has an area on its website that provides tools and resources for employers looking to develop a plan for their hospitals. The CDC states, "Maintaining a healthier workforce…will also positively impact many indirect costs such as absenteeism and worker productivity" (2021).

One of the best ways of ensuring that our hard efforts in creating a healthy and happy team of unicorns doesn't vanish is to create a healthy workplace environment centered around well-being. Every hospital needs to develop a plan. Simply talking about it is not sufficient. Your team needs to know that you are dedicated to their mental health. Many team members will probably embrace the idea and offer to help develop a program with leadership. Create a committee. The program needs to be evaluated yearly to see what else could be offered, what is working, and what may need improvement.

I'll pause here and call out those of you who believe that an employer creating a hospital centered on well-being is poo-poo hogwash. I can hear some of you saying, "In my day, we went to work and did our jobs. We dealt with our emotions at home." Good for you. I'm here to tell you that it likely wasn't the healthiest way of managing. When employers invest in the well-being of those who work for them, productivity increases, and turnover and negativity decrease. It's that simple.

During the pandemic, many veterinary hospitals started seeing clients by curbside only. Clients needed to wait in their vehicle while a veterinary assistant or technician brought the pet inside for medical treatment and care and eventually returned the pet to the car. By decreasing the number of people entering the hospital, veterinary teams found they could keep themselves safer. Curbside had some pros but some cons as well.

Since exam rooms were no longer being utilized, many hospitals got creative and turned them into wellness rooms. These rooms contain soft chairs, dim lighting, sound machines, aromatherapy, and, in some cases, punching bags. The leadership that created these rooms for their teams showed a dedication to preserving their mental health during such a stressful time. I challenge all hospitals to find a place to create a calm, inviting, well-being room that allows the employees to unwind.

I would encourage all leaders to develop a committee focused on the health and well-being of the team in the hospital. Meeting a few times a year to evaluate the plan is a good way to keep the committee engaged. Every veterinary employee should feel like their hospital genuinely cares about their health and well-being.

The CDC offers a comprehensive list of resources to create your hospital wellness plan. It first suggests starting by performing a workplace health assessment. The CDC has surveys and assessment tools on its website to help you assess your hospital. You can find these resources on cdc.gov/workplacehealthpromotion. Click on Workplace Health Model to find the assessment tools. You can also be directed to the website by scanning this QR code:

The second step is to create your wellness program. This is usually fun and should involve a diverse group of hospital team members. Brainstorming and developing a plan is also a great team builder. People get excited about creating a program that will help to reduce stress and promote health in the hospital. While there is no perfect wellness plan that will fit every hospital, here are some suggestions to start developing your own. You can find an abbreviated checklist in Appendix Three of this book to help you check off all the boxes in creating and implementing a wellness plan in your hospital.

Provide Health Insurance

It's probably not what you thought I would list first, but it's important that all employees have a good healthcare program. Many bad health insurance options exist, so ensure your hospital's plan is top-notch. It should include prevention and treatment options. Many plans cover mental illness and mental health by including counseling in the plan. More and more health insurance companies focus on prevention by offering discounts to gyms, online well-being apps, and even wellness retreat discounts. Make sure your health insurance plan covers the big stuff but also takes care of the entire person, including their mental health.

Encourage Health

Even though veterinary employees are busy walking around and standing on their feet daily, many struggle with being healthy. Many veterinary professionals don't eat the best because they are constantly grabbing a quick bite to eat, usually centered around snacking. Creating healthy challenges in the hospital, so long as they are not focused on body shaming and are not mandatory, can be a great way to encourage individuals to get healthy. I know hospitals that have purchased physical fitness monitors (step trackers, Fitbits, etc.) for everyone. They encourage people to join teams, and they award prizes. It should never be mandatory but certainly encouraged.

Years ago, I had countless smokers on my team. As a runner and someone who scuba dives, I value my lungs immensely. I rely on them to do outdoor physical activity almost every day. For those reasons, I discourage people from smoking, but I also saw the veterinary technicians and assistants on my team spending their hard-earned money on an addiction. I knew that many of them struggled to pay their monthly rent or car payments. Watching them spend their money on cigarettes broke my heart. I wanted them to get healthier.

Despite my coming from a place of kindness, no one seemed to be budging when it came to ceasing their smoking habit. I informed the team that I would take them all out to a restaurant to celebrate if even one individual could stop smoking for an entire month. For one team member, this worked. She had talked about wanting to quit for years, and this was the kind of motivation that she needed.

Sure enough, she stopped smoking, and after 30 days, I threw the biggest party. The entire break room was decked out for the celebration, complete with tons of snacks to munch on. The entire team congratulated her, even those who were still smoking. The team was impressed with what she had accomplished. There was no shaming of those that had not quit yet. It was just pure celebration for this one individual that had. The party then moved to a restaurant where they overindulged with a lot of Italian food. To date, this individual has never picked up a cigarette since. Get creative and encourage teams to be healthier.

The Hospital Should Look Healthy

A neat, tidy, and organized working environment has been proven to decrease mental stress. Feng shui is a modern-day practice originating from ancient China, which claims to use positive energy forces to create a more Zen atmosphere between individuals and their surrounding environment. So why can't veterinary hospitals have a little feng shui?

The saying, "Cleanliness is next to godliness," has some truth in it. People feel less stressed when things are neat and tidy.

I certainly don't want the staff to get upset about every mess that occurs daily, but employees should recognize that an organized and clean work environment will improve their mental stress. This includes the owners recognizing it too. When I walk into a hospital that is falling apart and is filthy, I feel more stressed. The workplace environment should be kept up to date, modern, and as clean as possible. Trust me; it improves mental health. The hospital should be an appealing place to work in, not gross and dirty.

Place visual reminders promoting health and well-being throughout the veterinary hospital. For example, the front office area is a wonderful place to maintain live plants or even an aquarium. Both have been shown to decrease mental stress.

To me, having visual reminders of joy and happiness help to decrease stress in any workplace environment. So why not have a unicorn on a shelf in the main treatment area? Then, switch it out every month. The next month it's a penguin. The month after that, maybe it's a panda. Just something to make the team smile.

I've always encouraged music to be played in the hospital so long as it's appropriate and everyone enjoys it. Angry music with lots of curse words probably should be avoided, but general pop and rock are diverse enough to make everyone happy and reduce stress.

Support Full Breaks

Yes! Veterinary medical leaders and professionals are terrible at this. This is a two-fold problem. First, I can't even believe that some veterinary managers and supervisors tell their teams that they cannot take breaks. It's inexcusable and illegal. It makes me angry. Yet, at least several times a year, I read either online or hear directly from veterinary employees who have been told that they are not permitted to take a break unless every veterinary patient and client has been cared for. Since it is a constant revolving door of never-ending patient tasks and client interactions, teams never get any breaks. Report these employers to the labor board if you're reading this.

I know of even more than just a few hospitals that have required their employees to sign forms stating that they are "giving away their breaks" so they cannot be sued. After all, if employees willingly give up their breaks, it must be legal, right? Just stop. I hope no one who is reading this is telling their teams they can't take breaks. You are breaking state laws. Even if your state allows some crazy horse-dung such as this, you are morally and ethically illegal.

Breaks need to be mandatory, and they need to occur. Everyone in veterinary medicine recognizes that they may have to forgo their break at some point. This is particularly true in emergency medicine. When you have emergency after emergency barreling down upon you and patients are legitimately dying, you may not have time to sit down and enjoy a real formal break. There are countless times when I have worked and never sat down because the pets in my care were critical. However, those days need to be few and extremely far between. When they do occur, leadership needs to acknowledge that it's not ideal. They need to work towards solutions for the future so that when another busy day occurs, employees can take breaks.

The other part of this problem is the veterinary professionals themselves. In every hospital I have ever worked, a particular number of veterinary team members refuse to take breaks. They claim they cannot because they need to be there for their veterinary patients. They feel guilty when they step away from the hospital floor to care for themselves. They feel they are inadequate team members because they have decided to ingest food. Ultimately, part of the blame must lie with the employee when they fail to take their break if leadership has done their best to provide one.

Veterinary leaders need to talk to individuals who are not taking breaks. They also need to lead by example. When technician managers don't take breaks but encourage their team to, the team worries that their manager may think less of them. After all, their boss doesn't need to take a break, so why should they? Leaders must lead by example by taking a break. Show them it is okay to take a break and take care of yourself.

Leaders should teach teams how to relax during their break time. This includes getting off the clinic floor, not talking about work, reading something fun, taking a brief walk outdoors, or playing an online game. Teaching teams how to quickly get their mind off of work is important. When teams are quickly eating food but still thinking about work, they're not taking a break; instead, they are doing a disservice to themselves. Taking a break means making a conscious effort to stop thinking about work. When the brain stops thinking about work, it can relax. When teams don't take care of themselves, they are more likely to make medical mistakes, suffer burnout, snap at each other, and disengage from their job.

Consider making your breakroom more inviting. Several years ago, I visited a hospital whose breakroom consisted of three hard plastic chairs, a small mini fridge, and a dirty old microwave. The breakroom was in a hallway that contained the freezers where deceased pets were stored before the pet cemetery picked them up. It was no wonder why no employee ever wanted to go sit in the "breakroom." They were eating off of the freezers! I wish I could say this is an extreme example, but it is not. Sadly, I've run across this type of atrocity in multiple hospitals.

You need to have a welcoming break room. It needs to be centered around relaxation, with comfortable chairs and tables for food and eating. Lighting should be warm and inviting and if possible, having windows that show the outside is important in a healthy break room environment. Nice photos on the wall, maybe an aquarium, or even some live plants will help encourage employees to find true relaxation during their break time.

Supply Healthy Snacks/Meals

No matter where the veterinary hospital is in the world, there are snacks on the break room table full of sugar and fat. The veterinary break room is a cesspool of unhealthy food. I will admit that I am a chocoholic and love sugar as if it should be an actual food group, but the reality is it's not a healthy diet.

When hospitals create wellness programs, they need to make a conscious effort to fuel their team with healthy food such as vegetables, fruits, and nuts instead of unhealthy snacks and candy. Most vending machine companies offer healthier options, so request that your company stocks the machine with granola bars, nuts, and water. While pizza is an easy and often cheap meal that leaders buy for their team, it's not healthy. Instead, consider salads and other less processed foods if you are inclined to buy a meal for the team.

Promote Work-Life Balance

Leaders must advertise the benefits of focusing on mental health and wellness. These same leaders must be fully engaged in all aspects of the well-being program to ensure the best buy-in from the hospital team. Too often, leaders poo-poo wellness programs. Leaders must lead by example and buy into creating a healthy workplace environment.

Employees should leave work at the door when they go home for the day. This includes leaders. It's not natural to be on call 24 hours a day, seven days a week. If leaders catch employees responding to emails while off the clock, they should discourage them from doing so in a kind but firm way.

Leaders also need to respect employees when at home. I just read through a post on Facebook where over 50 overnight employees said their managers would regularly call or text them while they were sleeping during the day. This is completely disrespectful. Don't bother your employee outside of work unless it's an emergency!

When employees come to work in the morning, leaders should ask what they did that was fun the night before. Checking in to ensure that your employees are taking care of themselves is important. They may not engage in something relaxing and fun every day, but it's important that leaders encourage this. They can show teams that it is important to promote a healthy work-life balance by taking care of themselves.

Leaders should talk to their teams about how they had a weekend to relax or did something ridiculously fun and silly. When leaders only talk about how they live and breathe the veterinary hospital every waking moment, they discourage others from taking care of themselves. Leaders must encourage themselves and their entire team to relax and enjoy life outside of work.

Too often, we see team members that go away on vacation and feel guilty about it. Then, they return to work and don't want to talk about the fun time they just had because others were working. They're embarrassed because they enjoyed life outside of work. Leaders need to celebrate when people take breaks, go on vacation and enjoy life. The team should be excited to hear about what others are doing to enjoy life outside of work. Leaders need to promote a healthy work and life balance every day.

Implement the Program

There are probably countless other fantastic ideas that you can incorporate into your wellness program. I hope that the ideas listed inspire you to start creating your own. However, no matter how well-thought-out it may be, implementing a program can be a struggle in a hospital. Let's face it. Many veterinary employees are a bit salty and snarky. When you tell them they need to take care of their health and well-being, you are often met with, "I'm fine," or, "If you force me to meditate, I'll quit." Yet, veterinary medicine has one of the highest burnout and suicide rates of any profession in the world. Clearly, veterinary professionals are not okay despite them saying, "they're fine."

As previously stated, leadership needs to be 100% bought in for any program to be successful. If leaders are dismissive or think it is unnecessary, so will employees. Rolling out a program will require meetings and sometimes even incentives. If leadership is excited about it, then their enthusiasm is usually contagious. The hospital is not forcing employees to do anything, merely providing them resources if they choose to partake in them.

I have seen wellness programs fail because they make things mandatory for employees. In this past year alone, I watched countless hospitals make yoga sessions mandatory for all employees. Some employees embraced the sessions, but many felt it was a burden and became even more disgruntled and disengaged.

If the wellness program stresses out the employees, it has the opposite intended effect. Everything in the wellness program should be made available to all employees but not be mandatory. This will help with the buy-in. If only a few employees partake in a certain event and enjoy it, the word will spread. I do think that offering yoga classes or meditation classes to veterinary employees can be hugely beneficial. Hospitals just can't make them mandatory.

Instead of rolling out the entire program in one lump sum, introduce one concept at a time. Commit for an entire year that the hospital will focus on well-being. Throughout the year, roll out different aspects of the program for employees to enjoy.

Review the Program

Lastly, hospitals need to plan to evaluate their well-being program. There is no sense in dumping money and resources into something failing or not being utilized by the team. Instead, hospitals need to figure out what would work better. Not having a well-being program is not an option. It's the year 2022 or later, people. Every human healthcare facility and moderate to large size company has a well-being program for their employees. Veterinary medicine needs to get on board.

The CDC offers a workplace health program checklist to review and monitor your program's progress. You can find it in the same link which I listed before. Programs should be evaluated for sustainability over time, how employees and leadership view them, and the return on investment. All hospitals should want to invest in the well-being of their employees, but there is a difference between investing and wasting money. For example, if a hospital pays for an online app centered around health and well-being and no one uses it, it's a waste of money.

Survey the team to gauge whether they feel less stressed, anxious and feel their work-life balance has improved. The survey should focus on questions centered around how people feel, whether or not they are using particular resources, and identifying potential gaps in the current offerings.

There is no perfect well-being plan for every hospital, but we must start by developing one and then modifying it to fit our hospital's needs. One of the most important steps in changing a hospital's culture from toxic to one full of unicorns is when leaders create a healthy workplace environment because they show they care deeply about the team.

End Notes

Turning a toxic team around takes a lot of time and effort. There is no magic wand that will fix your team overnight. The key is to start with the acknowledgment that the team is broken. When we can admit there is failure, we can then work towards solutions.

Figure out what is wrong. Work to identify the issues. Analyze what should be worked on first. Leave the emotion out of it. Admit there's a problem and develop a plan to solve it. Communicate the plan to your team. Now that you have got their attention, that change may happen.

Educate your team on how to communicate kindly to each other. They need to embrace the strengths of each one of their team members and learn to provide healthy criticism when necessary.

Start by developing the individuals. Then, focus on that individual's career in the future. Manage the toxic traits that an individual may have and for those who are already unicorns, elevate them further. Use not only the tools and resources provided in this book but continue to build upon them with even more knowledge.

It may seem like an impossible task to turn a toxic team around, but I can assure you it is not. It can be one of the most rewarding parts of your career if you're willing to put in the work. Once your hospital is in a good place, keep it that way. Perform routine maintenance throughout the year. Keep developing each one of your team members. Identify issues early, so the team doesn't fall into a vat of poison.

In the end, you will have a team of unicorns. And who doesn't want unicorns? Only the toxic people don't want them, and we don't want the toxic people in our hospitals.

Conclusion

Throughout this book, I thought I must be mad to ever start embarking on a second book right after finishing the first one. There were moments I flat-out hated this book, but one thing kept me going: the veterinary professionals. Every post I saw and every article I read centered on toxicity are the very reasons I kept writing this book.

I wrote this book for everyone who has found themselves in a bad working environment. Even if you are not in one now, I hope you found a bit here or there that inspires you and helps you on your veterinary journey.

Stopping toxicity and negativity starts with each one of us. We must stop and look inward when we struggle to enjoy this beautiful profession. It's up to each one of us to figure out what we need to be happy. We can no longer wait for individuals to create our happiness. This is the time we make our own.

If you're in a leadership role and are currently working in a less-than-desirable hospital environment, I hope this book empowers you to solve the issues. You have an immense responsibility to be the driver of change in your hospital. It's not just you that needs to help the hospital; it's up to each one of your employees as well. It is imperative you find a way to get them on board with wanting change and helping you to obtain that change.

We have all experienced some shit since the year known as 2020. But, we have also built resiliency and overcome some fairly large obstacles. We know now, more than ever, that things can get better even in the darkest of times. Each one of us can make a difference in our hospitals. I want every veterinary employee to strive toward eliminating toxicity in our hospitals.

I stand by my continued statement that we all work in the best career in the world. We get to save pet lives. Let's all do that in healthy workplace environments. This job is hard enough, so it's imperative we come together and work to improve the culture we work in.

I want to thank all of you for your work, the endless emotional and physical toil you give to save pet lives, and the amazing gifts you give to every pet owner. I stand in awe of this entire profession and am humbled to be just a small part of it. This book's only purpose was to help, even if it is just a tiny bit, the very profession that I love so deeply. You are all the inspiration for this book. Keep on being the unicorns you are.

Definitions

3-1 Development Plan: A year-round development plan that focuses on meeting with the team member three times a year to develop the individual and once to present the 360-feedback compiled. p. 273

3F & 3Cs: Importance of incorporating these into each coaching conversation: Clear, Collaborative, Coordinated and Frequent, Focused, Future-Oriented. p. 267

360-Feedback: A feedback development system focused on the employee receiving feedback from coworkers, the manager reviewing the employee, and the employee reviewing themselves. The manager receives all feedback and compiles it in a document to present to the employee. p. 276

Behavior: Defines a person's conduct and is learned and developed over the years. It can change and be modified. Personality may play a part in driving behavior. p. 226

BRAVING: An acronym Brené Brown created to remind you of the seven elements every leader needs to create trust with their employees. p. 74

Clubhouse Rules: Agreed upon rules on how individuals want to be communicated to during a conflict. p. 208

Cycle of Toxicity: This cycle starts when a new hire enters the hospital and starts to feel an increase in workload without any praise or acknowledgment for their work. They then feel unappreciated and conclude they aren't being compensated enough. p. 13

Emotional bank account (EBA): Each person has a bank account we can deposit into (by providing kindness) or withdraw from (harsh/negative statements). p. 106

Emotional Intelligence (EQ): The term for all the feeling, processing, and communicating of emotions that one does between themselves and others. p. 162, 225

Intellectual Humility: The acceptance that one's beliefs, opinions, thoughts, and intellect could be wrong. The ability to be open to new ideas and thoughts from others. p. 198

Personality: This is what makes an individual unique and different from others. A personality helps to drive a person's behavior and is influenced by genetics and the environment in which they grew up. p. 224

PKH: Polite, Kind & Honest: A form of communication that promotes kindness and compassion while communicating effectively by being honest. p. 93

Psychological Safety: When members of a team do not embarrass, reject, or punish others for speaking up. It's a safe environment for people to share ideas and be themselves. p. 349

Silo Statements: Statements that separate employees or groups away from others by putting them into a "silo." p. 232

Ten Commandments of Confrontation: Ten rules of how to treat one another during a conflict. p. 210

Toxic Positivity: An unhealthy obsession with positivity where the individual cannot tolerate anything negative or uncomfortable. p. 346

Appendix One:

Changing the Culture Steps

This is an abbreviated step-by-step guide for Chapter Seven.
For full details, please review Chapter Seven.

STEP ONE: Admit There's an Issue in a Meeting

Host a meeting centered around acknowledging the issues. Leaders must listen only. The goal is to hear from the team what needs to be improved upon.

Method one: Hybrid method at a Meeting
Team voices their concerns but has written option if preferred.

Method Two: Silent Conversation at a Meeting
Team writes down their concerns and turns them in. Leadership compiles information and looks for trends.

Method Three: Engagement Survey Online
Leadership first conveys their commitment to change and informs the team that they will be sent an engagement survey that will be anonymous. Then, leadership compiles the data and provides detailed responses at an in-person meeting.
Click this QR code to be directed to an example of an engagement survey.

After Obtaining the Information

Thank them for sharing, and set a follow-up meeting as the next step. Schedule the next meeting no more than three weeks from the first one.

Review the Concerns

Have the leadership team review all the concerns. Identify trends. Choose 2-3 concerns you will be committed to improving first. One of those issues will be communication. Write down plans. I would suggest adding in communication as one of the first things to start working on.

STEP TWO: Tackle a Few Concerns

Host your second meeting. Review the trends with the team and discuss which 2-3 issues the leadership team will work to improve first. Likely one of those concerns will be communication. To get buy-in, ask the team, "Do you think we need to work on our communication as a team?" The answer will likely be a unified "yes." This will open the door to introducing PKH communication. Address the other concerns during this meeting and share a detailed plan with the team.

STEP THREE: Receive & Share Feedback About Yourself

One step in change is allowing yourself to be vulnerable and open to feedback from every team member. Changing a team's culture starts with you wanting to be the best leader you can be. You may want to start attacking the needed change, but it's always better to start with yourself. Get feedback from the team and share that feedback with the entire group. Let them know how you are going to tackle your own growth. Consider a book club requiring them to read a book focused on developing their communication skills.

STEP FOUR: Teach the Team to Give & Receive Compliments

There are various ways to teach your team to give and receive compliments. Review Chapter Seven for examples. The goal is to teach teams how to give and receive compliments. It feels good and boosts morale. Unfortunately, while this skill seems simple enough, many toxic teams have lost the ability to provide praise to each other.

STEP FIVE: Start Bringing in the Honesty

Host 1:1 individual meetings in which you talk about areas of improvement and career development plans. This can be done in group meetings in which you act as the mediator, and each team member is coached on how to deliver and receive healthy criticism.

Coaching a team about how to have healthy communication never stops. Practice, practice, practice! Keep your team thinking daily about their interactions with each other while striving towards healthier communication.

Throughout these steps, you are revisiting your plan to impact change, reevaluating what is working or needs improvement, and keeping the team informed.

Timeline for Change

First Month

1) Hold a team meeting. Focus on the needed change. Choose a method to collect and analyze data.

2) Meeting with Leadership: Compile data, analyze and look for trends. Choose 2-3 items for change. Develop a detailed plan for each item.

Second Month

1) Meet with the team to share the data collected and the items that will be focused on.

2) Have 1:1 conversations with the team focused on what leaders could do better. This is leadership's time to listen and the team's time to help coach the leader.

3) Compile the information from the meetings, look for trends and identify 2-3 items you commit to improving for yourself.

Third Month

1) Hold a team meeting. Provide the feedback you received for yourself and share your commitment with them about your leadership change. Allow the team to ask any questions. Prepare them that the next step is for them to take on the challenge discussed at the next meeting.

2) Revisit where the team is in the original 2-3 items and how the change is coming along.

Fourth - Fifth Month

1) If you require them to read a book on communication, provide them two months to finish it. Reading a book will only make this next step easier.

2) Review Chapter Seven on various ways to coach your team on how to deliver and receive praise. During this meeting, you will encourage each team member to participate in a praise activity.

3) Revisit where the team is in the original 2-3 items and how the change is coming along.

Two Months Later (Months Six – Seven)

1) The team is now prepared to have honesty introduced. Chapter Seven has various ways to coach how best to receive and give healthy criticism.

2) Revisit where the team is in the original 2-3 items and how the change is coming along.

Seven – Twelve Months

1) Change never stops! Keep reevaluating your plan. What other items identified by the team should you start tackling? What about another engagement survey? Keep analyzing, asking the team for feedback, and developing plans. Focus on the unicorns.

Appendix Two:

3-1 Development Plan Steps & Example

STEP ONE: Three Meetings Throughout the Year

The three in the 3-1 involves you as a manager meeting three times a year for 30 to 60 minutes to focus on the employee's goals and performance. Ideally, meet once a quarter.

STEP TWO: 360-Feedback

You must have a team dedicated to helping each other by offering kind feedback, not cruel feedback. If you do not, then fix the communication of the team first. The 360-Feedback can backfire if the team is not in the right place to give or receive it.

How to Perform 360-Feedback

First part: Employee reviews themselves

Questions should be centered around their performance and goals for the future.

Second part: Employees review each other

Using a point scale system to calculate the average per section will make it more objective. The review should be no more than 25 questions in length but allow employees to provide more detail if needed.

Third part: Manager reviews employee

Manager uses the same form as employees. You should compile all the data, pull out any harsh comments, look for themes and deliver the information politely and kindly to the employee.

POSSIBLE STEP THREE:

Consider one follow-up meeting focused on the 360-feedback. This meeting may be where you coach a particular area or present a change in salary with an explanation as to why.

Sample Questions for Veterinary Employee Self-Review

1) Please list your top three strengths.

2) Please list your top three areas for improvement.

3) How satisfied are you with your overall job performance here?

     Scale: 1 (not at all) 2 3 4 5 (very happy)

4) What do you want to learn more about?

5) Where do you see your career taking you, or what is a goal you have for yourself here?

6) How satisfied are you with your career?

     Scale: 1 (not at all) 2 3 4 5 (very happy)

7) What is one thing you want to improve upon?

Sample Questions for Employee Hospital Review

This can act as a mini-engagement survey once a year.

1) What are your three most favorite things about working here?

2) What are your three least favorite things about working here?

3) Name one thing you would want to change here and how you would fix it.

4) Do you feel like your skills are utilized here?   Yes No

5) How stressful do you feel your job is?

    Scale: 1 (not at all) 2 3 4 5 (super stressful)

6) Do you feel appreciated here?

    Scale: 1 (not at all) 2 3 4 5 (yes, definitely)

7) Do you feel your direct manager supports a healthy working environment?

    Scale: 1 (not at all) 2 3 4 5 (yes, definitely)

8) Do you feel there is a healthy working environment?

    Scale: 1 (not at all) 2 3 4 5 (yes, definitely)

9) What could be done to make your job better/easier?

10) Do you have any other feedback?

Manager & Coworkers Review Employee
Sample Questions

Recommend having a minimum of 3 employees fill out a survey for a particular coworker. Survey is broken down into 8 categories of the top competencies.

Point Scale:
1 (Not at all)
2
3
4
5 (Yes, definitely)

Dependability

- Calls if running late for a shift
- Is a teammate I can depend on

Initiative:

- Able to complete tasks with little or no supervision
- Is a teammate who I consider helpful
- Asks questions when they don't understand something

Job Knowledge

- Continuously improves their knowledge
- Overall medical knowledge is great
- Provides excellent nursing care
- Has excellent technician skills

Problem Solving

- Deals well with stress
- When it's busy, this person is organized and focused
- Is someone who is a great problem-solver
- I go to this person to ask for their opinion if there is a problem
- Delegates work when necessary and does so appropriately

Client Skills

- Polite to all clients no matter the situation
- Able to handle difficult client interactions with ease

Teamwork/Leadership Skills

- Willing to train others
- Has a positive attitude
- Helps to resolve conflict
- Demonstrates compassion and care to all pets
- Open to other people's ideas and opinions.
- Exhibits friendliness, politeness, and respect to:
    - Technicians/Nurses
    - Veterinarians
    - Client Service Representatives
    - Leadership
    - All Others

Areas This Employee Excels In

This is an open area for them to convey their thoughts.

Areas for Improvement

This is an open area for them to convey their thoughts.

Appendix Three:

Wellness Plan Checklist

☐ Provide Health Insurance: Is it the best? Can it be better?

☐ Encourage Health: Provide healthy food. Create voluntary health challenges.

☐ Hospital Should Look Healthy: Tidy up your hospital space so it looks and feels better. It should be an appealing place to work in, not gross and dirty. Place happiness throughout the hospital. Consider plants, stuffed animals, or other things to spark a smile.

☐ Support Full Breaks: Breaks must be mandatory in every hospital. Stop allowing employees to skip theirs. Ensure you have an inviting breakroom.

☐ Supply Healthy Snacks And/Or Meals: Fuel the team with healthy options.

☐ Promote Work-Life Balance: Praise individuals who take time off. Have conversations centered on enjoying life outside work. Don't bother employees on their time off.

☐ Implementing the program: Have a systemic way to roll out aspects all year long. Get your team excited. Don't make anything mandatory.

☐ Review the Program: Continuously review the program. What's working? What needs improvement? How are the employees feeling?

Appendix Four

Conflict Management Style Quiz

Review the Questions and Assign a Point Value

1 Rarely   2 Sometimes   3 Often   4 Always

15 QUESTIONS
1. I try to listen to everyone and find something that works for the group.
2. When there is a disagreement, I gather as much information as I can.
3. I try to see the conflict from both sides.
4. I keep my disagreements with others to myself.
5. In general, I do not like disagreements.
6. It is best to end disagreements as quickly as possible.
7. During most conflicts, I have a clear picture of what needs to happen.
8. I don't mind conflicts. I welcome them as they are a good challenge.
9. I pride myself on being able to get my point across in a conflict.
10. I'm an easy-going person. In a conflict, I'm usually the one who can keep the peace.
11. I may not get what I want, but it's better to maintain the relationship.
12. I try to understand where the other person is coming from.
13. Negotiation is a great way to manage a conflict.
14. I think meeting halfway is the best way to end a conflict.
15. I don't mind giving in a little during a disagreement as long as I get something I want.

This quiz is meant to provide some insight into how you may handle conflict. It is not a perfect, one-size-fits-all resource. It's meant to allow you some self-reflection and help guide but not dictate or direct your behavior. This quiz is meant for general information purposes only. You should not rely upon this information as a basis for any legal decision.

How to Grade the Quiz

Please refer to Chapter Nine to review the Different Conflict Styles

Many people have more than one style they will use depending on the conflict.

Please add up the points correlating to the questions:
Collaborating (Questions 1, 2, 3): _____
Avoiding (Questions 4, 5, 6): _____
Competing (Questions 7, 8, 9): _____
Accommodating (Questions 10, 11, 12): _____
Compromising (Questions 13, 14, 15): _____

Preferred style: >9 Points:
 This is a style you likely prefer to use in most situations

Second style: 5-8 points:
 You may use this conflict style in some situations

Rarely used style: 1-4 points:
 This is the style you likely will rarely use

References

Aguilar E., (2016, February 29). The Art of Coaching Teams: Building Resilient Communities that Transform Schools. John Wiley & Sons

Ashkanasy, N., Wilderom, C., & Peterson, M. (2010). The Handbook of Organizational Culture and Climate Second Edition. Sage Publications.

BetterTeam. (2020, August 26). 5 Traits of Gen Z in the Workplace: A new generation is making its way into the workplace. BetterTeam. https://www.betterteam.com/5-traits-of-gen-z-in-the-workplace#:~:text=5%20Traits%20of%20Gen%20Z%20in%20the%20Workplace:,employees%20prefer%20to%20work...%203.%20Mobile-first%20habits

Brown, B. (2018). Dare to Lead. Random House.

Cain, S. (2013). Quiet: The Power of Introverts in a World that Can't Stop Talking. Cain Publishing.

Carnegie, D. (1936). How to Win Friends and Influence People. Pocket Books.

Center for Disease Control (CDC). (2021, January 7). Workplace Health Model. CDC Website. https://www.cdc.gov/workplacehealthpromotion/model/index.html

Clark T. (2020, March 9). The 4 Stages of Psychological Safety: Defining the Path to Inclusion and Innovation. ReadHowYouWant

Colella-Graham C. (Aug 10, 2022) The Rise of Toxic Positivity. Forbes. www.forbes.com/sites/forbeshumanresourcescouncil/2022/08/10/the-rise-of-toxic-positivity-and-what-you-can-do-about-it/?sh=61261ed5bf8a

Connley C. (2020, September 3). 45% of Women Business Leaders Say It's Difficult for Women to Speak Up in Virtual Meetings. CNBC Making It. https://www.cnbc.com/2020/09/03/45percent-of-women-business-leaders-say-its-difficult-for-women-to-speak-up-in-virtual-meetings.html

Daum, K. (2015, February 20). 11 Qualities Shared by Superstar Employees. Inc.com. https://www.inc.com/kevin-daum/11-traits-of-extremely-valuable-employees.html

Davey, L. (2013). You First. John Wiley and Sons.

Dvorak N., Pendell R. (2019, March 6), Want to Change Your Culture? Listen to Your Best People. Gallup Workplace. https://www.gallup.com/workplace/247361/change-culture-listen-best-people.aspx

Ekman, P. (1957, January). A Methodological Discussion of Nonverbal Behavior. The Journal of Psychology, 43(1), 141–149. doi: 10.1080/00223980.1957.9713059

Felps, W., Mitchell R., Byinton E. (2006, December). How, When, and Why Bad Apples Spoil the Barrel: Negative Group Members and Dysfunctional Groups. Research in Organizational Behavior. Volume 27, 2006, Pages 175-222. DOI:10.1016/S0191-3085(06)27005-9

Feltman, R. (2014, July 3). Most Men Would Rather Shock Themselves Than be Alone with Their Thoughts. Popular Science Magazine. https://www.washingtonpost.com/news/to-your-health/wp/2014/07/03/most-men-would-rather-shock-themselves-than-be-alone-with-their-thoughts/

Forbes Workday. (2019, September 12). Generational Differences and The Shifting Workplace. Forbes Inc. https://www.forbes.com/sites/workday/2019/09/12/generational-differences-and-the-shifting-workplace/?sh=f1fc6ff53ce7

Gee, D. (2010). How Does Sport Psychology Actually Improve Athletic Performance? A Framework to Facilitate Athletes and Coaches Understanding. Behavior Modification, 34(5), 386–402.

Gleeson, B. (2013, October 2). The Silo Mentality: How to Break Down The Barriers. Forbes. https://www.forbes.com/sites/brentgleeson/2013/10/02/the-silo-mentality-how-to-break-down-the-barriers/?sh=71997fe38c7e

Goldsmith M., Reiter M. (2007, January 9) What Got You Here Won't Get You There: How Successful People Become Even More Successful. Hachette Books

Grenny J., Patterson K., McMillan R., Switzler A., Gregory E. (2021, November 3). Crucial Conversations. McGraw Hill

Hanson, B. (2020). Sport Psychology for Sport Coaches: What you Need to Know. Athlete Assessments. https://www.athleteassessments.com/%ef%bb%bfsport-psychology-for-sport-coaches/

Holland, M. (2020, June 30). Steve Jobs: Your Work is Sh!t. SynergyIQ. https://synergyiq.com.au/steve-jobs-your-work-is-sht-8/

Kellerman, B. (2006, April). When Should a Leader Apologize—and When Not? Harvard Business Review. https://hbr.org/2006/04/when-should-a-leader-apologize-and-when-not?registration=success

Kuppler, T. (2015, May 13). Workplace Culture vs. Climate: Why Most Focus on Climate and May Suffer for It. Human Synergistics. https://www.humansynergistics.com/blog/culture-university/details/culture-university/2015/05/13/workplace-culture-vs.-climate-why-most-focus-on-climate-and-may-suffer-for-it

Kurtzleben, D. (2020, October 3). How Gender Shapes Presidential Debates — Even When Between 2 Men. NPR. https://www.npr.org/2020/10/03/919093731/how-gender-shapes-presidential-debates-including-between-two-men

Lighthouse. (2021). Essential Tips for Managing Generational Differences in the Workplace. GetLightHouse. https://getlighthouse.com/blog/generational-differences-workplace/

Lencioni, P. (2002). Five Dysfunctions of a Team. Jossey-Bass.

Lencioni, P. (2012). The Advantage: Why Organizational Health Trumps Everything Else in Business. Jossey-Bass.

Maxwell, J. (2016, October 4). The Ten Commandments of Confrontation. John C. Maxwell. https://www.johnmaxwell.com/blog/the-ten-commandments-of-confrontation/#When:15:00:00Z

Meinert, D. (2017, April 18). Why Workplace Conflict Can Be Healthy. SHRM. https://www.shrm.org/hr-today/news/hr-magazine/0517/pages/why-workplace-conflict-can-be-healthy.aspx

McDuff, D., Kodra, E., Kaliouby, R., & LaFrance, M. (2017, April 19). A Large-scale Analysis of Sex Differences in Facial Expressions. PLOS ONE. http://doi.org/10.1371/journal.pone.0173942

Obama, M. (2018). Becoming. Crown Publishing Group.

Paley, A. (2015, September 18). This is Why You Should Focus More on Your Top Performers Than Your Low Ones. Ladders. https://www.theladders.com/career-advice/this-is-why-should-you-focus-more-on-your-top-performers-than-your-low-ones

Porter, T. (2018, April 30). The Benefits of Admitting When You Don't Know. Behavioral Scientist. http://behavioralscientist.org/the-benefits-of-admitting-when-you-dont-know/

Purdue Global University. (2020). Generational Differences in the Workplace. Purdue Global University. https://www.purdueglobal.edu/education-partnerships/generational-workforce-differences-infographic/#:~:text=Generational%20Differences%20in%20the%20Workplace%20[Infographic]%20For%20the,of%20challenges%20does%20this%20present%20for%20today%E2%80%99s%20employers?

Regier, N. (2017). Conflict without Casualties: A Field Guide for Leading with Compassionate Accountability: 2nd ed. Berrett-Koehler Publishers.

Riegel, D. (2020, November 3). Talking About Mental Health with Your Employees — Without Overstepping. Harvard Business Review. https://hbr.org/2020/11/talking-about-mental-health-with-your-employees-without-overstepping

Sanburn, J. (2015, December 1). How Every Generation of the Last Century Got Its Nickname. Time Magazine. https://time.com/4131982/generations-names-millennials-founders/#:~:text=The%20next%20cohort%20%E2%80%94%20Generation%20X%20%E2%80%94%20gained,a%20Robert%20Capa%20photo%20essay%20from%20the%201950s

School of Babel. (2020). Building Better Communications in Team. School of Babel.

Scott, K. (2019). Radical Candor: Fully Revised & Updated Edition: Be a Kick-Ass Boss Without Losing Your Humanity. St. Martin's Press.

Smola, K. W,. & Sutton, C. (2002). Generational differences: Revisiting generational work values for the new millennium. Journal of Organizational Behavior, 23, 363–382.

Spalek, K., Fastenrath, M., Ackermann, S., Auschra, B., Coynel, D., Frey, J., Gschwind, L., Hartmann, F., Maarel, N., Papassotiropoulos, A., Quervain, D., & Milnik, A. (2015, January 21). Sex-Dependent Dissociation between Emotional Appraisal and Memory: A Large-Scale Behavioral and fMRI Study. Journal of Neuroscience, 35(3), 920-935. https://doi.org/10.1523/JNEUROSCI.2384-14.2015

Sutton, R., & Wright, B. (2019, May 6). More Harm Than Good: The Truth About Performance Reviews. Gallup. https://www.gallup.com/workplace/249332/harm-good-truth-performance-reviews.aspx

Tang, T.L., & Tzeng, J. Y. (1992). Demographic correlates of the protestant work ethic. Journal of Psychology, 126, 163–170.

Tolbize, A. (2008, August 16). Generational differences in the workplace. University of Minnesota. https://rtc.umn.edu/docs/2_18_Gen_diff_workplace.pdf

Vechy, J. (2012, March 22). Keep Turf Wars from Destroying Your Company. Inc.com. https://www.inc.com/john-vechey/how-to-keep-turf-wars-from-destroying-your-company.html

Wigert, B., & Harter, J. (2017). Re-Engineering Performance Management. Gallup. https://www.katherinespinney.com/wp-content/uploads/2018/01/Re-Engineering-Performance-Management_012517_v11_rj.pdf#:~:text=Re-Engineering%20Performance%20Management%20This%20approach%20aims%20to%20hold,ratings%20is%20that%20managers%20often%20choose%20them%20based

Wpengine. (2020). Motivation in Sports Psychology. Peak Performance. https://www.peakendurancesport.com/endurance-psychology/coping-with-emotions/motivation-sports-psychology/

Zenger, J. (2017, October 12). What Solid Research Actually Says About Performance Appraisal. Forbes Leadership Strategy. https://www.forbes.com/sites/jackzenger/2017/10/12/what-solid-research-actually-says-about-performance-appraisals/?sh=385b1f5f2b59

INDEX

Acknowledgments

I need to acknowledge everyone who was kind enough to believe and support my first book. I am humbled and in awe of the outpouring and overwhelming praise my first book with a unicorn on the cover has received. You have left me all speechless. It is because of you that this second book exists. I am eternally grateful to be in the best profession in the world. I owe a debt of gratitude to all of you. You are true unicorns.

To my friends and family, I could not have done this alone. Because of your unwavering support, I continue to survive and thrive in this crazy journey called life. When I tell you about some nutty idea I have your only response ever has been, "You should do that." I am so lucky to be aligned with some of the best human beings on the planet. You tolerate my insane schedule and demands to pick your brain, and you provide me with the best honest love when I need it the most.

Lastly, I would not be writing about veterinary team dynamics and culture if it weren't for the pets that shaped my life. There have been some amazing animals that touched my life and paved my path to veterinary medicine. I chose this career to save animals. My career evolved because I wanted to help the people in the teams I worked in. Eventually, I found myself wanting to help the entire veterinary industry. This entire crazy journey started because of a dog named Molly.

Pinch me.
I am one lucky human being.
All I can do is to say thank you.

We Want to Hear from You!

Whether you loved, liked, or hated this book, we want to hear your thoughts. We want to hear what topics you thought were missing from the book, what you felt was particularly useful, or anything you felt was utter rubbish.

Scan this QR code with your phone
to be taken to a brief survey where
you can share your thoughts and ideas.

This anonymous survey will be sent
directly to Amy Newfield.

We Need Your Amazon Review!

Help get the word out about this book.

Follow Amy Newfield through her website: VetTeamTraining.Com
Sign up for exclusive member-only content, including podcasts!
Email: VetTeamTraining@gmail.com

#BeaUnicorn

Made in the USA
Middletown, DE
25 March 2024

52070468R00239